OFF COURSE
From Truman to Nixon

OFF COURSE

From Truman to Nixon

Rexford G. Tugwell

PRAEGER PUBLISHERS   New York · Washington

BOOKS THAT MATTER

Published in the United States of America in 1971
by Praeger Publishers, Inc.
111 Fourth Avenue, New York, N.Y. 10003

© 1971 by Praeger Publishers, Inc.

Library of Congress Catalog Card Number: 70–131945

Part of the first section on Franklin Roosevelt appeared
originally in a very different form as "FDR: Living Memorials"
in *The Nation*, April 7, 1956.

Printed in the United States of America

To
the Class of Forty-two
in Puerto Rico
Associates, Friends

Contents

OFF COURSE
From Truman to Nixon

I
Introduction

1. *The Unlikely Appointment*

Whether anyone is indispensable is not an abstract question. What has to be asked is: how much will he be missed? is there no one else? is his work done? does he have further intentions? does he possess unique talent for seeing them through? and will they never come about if he is taken away? There is momentum in events themselves; but is there reason for apprehension that with him gone there may be a slowing down or even that courses may be altered?

This is what happened when Roosevelt died. His plans died with him. The war went on to its prepared end—so much for momentum; but what happened after that was drastically different than it would have been if he had lived. He survived in people's memory, a standard for his successors; but, much as they might be granted for effort, they failed.

Most men and women now grown cannot actually recall Roosevelt even in the places where he was known while he lived. Those who did know him grow fewer year by year; but people and things have been slow to surrender his influence—

3

slow, that is, as these things go. Time's erasing effect is no doubt inexorable, but some recordings have been made; and institutions do remain whose start was owed to him. In this sense he has lived on among Americans, becoming, like Washington and Lincoln, heroes of their history, rather than mere political leaders elevated to the White House.

It is only factual to say that some of his bequests appear in American annals like mountains seen from a plain. Because he was not only a man who meant to do things but also politically skillful, he saw some of them well begun, and these have gone on growing. Of some it can be said that they could not conceivably be dispensed with; and of some, let go by his successors, that they should have been kept and may have to be restarted; all, even those no longer needed, served a purpose, even if it was for their own time only. They helped the nation through as bad a time as it had ever experienced.

Of the more permanent, there is, for instance, the banishment of depression; there is social security; there is industrial peace; there is national planning; there are public enterprises; there are regulatory agencies for power, communications, banking, and the exchanges; there is no more child labor. Then there is the conquest of polio; and there is immense progress toward equal opportunity. These were for Americans themselves. For the world there was the extirpation of Nazism and fascism, the Good Neighbor policy, the United Nations, great peace-keeping bombers followed by satellites. More than anyone else in modern history he pushed the world toward oneness.

Seen from a time when none of them existed, amazing achievements did spring somehow from his mind. They were not acceptable to most older Americans. He had to contend for every one of them, sometimes against opposition rooted deep in the rugged individualism Hoover had so lately spoken for. It is the more remarkable to recall that they originated with a man who was rated by contemporary intellectuals as not much more than mediocre and who was a physical cripple as well.

Perhaps his greatest contribution was the demonstration that experiment was the way to progress in government and governmental policy, just as it is in science and technology. To experiment means to try and to discard what does not succeed. Critics like to call such failures. mistakes; but error is a way of learning. The real mistake is not to leave open the way to retrieval, to persist in what fails. This Roosevelt did not do. He was not infallible. He did not pretend to be. In his message to the Congress asking for the passage of the Agricultural Adjustment Act he said this:

> Deep study and the joint counsel of many points of view have produced a measure which offers great promise of good results. I tell you frankly that it is a new and untrod path, but I tell you with equal frankness that an unprecedented condition calls for the trial of new means to rescue agriculture. If a fair administrative trial of it is made and it does not produce the hoped-for results I shall be the first to acknowledge it and advise you.

It was a passage not written *for* him; the original was set down *in his own hand*. It hangs now, framed, in the Library at Hyde Park. More than any other short passage from his many messages, speeches, and other official papers, it characterizes his approach, his method. It describes the way he persuaded the nation to accept its responsibilities in a changing world.

Since his death Americans have needed to go on to new achievements; but they have not been urged, and they have not been given leads. No one has assembled an overwhelming push; no one has bargained and maneuvered to get things going in the way they must go. When Roosevelt died there were not many who felt that their government was failing them—except, of course, the more affluent. Even when the reluctant had been called to war, it had soon become *their* war. There were many still who were unemployed; but much was being done to find employment for everyone. There remained the lingering shame of racial discrimination; but even this was beginning to torment the consciences of those who, if they had not condoned it, had done nothing active to alleviate it. There was still poverty; but there was a good deal less of it, and the conviction had spread that it was unnecessary.

Few doubted—even Roosevelt's detractors—that he was urging them to worthy endeavors. Some disliked paying the bill; but they had more to pay it with, and their objections were suspect. Worst of all there were the fearful; and the holding back was so successful that an accumulation of neglects would finally cause doubts about survival itself; that would be the situation in 1970.

From March 4 in 1933 until April 12 in 1945, there was no such uncertainty, no such sickness. Everything *could* be done, and there was no doubt that it would be done, if not right now, then when the time was right. Roosevelt would see to it. It might come slowly. He had much overcoming to do; but he was on the side of those who were oppressed and discriminated against; and, in the long run, he would have his way. They knew it would happen.

In the quarter-century after 1945, there were only two moments when Rooseveltian progress seemed about to begin again. One was when Kennedy called on Americans to ask not what their country could do for them, but what they could do for their country. But Kennedy was inexperienced and made grievous mistakes. He failed to establish momentum, and then was tragically assassinated. The other moment was when Johnson defeated Goldwater so decisively, and carried with him into the Congress such a liberal majority that a flood of catching-up legislation was passed. It lasted two years, until another election went against him. The Congress, for the rest of his time, had a majority of objectors. His program was badly fragmented and badly administered. He had deepened the involvement in Southeast Asia and lost the supporters who might have made the legislators more tractable. For this and other reasons he left the Presidency with far less solid accomplishment than might have been expected from such a beginning as he had made. Besides, the implementation of his program was impossible with half the budget devoted to anticommunist military ventures.

Beginning in 1948 the Republicans still rather fondly ran against Roosevelt more than against their nominal opponents. And the Democrats, down into the 'seventies, with or without justification, were still claiming to have inherited his policies. As for the ordinary individuals from whose approval his strength had come, the sense of loss they felt in April of 1945 has, of course, been deadened; most of them, in fact, are no longer here; but "What would he have done?" is still a relevant question in crises.

It is sometimes said that he was not really elected in 1932; it was, rather, that Hoover was defeated. There is a good deal of truth in this, but what is also true is that, from the moment in his inaugural when he called his fellow Americans back to courage, telling them they had only fear itself to fear, he was the great and central figure they had needed to form behind. From that moment, no person in the nation had stature such as his; no one commanded such respect and confidence. After its long paralysis, the nation lived and moved and had purpose.

His successors won their elections truly enough; and Eisenhower at least was trusted; but none afterward commanded such steadfast support reaching out into the hinterlands and deep into the crowded cities. There was lethargy instead of excitement; there was a sense of holding instead of moving. Even when Roosevelt maneuvered and made doubtful deals his following judged them to be in good causes. The credibility gap, so devastating for Kennedy, Johnson, and Nixon, was not heard of in his time. He had his hidden intentions; he liked favorable interpretations of his behavior as well as they; but when he refused answers or made things look a little better than they were, it was allowed as harmless deception. Most people laughed. They did not resort to violence. Unhappy objectors were neglected. Even the press, eighty-five per cent of it devoted to derogation, found its castigations disbelieved. If they said it about Roosevelt, it simply could not be true.

His presence seems especially to linger at Warm Springs and at Hyde Park; but it also survives in Albany and Washington; and it reaches too into more remote places. For as a people Americans after a quarter-century do have terrible problems, and there is no one who is trusted to meet them.

This long shadow of Roosevelt has its own special irony. He was so seriously stricken with polio in 1921 (when he was 39) that he almost died; and for several years afterward his struggle back toward reasonable management of his body was so severe as to monopolize most of his time and require most of his energy. He was, it seemed, a stone refused by the builders. He became the headstone of the corner by an effort so heroic as to be an example for all the future to those sunk in self-pity and inclined to shrink from the duties of common living.

The permanent paralysis of his lower body might well have ended any thought of a career and especially one in politics; but he was not content to become merely a country gentleman as fate seemed to have determined and as his imperious mother demanded. He had meant to go on. He had meant to become President. Presently he did go on and did become President.

His last intention—the creation of the United Nations— slipped from his grasp as he passed away and it was not shaped as he hoped it would be. This is one of the reasons he could have gone on being useful. Still, Americans had rounded a bend of history with him and had seen ahead of them freedom from want instead of the poverty they had been living in; freedom too from many injustices; and finally an end to recurrent wars among the great powers. They saw, beyond this, unimaginable achievements as their productivity increased.

2. *The Long Shadow*

Richard M. Scammon, the political analyst, responding to a question asked by an interviewer after the election of Richard M. Nixon in 1968, said this:

> One interesting thing about the election was the survival of the Roosevelt coalition. It's one of the myths of American politics that the coalition is dead. In each four-year period we spend forty-seven months talking about its death and then one month commenting on how it's really alive. And we saw that this time. The columnists announced that with the disaffection of the young, the poor, and the blacks, the coalition had fallen apart. But the coalition survived—with the one major exception of the South. I don't say it *will* survive in the future—I say it has survived up to now. . . . You have today very much what you had in Roosevelt's day. There are modifications, of course, but basically the better-educated and those with more income tend to vote Republican. People with less income and less education tend to vote Democratic. The countryside and the rural areas are Republican. The cities are Democratic. Normally, Roman Catholics vote measurably more Democratic than Protestants. Jews vote measurably more Democratic than Catholics. Slavic-Americans, Italo-Americans, Latin-Americans, Mexican-Americans vote measurably more Democratic. Negroes vote the most Democratic of all. Suburbia is perhaps less Republican than it used to be a generation ago. But this is interesting, because it may be the exception that proves the rule. . . . As its white

working class moves more and more into the middle class, suburbia becomes more and more a mirror of white America.*

He had said they must no longer fear fear itself, and believing him, they almost banished it; but after his death fear
crept back into their lives and no Roosevelt showed them
how it might be overcome. His recovery from paralysis and
his political successes were not enough; nor was all he was
able to do as President and commander in chief. There was
more to be done when he died, and he had no successors who
understood his intentions or who could have carried them
out if they had understood. So far as any man could have
been he was indispensable.

It is tragic to consider that Roosevelt might have been here
to have energized this coalition and direct it to the ends it
was deflected from as soon as he was gone.

He was born in January, 1882. He died in April, 1945. He
was therefore a little short of 64. In 1970 he would have been
88. Going on to such an age was not, of course, expectable;
but if twelve more years had been added to his sixty-four, he
would have been only 76; and his going on until then is
credible. He would have finished out his fourth term and
had a fifth and sixth. But suppose he had only finished his
fourth term and had a fifth—eight years—he would have been
only 72.

Those eight years might have seen the coalition gather
power and do much of what still had to be done; they will be
spoken of again; but it may be noted here that, if he had gone
on, the nation would have been spared the ministrations of
Truman and perhaps Eisenhower. Churchill, de Gaulle, and
Chiang Kai-shek, his contemporaries, all lived to such an age,
and all presided over preventable postwar disasters. For him,
death may have had no sting; for those who were left, it did.

* Quoted by William Whitworth in *The New Yorker*, September 20, 1969,
pp. 50 ff.

3. *What Was Needed*

It will perhaps be granted that the disarray to be called in reference here is real and hardly at all exaggerated. Exception may be taken to omitting much account of achievements. The twenty-five years after Roosevelt have certainly seen some. It is just being realized, however, how small the *net* gains have been. The credits would nearly all be economic —higher average incomes and consequently a wider stock of goods and more services. But even these have immense deductions of unnoticed costs to be made from their apparent utility. The goods have often been shoddy, unsafe, and misrepresented; the services, more and more undependable and grudgingly rendered.

Then there have been hidden, more distant costs to be deducted. The automobile has been suited to the aggressions of the erratic and so has caused a slaughter on the highways that would be intolerable in a war; and it has laid a deadly blanket of smog over all the cities. Pesticides have "revolutionized" the cultivation of crops but have poisoned the soil and water and perhaps even people. Rebuilding has made living and working places much more useful and pleasing; but it has taken so little account of the community that structures often rise from the neighborhoods made untenable by decay; the broad land has been made usable for men's various enterprises, but the products they have produced may have been by methods incompatible with natural cycles necessary to life on earth. There has been no recognition of any organized sort that irreplaceable resources are being used at a headlong rate. They will be used up. This is a condition of earth, since it is small in the universe and finite. There are, of course, vast forces, many of them only guessed at as yet, still to be utilized. The human race need not disappear because of starvation; there are infinite sources of power; synthetic materials may be better than the old exhaustible ones; but poisoning and other ecological interferences may well prove to have been fatal. Or if not that, then contributory to a very possible calamity.

The question is one of juncture. Will the new come soon enough to replace the old? This is the caretaker's job. We have allowed exploiters to despoil the earth and cause an infinitude of suffering; and if they have their way, they will own the future resources too. What can be learned from the quarter-century just past is not reassuring. The balance of gains and losses during this time are at last being struck; and all who know the result—and that is nearly everybody now—are appalled. How could so little foresight have been used? How could such heedless exploitation have been tolerated? How was it that the rising nitrogen content of soils had not been seen as a threat? How could the thickened air have been allowed to become a whole generation's curse? How could irreplacable resources have been allowed to be used for such doubtfully useful products?

The preventive would have been the planning that was not done. Conforming to nature's imperatives, not to those of undirected enterprisers, is implicit in public plans; to go on as was done, it was necessary to be heedless, profit-minded, short-sighted, irresponsible. So the Congress, whose majority had these characteristics, angrily abolished Roosevelt's Planning Board. Leaders have been needed who knew about—or could learn about—these matters and who would have protected the public from self-interested exploitation. There have not been such leaders. It could not have been expected from such successors as those who followed Roosevelt: Truman, Eisenhower, Johnson, or Nixon. Kennedy might have been an exception; but his chance was a short one, and he wasted his energies on small conflicts with obstructors.

None of the other successors was of Roosevelt's caliber;

and they and their chosen associates have landed the nation in a double crisis of such proportions that recovery has begun to seem almost impossible. That crisis is both military and civil. Neither was tractable; policies were set; the way of escape from neither was visible as the 'seventies began.

So, surely, it is permissible to ask what Roosevelt would have done. It might possibly tell us what ought still to be done—if security and well-being are, indeed, still recoverable.

4. *Allowances Requested*

Much of what will be said here will not be provable by documentation. It could not be, because the documents do not exist. Roosevelt consistently concealed his intentions unless he sensed wide approval; and, except in crisis, wide approval was unlikely in his time for innovations of any sort in public affairs. He revealed them in good time when they had a chance of approval.

There were several reasons for this. One was that he meant to explore the great causes and experiment with the grand designs he was clear enough about in his own mind but would have to induce an uninformed electorate to accept in principle. Few of them were alien to American tradition, really, but many seemed to be. The end needed to be made so important that the means would be acceptable, even though it went against the grain; but this was Roosevelt's special talent. It was a matter of insisting on values already professed but often not supported in practice, and showing how they could be made operative. Because he was more often not certain about these means, or people's willingness to tolerate them, he kept his thoughts strictly to himself while he watched and waited for the right time to arrive, meanwhile maneuvering for approach to acceptance.

This was the method of a sophisticated politician. To reveal intentions was to risk their defeat by those who would be injured by them or who perhaps just disliked them or him. And lacking a sense of urgency to be counted on, a politician must approach his ends with a long preparation of people's minds. There must be no unpleasant surprises; the gains must be made visible; and whatever sacrifices would have to be made must not seem unfair.

There were, of course, many delays involved in this; but what would have been fatal to have advocated in his first Presidential campaign soon became a program enacted by a frightened Congress during crises and was gratefully welcomed by wearied citizens. Even then, however, he emphasized recovery more than the unaccustomed means he knew well enough would have to be used to achieve it or to make it permanent.

Similarly, he had repudiated the League of Nations during the campaign and concealed carefully his intention to advocate an organization for world order of a similar sort when it became possible. In another instance, no one could prove by anything he said publicly, or in any other way, that he meant to modify the business system responsible for the Depression or, as President, to propose continuing governmental responsibility for the welfare of the jobless and the handicapped. When he did reveal the first stage of these conceptions, the time was right. There was general recognition that it was possible and necessary.

This method of his makes speculation about what was there in his mind, and never materialized for public viewing, much more reasonable than it would otherwise be. Some—a few— knew a good deal about his later intentions and could see that vast changes yet to come were no more than an extension of his purposes. His helpers, not understanding until he instructed them, were impatient for revelation. They were cheerfully diverted. He had his own sensitivity; he meant all of it to be done; but only when his political radar told him it would succeed.

It is not unreasonable, perhaps—using even less certain evidence but extrapolating from what he was, how he did things, where he seemed to be going, and how he had always seen the American future—to state it for comparison with what happened after he was gone.

What is said here is to be taken in that way—as the projection of what is believed to have been in his mind for the years after the war—the quarter-century just passed. No apology is made for this; it is simply explained as that sort of thing. It will depend for its acceptance on readiness to believe that the author has a fair idea of Roosevelt's mind and to that extent knows what he is talking about. There will be some evidence, most of it inferential; but there will not be much proof.

An essay of this sort will perhaps be regarded as a tongue-in-cheek exercise. The war destroyed so much and began so much that projection beyond it seems problematical; but all the old cords to the past had not been cut. For the United States, there was nothing like the dissolution of empires, faced by Britain, France, and the Netherlands, to be accepted and adjusted to. The unexpected alliance with the Soviet Union could be projected into the peace if ideological objections could be compromised. Wilsonian self-determination partly, at least, responsible for the second war, was clearly modified in Roosevelt's mind by the need for disciplining some and assisting other neighbor nations. South America, like the Balkans, was bound to be dominated by the great power of the hemisphere. So a look at the international future *as it might have been* does have some credible sources.

The same is true of the American future. The principle abandoned when NRA was rejected had been reintroduced as an organization for war production. Ways were being found for establishing industrial peace; racial and economic equality were advancing; welfare had become a governmental responsibility. Other known points of reference to the past were numerous.

Some negatives were just as apparent: there would be no attempt to establish an American empire as a substitute for that of the British, for instance, and no irreparable breach with China and the Soviet Union; these changes and alliances had cost too much to be cast away in careless moments of annoyance at uncivilized behavior. And the development of nuclear energy would have been turned to peaceful purposes, not to poisoning relations with Asia for perhaps all the future.

It is a projection without assurance only if Roosevelt is supposed to have finished his work, and only if it is assumed that he had lost his talent for persuading Americans to do what their interests clearly called for. However unpalatable, agreement must be reached. At any rate, if these allowances are not wholly granted it still may be that they will be granted in part; and the alternatives they point to may at least be considered reasonable.

Roosevelt until 1952, at least, and perhaps until 1956!

5. *Continuation*

It should probably be said that what follows here is more or less an extension of the argument begun in *A Chronicle of Jeopardy*, published in 1956 by the University of Chicago Press. That book was a plea for the abandonment of containment and a resumption of efforts for coexistence.

In 1946, the nuclear scientists at the University—or some of them, Leo Szilard most actively—were trying to tell the legislators in Washington that the bomb was the product of a universally known body of knowledge and that it could not be kept from the Russians, who, indeed, already must possess most of the necessary technology.

Just at that time, the Congress was furiously debating the control of further nuclear activities and very much inclined toward military custody. The scientists wanted a civilian commission to manage the further development of nuclear force, particularly because of its obvious peaceable potentialities.

In that year, the *Chronicle* was begun; and a chapter was written at the same time in each succeeding year for the next decade. It was with grave fears for the future of mankind, overhung with such a threat, that what I recorded year after year was deeper involvement in weaponry based on the genocidal uses of nuclear energy.

The *Chronicle* was ended in 1956, partly because no change seemed to be in prospect and partly because there was such slight interest in further insistence that the cold war was suicidal. Almost no one read the book, and those who did, even old friends, offered only reproof.

There have been several direct confrontations since, and nuclear war was avoided only by what have seemed like miracles. The recurrence of these and the dying off or retirement of the xenophobes who controlled public policy so long, has led to the writing of this short account of the years since Roosevelt, so full of muted terror, so full also of promise unfulfilled. Having escaped a nuclear holocaust by some providential intervention, there is still time—not much, but some—for the nation to resume the course dictated by reason.

I have taken leave to describe briefly how it was and how it is—at least as I have seen and still do see it.

It remains to remind the reader that the author participated in the devising of a model for a world constitution published in 1957. Perhaps this indicates a bias for world order, still without doubt apparent in this essay.

II
How It Was
When He Died

1. *Hyde Park*

Springwood, at Hyde Park, the Roosevelt home, is now a national monument. Visitors who go there on a pleasant day find others, often too many for the outdoor paths, and there is scarcely elbow room as they push into the house. Many in the months and years after Roosevelt's death were something more than tourists who happened to be passing; they came to give thanks in decent silence for lives called in the past to renewed courage and determination to survive and keep their self-respect when it was all but lost. The common emotion was obvious; and the garden where the Roosevelts are buried was small for their deployment.

Many of those who came then were family groups. As time passed, fewer of their members had any actual recollection of the man who had lived here. His service merged, as was bound to happen, into the tradition of those who had been Presidents during crises before his time—Washington, Jefferson, Lincoln, that earlier Roosevelt who came of the same stock, and Wilson, this Roosevelt's mentor. If you followed one of these groups you might overhear an older person, perhaps a father or a grandfather, trying to tell the younger ones what he felt. Children are never easily impressed, but they recognize something they respect in the emotion of their elders in this place.

The monument as a whole is a creation deliberately planned and carefully executed to recall a past whose agonies had been overcome. It was meant to reach across the generations and ask respect for ancestors whose trials were hard but whose accomplishments were worthy. No doubt in subtler yet grander ways Roosevelt is reaching down the years through the institutions he caused to be created; they say plainly to the new man: you will have other fears than the ones we dispersed, and you too will be tempted to despair; but look what courage did when Americans were beaten into paralysis; and look how, only a few years afterward, we came to the defense of democracy when/ it was challenged. Are you the men and women we were?

Even these mementos at Hyde Park do not teach all that, but they do draw thoughts back to hard times and how they were escaped. Courage was summoned and did prevail. Roosevelt was not a superman, only one who loved his country and had a certain talent. He became what he was in no extraordinary way, only by growing up in this moderately grand house and among these fields, woods, and orchards, then going to school and on to college. It was an ample beginning, and he went to the best school and the best college, but there was no lavishness and no extravagance. There is no visible reason for greatness.

He left this place, his creation, to the nation. These domestic artifacts are not a reminder to posterity that he was a great man, but rather that he was one who studied his people, understood their needs, and used his talents for their improvement.

This estate in the Hudson Valley and the big house are not so ancient as they seem. The appearance of antiquity is illusory; only two generations of Roosevelts lived here. It was Franklin himself who rebuilt it and made it the pleasant house it now is. That was no longer ago than 1915, when Franklin was already thirty-three. So the solid elegance, of no recognizable style, but conforming well enough with all its surroundings, is not the creation of distant forbears any more than of an architect following a classic model. It is the product—a typical one—of this Roosevelt's mind. If it was built to furnish a background as well as a living place, it serves the purpose well. That it might be a reminder to later Americans that one statesman had cared more for simple amplitude than for the assertion of wealth was the after-thought of a President.

The house is generous, but no one would call it a mansion; only one room is of notable size—the library on the south with Italian marble mantels at either end. It is plain and rectangular but very just and gracious; nothing showy, it might be said, but planned with a feel for solidity and good proportion. Portraits of ancestral Roosevelts give it a sense of the past, as do prints of ships from old navies spouting broadsides. The central part of the original house is on a slightly higher level, and anyone coming down into this room has a sense that its accustomed occupant has only just gone away. Until those who lived when Roosevelt did became fewer, even children understood that a man their father or grandfather had listened to over the radio, whose being President had been a comfort in trying times—of depression, if you were getting to be old, or war, if you were younger— might very well just have wheeled himself down the ramp to sit at this table where books and papers are scattered.

He could be pictured there, sitting beside the fire, absorbed for an hour with his stamp collection, studying a paper, looking into a book, or entertaining friends after dinner. In glass cases along the walls were documents he collected, rare ones among them, having to do with local history or naval lore. Small objects in the room were ones he had liked to have near him, plastic donkeys, bronze statuettes, an assortment of ash trays for the cigarettes he smoked through long paper holders. Nothing had much value or could be called artistic; but what could not be missed was its homeliness.

Toward the southwest and down a wooded slope, the Hudson stretched, and far across it were the Catskills. In the other directions, there were lawns, well kept, but not over-orderly, merging into fields. It was countryside, decently kept by a dutiful proprietor.

It was easy to think of a man, recently crippled for life, sitting here when he allowed himself time off from the wearing exercises he hoped would give him back his legs. This indeed was where he did sit—here or on the adjoining porch, shirt-sleeved in summer or wrapped in a cloak against the chill of fall. But he could just as well be pictured in the dining room that seemed all old polished mahogany and worn silver. Those who had lived when he did had heard how he presided at table, never too weary or harassed to be the kind of host who drew out his guests or told them things they took to be confidential.

The stories about this room included other Roosevelts. Eleanor, his wife, was never at the table's other end. That was where the grand dame, his mother, sat, plainly resenting some of the crude political guests who had come to see her son. She was apt to inquire audibly about such "persons." They may have commanded majorities in Boston or Chicago or Omaha; but the old lady could not believe they were that important. Eleanor, somewhere in the middle, and embarrassed, would make small talk, allowing her voice to escape into high registers to save the situation. She had had some sense of politics. It was the elder woman's view that it was right for her son to be Governor or President, but such offices ought to be conferred on him, not striven for with such demeaning entertainments.

Upstairs, on the door of one bedroom, a plaque says it

was once occupied by the King and Queen of Britain; but a plain visitor may not think the royal visit so high a light in the history of this house as the custodians evidently do. Other royal persons stayed here, if it comes to that; also a succession of important Americans could be catalogued, if anyone cared to do it. But keepers of memorials have their own standards, and they are not too different from those of the matriarch who was so proud to entertain a Queen that Roosevelt's more irreverent assistants had conferred a title on her. Among themselves they called her "The Duchess."

Some of these guests, those who meant something in the furthering of Franklin's large designs, visitors are told, had sometimes gone further down the hall to his own bedroom at the end, invited to talk with him before he got up in the morning. He would be sitting up in bed wearing his old gray sweater, cigarette alight, a litter of newspapers on the floor, last night's detective story on the bedside stand. Persiflage might very quickly have given way to important matters before those conversations ended. Some maneuver being hatched still seems to linger in the air, and fathers smile as they imagine the deals made or the directions given.

These bedside conferences annoyed such fellow-Grotonians as Dean Acheson, who wrote about their similarity to the bedchamber attendances required by Louis XIV. Others had allowed for the President's crippled state, and anyway were not above conversing with a President in any circumstances. Later visitors noted the plainness of the room and dismissed the Acheson comparison with the Sun King. However Roosevelt had done what he had done, it was all right with them.

For anyone but a rare survivor, the Springwood establishment would have seemed an anachronism at any time after the Depression. It could only have been maintained because by 1928 Roosevelt had been Governor of New York and would never again be out of office. Official servants supplemented those the matriarch could no longer afford. The household was at least partly on the public account.

Roosevelt in office had expected to live until he could retire; but it would not have been in this house. During his third term, he had built a cottage several miles away, more suited to such circumstances. He called it Hill-top; and this older place was expected to be exactly what it is today, a monument, a reminder, as it is proving to be. Nearby, he had caused to be built the library-museum for his papers and artifacts.

He conceived and directed the building of the library-museum himself. This was to be, and is, a place of public resort. Like the house, it was to be the nation's, and his possessions were to be available to scholars as well as to those whose sentiment drew them here. He designed the complex in the Hudson Valley Dutch manner, one the Roosevelts could call their own.

In the library he had arranged a room to be the workplace where he would do the work on the inevitable *memoirs*. His friends and collaborators, Sam Rosenman and Harry Hopkins, were to live nearby and work there with him. Together, they would sort papers, make notes, and, as age descended on them and their participation in the world's events became less and less, they would watch their successors with critical sophistication.

He had sat a few times in the library room at the desk to be seen there; but the feel of him is not at all what it is in the house. There is a sense of arrangement; it is too elegant.

The rose garden, where he lies beneath the block of marble he had specified, is only a few yards from the house. Its surrounding hedge far outdates all the Roosevelts in this neighborhood. But then most of the trees outdate them, too. He had had a special feeling for trees; and actually he had planted many acres of them. Those, however, are in wood lots; the ancient specimens close to the house were already mature when Franklin had climbed them as a boy; they are now fast reaching a falling-down condition, and many are shored up in one or another way. But, although he was not responsible for them any more than he was for any of the other features of the original place, they merge so perfectly into the whole as to seem inseparable from it. He was on good terms with his surroundings.

At Mount Vernon it is difficult to think of a living Washington; Monticello seems too polished to be true; but Springwood is somehow not at all a frozen artifact. It seems not to be disarrayed by trampling feet, sullied by inane remarks, or dulled by the boredom of children. These are the Americans who raised Roosevelt to this supreme position and kept him there until he died. The house lives and glows in a modest manner, reminding visitors that one who understood the democratic process and had a talent for leadership lived here. The man who built this home and lived in it was wealthy; but he had been taught and never forgot the principles of noblesse. He had worked for the people; they knew it; and they took little notice of the critics who, because of Springwood, called him a country squire.

The sophisticated student might tell himself, as he watched the tourists, that it had been planned that way for the glorification of a personality, that it represented an attempt to manage history. What he might tell himself of this sort would, however, tend to escape his most determined skepticism. It would come over him that the effect is good. The man born to this place symbolized the American dream even better than he might if he had come to the grave in this formalized garden from birth in the traditional log cabin. A man may be a democrat, whatever his origin. He may also be an exemplar and teach what it is to be a patriot.

The lesson of this memorial is too plain to miss; and no one who comes here misses it.

2. *Warm Springs*

It may be that only those who make a conscious effort can conceive that the institution at Warm Springs could have grown out of one man's agony; but it did, and it continued to be enlarged even when he finally recognized that his wasted muscles would never again come to life in what he had hoped were curative waters. Its later uses demonstrated how a cripple may attend to more than his own selfish concerns, however, and this led on to the more important decision that if the disease could not be cured it must be conquered. Who can measure the pain avoided, the beginning lives made fruitful by the resulting preventive procedures? If Roosevelt had not fought a depression, or commanded armies, this alone should have given him a place in the grateful recollection of people everywhere.

Where once in a back-country corner of the South a man struggled in a tumbling pool of blue-green water to get back the use of his legs there were soon hundreds who had heard that there was hope and came there to struggle too. The rumor spread before anything was ready; but somehow very few were turned away. All were disappointed; but all were benefited too. Their crippling remained; but their health improved. So did their spirits; and this was important beyond measure.

Those who went to Warm Springs after more advanced techniques came into use received better care than Roosevelt, who had practically none; and the improvement was owed to the ferocity of his battle with the dead legs he was cursed with from 1921 until he died. Again and again he thought he could feel running down them the first faint tremors of feeling; he said many times that he hoped to wiggle a toe very soon. He was always betrayed. He never got back any command at all of his lower body.

He did get a magnificent torso as an incident of the strenuous exercise. His arms, chest, and shoulders, after years of hauling himself about, exercising in the pool, and swinging onto and off his wheelchair, were those of an Atlas. It was a kind of compensation. Those who sat with him at table—and especially if they were of the other sex—found it hard indeed to remember the withered unseen legs; and, if they saw him at his desk with his chin upthrust from his corded neck, muscular jaws gripping the long cigarette holder, the last thing anyone thought of was the reason he had not got to his feet when they had come in.

So he did conquer the legs in the sense that he got the best of them even though they never gave him back an instant of support. It was after years of trying one thing and then another, all of them calling for the toughest resolution and for physical effort carried to the exhausting limit, that he heard of warm-water therapy. It was after several winter seasons of this among the Florida Keys that he was told of Warm Springs and came to look and try.

There was a dilapidated resort hotel and not much else in the way of accommodations; but there was the amazing outpouring of water, warm and heavily mineralized from deep-under limestone ridges. It was a poor countryside. In that part of Georgia and over into Alabama, there are hills that grow weed trees and little else. The towns were shabby, the kind where poor whites came to work in textile mills; and Warm Springs itself was hardly even a village. But the water always poured upward in a barreling stream, mild and buoyant. He got into the old pool the first time he saw it and stayed for hours. He felt at once that it was good for him; and his hopes outran a skepticism owed to many disappointments.

Before long, as everywhere and always, his impulse to improve everything around him went to work. He sank more of his fortune in the therapy center than Eleanor thought he ought; but protests had no effect whatever; and presently it could be seen that there would be no lack of patronage. It was impossible to keep ahead of the rush as the news got around. The accumulated victims of polio saw the place as he had; like him, they asked what they could lose. Nothing else had done any good, and nothing else offered any promise.

He had first come to the Springs in 1924 and found that exercising in the water was at least less exhausting than hauling himself about on a railing, as he had done at Hyde Park, or setting himself to swing a little further on braces and canes one day than he had the day before. He invented exercises and made games of them when he could. The doctors and nurses he assembled learned as much from him as he from them. He was, indeed, the chief therapist. He played and worked with others under the Georgia sun; and as he exercised he planned. He visualized much larger pools and a rehabilitation center. He had only begun the improvements he meant to make when, in 1928, Al Smith, who was desperate about carrying even his own state in the Presidential race of that year, demanded that he help by running for the New York governorship.

This turned out to be a good thing for Warm Springs. Friends and supporters began to lift the debt. The March of Dimes was created, and the ramshackle place became a fine convalescent complex in the Georgia pines. The pools were refitted, new buildings went up, the staff was professionalized, and helping funds enabled many cripples to come who had felt themselves burdens to their families.

Roosevelt himself could not come so often after 1928, but he did not withdraw. He built a small house close by and bought a farm not far away. This he stocked with beef cattle; he also cultivated trees and undertook to find more productive crops. The farmers round about were in deep trouble; the boll weevil had finished a disaster begun by the exhaus-

tion of their old fields. He set out to see if something could
not be done.

He regularly came in November and again, when the
azaleas began to bloom, in April. Then he played with the
patients, went on picnics, drove the small car he could control with his hands about the country roads and into farmers'
lanes, inspected his cattle and trees, and, when he must, sat
at his table over the papers that came down from Albany in
great packets. Georgia, he said, was his "other" state, his
Southern home. Presently that would have political meaning.

Always at Thanksgiving and sometimes on other occasions, he presided over feasts in the new dining hall. His
tenor was as loud as any in the singing, and he claimed to be
a more skillful carver of turkeys than anyone around. His
presence braced everyone for ordeals that never ended.

All during the time the big man with the withered legs
was coming down to share the autumn or spring with his
fellow cripples, responsibility was settling on him more
firmly; and, almost before the Warm Springs colony realized
it, he was President of the United States, a living demonstration that polio need not be given into, even when it had
ravaged half a body.

He still came when he was President. The institution was
growing rapidly now, what with all the help from well-wish-
ers, and his own small house on the hill grew some append-
ages and was called locally "The Little White House." He
still played water polo and took his exercises, drove about
the countryside and presided over the Thanksgiving feasts.

Everyone got used to seeing a President about, but, now,
there were important people coming constantly to stay at the
visitors' quarters. They went back and forth, when summoned; the packets of paper grew to bulging pouches; reporters were always about, and secret service men were
never quite invisible. When the war came, there were marines to guard the commander in chief.

The place was very different now from the bankrupt re-

sort of the 'twenties. The institution had grown so large that
what had happened could be called a transformation; but
still nothing was finished. There was more to do. There were
hundreds of patients, dozens of doctors and nurses, and a
sense of permanence. It was still heartbreaking to see the
faces trying to be cheerful over twisted and tortured bodies,
and it was necessary to believe what was said about the
prospect of conquering the disease. It was even possible to
think that the Springs would not be needed for another
generation of polio victims.

About the countryside, there was more improvement as
his Presidency went on. The towns became sprucer, reflecting welfare benefits and assistance from federal funds for
schools, hospitals, water systems, and other public works.
Hard roads replaced the dusty yellow ones; and, just off one,
not far from Warm Springs, a state park named for the
President recalled the WPA, the Resettlement Administration, and the Civilian Conservation Corps. Nowhere had they
been more useful than in this poor area of the South, where
land and people both had such need.

It may as well be said that neither in the rehabilitation of
polio victims nor in the rescue of the West Georgia farmers
were his efforts at rehabilitation successful. Muscles wasted
would never serve again; fields gone to bush would never
again grow paying crops of cotton. Yet he certainly won as
well as lost. Polio was made incapable of crippling others;
and when he became President his first accomplishment was
to relieve the distresses of even the poorest farmers.

Death came to the President here in 1945, as he sat at his
table over the familiar pile of papers in the living room of
the cottage he had built. He was taken away in splendor,
riding in a railway car, as Lincoln had ridden back to Spring-
field, with mourning people everywhere along the tracks.

Visitors would continue to come and could imagine him
there in the Little White House. It was kept open as though
he might come wheeling in, his cigarette holder in his teeth,

talking as he rolled. He might still be swinging easily onto the chair behind his table, ready to deal with waiting papers, anxious to get rid of them so he could escape to drive along the familiar roads, go to a barbecue, or perhaps a picnic in some neighbor's yard or over by the river.

He went on being a presence at the Thanksgiving feast, and every newcomer heard the traditional stories about his galumphing in the pool, stopping to make a joke or give a word of advice; but the patients were no longer polio victims; some other catastrophe had crippled them; but polio had been conquered.

Visitors are as visibly moved here as they are when they look into his room at Hyde Park and see the books on his bedside table. Here they look out into a thicket of pines; but here, too, there is a shelf of favorite books.

The small paneled living room and the smaller bedroom next door have a nautical look; it might be the captain's quarters on a modest ship. There is a fireplace; but on its mantel is an unmistakable chronometer serving as a clock. The kitchen, where faithful Daisy Bonner cooked to his satisfaction—that is, simply, but with a Southern accent—is no larger than a galley. These reminders of the sea may seem strange without the knowledge that, if he had had his way, he would have gone to Annapolis. As a boy his one real accomplishment had been his handling of a sailboat in the fog and currents of the Bay of Fundy. He had tried to be an athlete but never won a place on a team; he had been too long and stringy. Besides, he had read Captain Mahan's essays on sea power with more excitement than he found in any other book. American ships were the warning to others that independence would always be guarded.

One of his first allocations of public-works money in 1933 had been a large sum for the modernizing of the fleet. Those who had been surprised at that must have forgotten his years as Assistant Secretary of the Navy. Those had been war years, and he had been the only appointed subordinate to

Josephus Daniels, the Secretary. His rapport with the officers had been of a kind Daniels neither had nor wanted. Roosevelt had meant to be an officer before the war was over, but he had not been allowed to leave his administrative job.

The evidences of his leanings were obvious enough at Hyde Park—his books on naval history, his pictures—and even more conspicuous in his own rooms in the White House. The walls of his office, for instance, were nearly covered with naval prints. But here in Warm Springs, the cottage-ship had been grounded in a forest. True, there was a deck, a large circular one, thrusting out into the trees; and there he had often sat, especially in his last days, his tired face animated only when he made a visible effort.

In that last spring he was dying on his own vessel. But, as he passed into eternity, the war was being concluded and he had brought the allies reluctantly to concurrence in a treaty that included the United Nations. If his work was not done, it could have been thought well begun.

He had emerged from the Presidency of his own nation to be a sort of President to many other peoples; but his last days, his last hours, were passed in this small cottage. It was not a death appropriate to royalty or even to a hero. A petty officer had carried him from the chair where he had slipped into unconsciousness and had laid him on his narrow bed. With him in the room had been his two maiden-lady cousins, Margaret Suckley and Laura Delano, together with Lucy Rutherford, a dear friend from his younger days in Washington. There was, as well, a Mme. Shoumatoff, who was there to make a portrait for Lucy. That Lucy was there lends a sentiment to his last days that no one would have grudged him. She had once been a passionate friend and had remained a helpful one. They had turned away from the disruption of other lives; and if their friendship continued it was to no one's hurt.

Lucy and the others went away, and the business of a Presidential burial began, irrelevant now but necessary for a nation's mourning. Those who loved him had not always been so many; but now they seemed to be everyone. Graham Jackson, who had so often entertained him at picnics and barbecues, now played "Going Home" when his funeral car paused for one last time before Georgia Hall. His simple accordion music was heard round the world. So indeed were the spirituals sung by those crowds lined along the railway, as the train bearing him to a Washington ceremony proper for Presidents who had died in office passed slowly northward in the night. He had had no ear for music, really, but these were sounds he had wanted to hear again and again.

A vast void evades description; it is not exactly a fear; it is a sense of having lost a powerful and steadfast friend. Even those who disliked him were so adjusted to his presence that they hardly knew how to behave. What would happen now? The question would have its answer; but the answer would always be measured against what it might be guessed he would have done if he had lived even a short time into a world without war.

3. *Albany*

One popular political philosopher would be remembered in future for an incautious comment made in January, 1932. Roosevelt had then been Governor of New York for three years and this was a Presidential year. Journalists, somewhat belatedly, had become aware that the New Yorker had a long lead over other contenders for his party's nomination, and that a Democrat was likely to be elected. The thought of a Democrat as President did not disturb Walter Lippmann; it was the specific prospect that an old acquaintance

of his, from Harvard days, might be the nominee. His estimate of Roosevelt had not been a high one, and he was appalled by the possibility that his fellow graduate might
succeed to a position of such power in time of crisis.

Roosevelt, he had said, was "an amiable gentleman lacking
conviction of any kind" and had gone on to remark that his
only qualification for the Presidency was a desire to have it.
This estimate had been fairly prevalent among liberals; it
was felt and said that Roosevelt was evasive, that he took
no stand on issues they felt important; and they suspected
that he had no stand to take. They would not—or anyway did
not—grant that a candidate who knew he was in the lead was
wise not to offend anyone, and they were not very kind in
appraising his conduct.

Ruling party politicians, anticipating victory, are much
tempted to choose an outright nonentity they can be sure of
managing. Roosevelt was not this; but he had known better
than to be aggressive and difficult. The politicians' estimate
was that the vote was going against Hoover anyway—provided, of course, his opponent was reasonably acceptable.
Roosevelt, they thought, was about right—moderately progressive but not committed to controversial policies. That
this would seem to have been a strange judgment in view of
his behavior as President has tended to obscure its justness
at that time. He was a man who knew how to run for high
office in a democracy. This meant that he did dissemble, as
the journalists said he did, and that he did avoid talking
about what he knew ought to be done but would arouse
controversy if spoken about. He did not yet have such a following that he could risk offending any considerable group
of voters. The advantage of getting a mandate he weighed
carefully against the disadvantage of awakening distrust. He
chose discretion. It was a professional decision. He said
frankly to those of his helpers who would have liked more
forthrightness that none of what they—and he—wanted could

be had unless he became President; and *that* he meant to do at whatever sacrifice of frankness.

What had deluded Lippmann, along with so many others, was the outward appearance of agreeable conformity following from this. Then too he had a deceptive habit of nodding as he was lectured by earnest proponents of schemes for curing the ills then so painfully affecting the country. Lippmann was quite right to speak of him as an agreeable gentleman, but he was quite wrong to judge that he had no ideas of his own and no stubborn intention of seeing them materialize in public policy.

The booming business of the 'twenties had had an inner disease that, after a period of incubation, had brought the economy near to death. A belief in permanent prosperity had been put about by business propagandists in an excess of euphoria, and even those who invented it had come to believe it. They were grievously mortified when conformity to their construct abruptly faded; and they harangued any official who would listen. Roosevelt had been as much at a loss as anyone about causes and cures; but he had suspected, as most others had not, that the sickness was systemic, that business had an inner tendency to destroy itself. It was not a discreet thing to say, however, to a people who wanted the good days back on the same terms as before. So he nodded; but if they thought him persuaded they were mistaken.

He had a political sophistication that was generally overlooked. He had indeed been wary and meant not to say something he might regret even if his progressive friends should be offended. He had been a candidate, actually, since 1910, something known well enough by observant professionals but not, evidently, by many others. That some serious party elders were prepared to be his sponsors had already been shown by their response to the open solicitations since 1930 of Louis McHenry Howe and James A. Farley, Roosevelt's representatives. By January, 1932, when the famous Lippmann paragraphs were written, a long and carefully conducted maneuver was coming to its climax with the active concurrence of many old and experienced operators.

There were some historians even then, who, belatedly discovering that the New York Governor might be tagged for greater things even though they had not anticipated it, had looked back over his governorship and decided that, since he had obviously had his eye on the Presidency all along, his governorship could not of itself have been of any importance. It had been merely "a stepping stone," they said. This had been mistaken, too. If they had known their political history as well as they should, they would have been aware that Roosevelt had not wanted to be nominated for the governorship in 1928 and that he had done everything humanly possible to escape it. Both he and Howe had judged, at the time, that winning was most unlikely and that losing would be fatal to further progress. It had not been part of his scheme to have an interlude as Governor of New York.

What was only seen afterward was that, with a seat in New York and with a "home" in Georgia, he had become a kind of national Democratic favorite. Ever since his defeat for the Vice-Presidency in 1920, he had maintained contact with the party's leaders in every state. The correspondence in his name, supervised by Louis Howe, was immense. There was always a country welcome for political leaders of all ranks at Springwood or at Warm Springs; and they always went away speaking of his friendliness and practical sense. Moreover, he had worked hard for Al Smith. He had not only made the famous "Happy Warrior" speech at the New York convention of 1924—when Smith had failed to get the nomination—but had repeated the service at Houston in 1928, when he had got it. He had become a big man in the party, and bigger because he seemed so willing always to help without asking anything in return.

His plan had called for waiting until 1936 to make his try for the Presidency. Hoover by then would have finished his second term, and the Democratic candidate would be running against a new man—just possibly, Roosevelt may have thought, Ogden Mills, his upriver neighbor, Hoover's Secretary of the Treasury, and the obvious favorite. All this might be long range; but, as would be seen afterward, it was neither nebulous nor unrealistic. It was the planning of the most successful political strategist of his generation.

His reluctance in 1928 was real. He had been a Vice-Presidential candidate and was therefore beyond the governorship stage. Why should he risk a rocky detour by way of Albany? Even if he won—and how could he with Smith losing?—he could not hope to make a striking record following a personality so popular in New York as Al Smith. No! It was all wrong!

Pressure had then been applied. He was told, and not too politely, that if he ever expected anything from the party in future he must serve it now. Howe, who might have stiffened his friend's resolve, happened to be in New York, and Roosevelt, alone at Warm Springs, although he managed to stay incommunicado for two days, was finally compelled to answer a waiting recessed convention. He had no real choice. He had to say "yes."

When, amazingly, he won, at the same time that Smith failed to carry the state—his own state—against Hoover, Roosevelt had a difficult problem. He would have to convince the New York bosses that he deserved renomination in 1930, in 1932, and in 1934; and he would have to be re-elected. This would be necessary to maintain his franchise on the opportunity in 1936, when Hoover, according to expectation, would have finished his two terms. How could he make a decent record and still get along with Tammany for six years? It seemed impossible for an independent upstate Democrat.

When, a little startled at where things had got to, commentators had surveyed the situation in early 1932, they had too easily attached the label "commonplace" to Roosevelt's performance; moreover, they had strongly implied that there

had been indecent compromise in what appeared to be—
even if it was not—kowtowing to Tammany.

The counts against him were political as well as administrative, mostly that he had appeased not only Tammany but
also the conservative party elders. How that came out in the
end, everyone would learn who had ever heard of Sheriff
Farley and his little black box or of the playboy Mayor
Jimmy Walker and his forced retirement. Such a reckoning
could not very well occur until the renomination and re-
election in 1930. Breaking with Tammany earlier would have
ended his career. So his circumspection was easily explained
as essential if he was to have any political future at all.

When his accomplishments were looked for later, it could
be seen that, even if he had been a reluctant gubernatorial
candidate, he had soon begun a fruitful love affair with the
Empire State. Perhaps such a passion was latent all along;
after all, Dutchess County had sent him to the Legislature—
and so given him a start—in 1910; and he was a man who
regarded his native land with deep respect.

In his first legislative term he had become well known far
beyond the state for heading a conspiracy against "Blue-
eyed Billy" Sheehan, the utility lobbyist and Tammany's
candidate for the United States Senate. Howe, then an Albany newspaper man, had seen to it that Roosevelt's part in
Sheehan's (and Tammany's) defeat was well publicized.
What was not so well known was that he had worked hard
on conservation measures, had favored labor legislation, and,
in fact, had become a professed progressive, with all that had
meant in the period 1910–12, so much so that Josephus
Daniels had taken him from the Legislature and made him
Assistant Secretary of the Navy, a post he held throughout
Wilson's Presidency.

His governorship, two decades later, had resulted in extensions of these efforts. Most of them were in the Smith tradition and so not especially noted; but no one before him had
ever paid so much attention to the farms, the forests, the hills,

the lakes, and the streams. He watched over them and saw
to their improvement. He journeyed across the state on the
Erie Canal, stopping to take side trips; he talked with politicians, farmers, and businessmen while Eleanor looked into
the dormitories and the kitchens of the state institutions. And
his governor's car, at other times, was seen often in the vicin-
ity of Binghamton, Jamestown, Buffalo, and Watertown.

He had talked the language of the upstate counties. In the
first campaign, Sam Rosenman—who had been assigned by
Al Smith to write Roosevelt's speeches—was amazed when
the candidate spoke extemporaneously on agricultural issues.
He was not so much at home when it came to labor's problems
in Buffalo and Rochester; but he soon improved. Nothing in
New York was alien to him. He cared; and New Yorkers
knew it.

It was sometimes said that he responded feebly to the
Depression; but for handling relief he had Jesse Straus and
Harry Hopkins—Straus, the successful businessman, and
Hopkins, the social worker. The mention of these names is
evidence that he was quicker than most to assess the consequences of the crash in 1929, even if no wiser than others
about what must be done about the following depression—
except to use every resource he could find to help those in
trouble.

Hard times altered the political timetable. Hoover was no
longer a certainty for a second term. The target year for
Roosevelt became 1932 instead of 1936; and this naturally
affected his subsequent conduct in Albany. Even if he had
not understood at once how little one governor could do about
the economic disaster, and consequently had attempted more
than could be accomplished, he quickly had formulated the
rule that the state and its government existed to foster and
to further the well-being of its citizens. In deciding this, he
committed himself to what afterward became the New Deal.

Almost at once his attempts to provide relief for the distressed in his own state were overwhelmed by the vast num-

bers of those who week by week were losing jobs, being put
out of their homes, and finding it hard to provide for their
families. Nothing he could do was enough. Only the federal
government, he was reluctantly forced to admit, had the
necessary resources. Hoover insisted that charity must be
relied on without involving government. Anyone in office
while things are going badly finds it hard to explain why he
cannot find a cure; and it is worse if he does not relieve dis-
tress. Hoover could be held accountable. This was Roosevelt's
opportunity.

During his last term in Albany, it was a matter of luck that
he escaped criticisms for bank failures and the excesses of the
stock exchange. The state's responsibility for regulation had
never really been taken seriously in the past; and, if a governor did little remedial now, he was not much blamed. He
did not understand such matters very well, to tell the truth;
but there were not many others who understood them either.
When factories closed, bread lines extended around city
blocks, and Hoovervilles began to spread, he at least established an emergency relief system. If its insufficiency taught
him how little one state could do, it was a lesson he did not
forget when he became President.

With depression to contend with and a Presidential nomination now imminent, his life as Governor in Albany after
1930 can be imagined. Besides the immense new administrative problems, there were innumerable political conferences
and continuous visitations. These last were not so much of a
change as might be thought. Involvement in national politics
had been quite unavoidable since his first unexpected election, and the pressure increased after his spectacular re-
election in 1930, with the largest majority in the state's history.
At any time after this he was a likely future President; and
his behavior in Albany had to be adjusted to this probability.

Governors would succeed Roosevelt—Lehman, Dewey,
Harriman, Rockefeller. Some would be potential Presidents.
Before Roosevelt, Al Smith had been a candidate; and, fur-

ther back, there had been such others as Hughes, Cleveland, and Seward. Naturally Roosevelt recalled that "Uncle Ted" had begun that way. Albany was, in fact, a possible prelude to Washington for any governor. It became an actual one for Roosevelt.

The glamour of accreting power had often been felt here. The old mansion (there is a new one now) had been built merely to be a convenient place for living, not to be a staging place for national campaigns. It was comfortable in winter, and its porches were cool in summer. They were defaced by wheelchair ramps for Roosevelt's convenience; but then there was no pretension to architectural quality.

Although there were solemn, sometimes desperate, and conniving visitors during his governorship, intent on joining up before too late, there were also Roosevelt children to make a stir, and there were, as well, and perhaps strangest of all, visitors to whom politics was a low trade but to whom a governor in office was a member of the ruling class.

It was in the brownish plush *décor* of the Albany mansion that Roosevelt received reports and gave directions while the Chicago convention went on. When it was over and the campaign had begun, the house was jammed to the roof with party workers and their staffs. Summer ran into fall as the frenzied activities went on. The house was a hopeless shambles; and, when the election was won and the Roosevelts were about to depart, disorganization was complete. When they were gone, the silence was like a physical weight. The house fairly echoed with emptiness. The Lehmans moved in quietly and had a quiet administration.

If ghosts walked in the old house perhaps one of them glided by in a wheelchair, taking an upgoing ramp with deceptive ease, great muscles working under his jacket. Since the house is gone now, the ghost must be gone too; but it is not difficult to imagine this particular wraith, trailing cigarette smoke, pausing an instant, big hands on the wheels, and saying to a visitor: "Know Walter Lippmann? Ask him what he thinks now about that well-meaning fellow in Albany."

Contemporary theorists talk of the states as about to be merged in more rational administrative regions, ones suitable for modern management purposes. Albany may not be the capital of one of these; and for this as well as other reasons it will not then be a staging base for the Presidency. Future Presidents will not be chosen, as have so many in the past, because of being governors of states with large blocks of electoral votes. There may be no more electoral votes; and television will give others with national exposure an advantage. Harriman and Rockefeller lost bids for nomination to such competitors.

Cleveland, who moved on to Washington after a brief tenure in Albany, had no more to recommend him than a reputation for simple honesty, a peculiar virtue in the Buffalo and Albany of his day; Theodore Roosevelt, who became President, did so only because he happened to have been made Vice-President by politicians who wanted to get him out of the state. They were dismayed when McKinley's death promoted him to the White House.

Qualifications had changed. Being Governor of New York was not even Roosevelt's best claim. The Depression had done it. A Presidential candidate, after Roosevelt, would have to say what Roosevelt had been the first to say—that it was the business of government to take care of people and that the federal government must do it. This was made specific during his time. There must be no more spells of national paralysis, the kind that Cleveland had sat out in 'ninety-three and 'ninety-four and that even Theodore Roosevelt had seen no way to do anything about in 1907. It was the President's business to make sure that nothing of the sort happened again. Roosevelt expanded this into what became known as Social Security, a cradle-to-grave insurance for everyone; and even his conservative successors would be forced, not only to accept it, but to extend its coverage.

A governor in 1932 could become President because he had made such promises and had tried to carry them out in one state. Albany was years behind him when he died, but he was the most famous of its Presidential pretenders. It might no longer be so usual for governors to become candidates; but his successors were still measured by his record.

4. *The White House*

The evolution of the Presidency into a ramifying and ever more complex office center went on very rapidly under the compulsions of the 'thirties and was elaborated during the war by emergency administrators, some of whom were even spoken of as Assistant Presidents. Roosevelt himself had to concentrate on strategy; domestic progress was put off until peace should return. The repair after depression, the assumption by government of wholly new duties, and, later on, the world war and the responsibilities of world leadership—all these made the transformation inevitable.

Kennedy's Dallas speech in 1963—the one he never made —would have proclaimed that Americans were "the watchmen on the walls of liberty." He was recognizing something carelessly undertaken and by then in deep trouble. There had been a Marshall Plan for Europe, an Alliance for Progress in South America, and even the remotest countries were being aided in one way or another; but there were accumulating problems, and they were getting worse every year. Kennedy could be thankful for Roosevelt's beginning of governmental rationalization for what was becoming a welfare state. The expansion of White House personnel from a few hundreds in a short time had been somewhat disorderly but no more than was inevitable in the circumstances.

Roosevelt was the bridge—quite a long bridge—from the old to the new. When he took over from Hoover in 1933, the White House itself still overshadowed the offices in its West Wing; when he died in 1945, the house was still the place where the Presidential family lived, at least officially, but the offices had become the center of an immensely expanded operation. There was now an East as well as a West Wing and the new area had housed Byrnes and Hopkins, among others, both of whom, regardless of titles, were regarded as sharing the Presidential power and had their own establishments. Not only that; expansion had inundated the old State, War, and Navy Building across the street.

During the first Roosevelt term, this had still been the State Department's home. Moley and Welles had found it easy to cross from one basement door to another, unseen by newspaper men upstairs; but the expanded Department was intolerably cramped, and a new complex of nondescript buildings was being prepared for it where once there had been only marshes. It would continue to be spoken of as Foggy Bottom. The old building became a White House annex—the Executive Office Building.

In later days, when repeated examinations of the executive establishment seemed to result in almost continuous reorganization, the earliest of these serious appraisals—that made by Merriam, Brownlow, and Gulick in 1937—is only recalled by students of public administration; other studies soon superseded it; but disturbance of old customs was more considerable than resulted from later, more elaborate ones, if only because it was the first that used the apparatus of modern research and had the intention of making the Presidency effective for what had now to be done.

Roosevelt's own conception of the Presidency when he took over from Hoover was well formed. He believed—as Wilson, Theodore Roosevelt, and other "strong" Presidents had—that he must be a strategist as well as an executive; he had, in fact, learned much of this from them. To do everything well he needed a better "office." He thought of an enlarged Cabinet with a small inner group to meet with him, somewhat after the British model; and this was what he developed. It was, however, foreshadowed by various interim devices—the National Emergency Council at first and, later on, the Executive Council and other groups of a similar sort, including the Council of National Defense, with its Advisory Commission.

Then there were many auxiliary services no President had had before. It was he who set up new statistical and reporting agencies, moved the Budget out of the Treasury and made it subordinate to himself, and accepted a like suggestion for the National Resources Planning Board first set up by Harold Ickes as an adjunct to the Special Board for Public Works. He surrounded himself with experts to make the executive reach more knowledgeable.

Besides he sometimes spoke of the President as being a teacher; and this duty too he took seriously. He had the radio for his instrument. He was the first public man who really learned how to use it, speaking to people all over the land when something needed to be said; "fireside chats" became an institution. He knew that a President could count on a vast interest and, indeed, good will, and that he must not allow these to diminish. The confusion, in the American system, of the chief of state with party leadership brought him some criticism; education could easily become politicized; but this was inevitable.

A President, to his mind, must see too that laws were written and passed as well as executed, and that the passing and the executing made the country safer, and more productive, and more just in sharing. Presidents before him had been guided by the conception that productivity was a matter for business alone and that sharing was to be arranged by bargaining. None ever would in future—witness Eisenhower, who tried it and had to reverse himself, and Kennedy, who knew his responsibility but could not find the support he needed. The poor people—black and white—who grieved at Roosevelt's death were evidence of his success.

One of the most unforgettable photographs of the funeral procession down Pennsylvania Avenue showed a black woman standing among the crowd along the curb with tears streaming down a ravaged face. His going was a personal thing for her. Behind those tears was a deeper knowledge than more sophisticated watchers possessed. She sensed intentions he had not said much or done much about. Only a few of those closest to him knew as much as she or others of her kind. Many of those who would come to Hyde Park and Warm Springs as to shrines had the same secret knowledge.

The President who wakes now in the morning to the routines of his office must be conscious of following ones begun by Roosevelt. He must sometimes consider ironically the Roosevelt reputation, while he still lived, of being an inefficient executive, a reputation deliberately risked in the interest of the office he enlarged. Any such change must arouse opposition, cause confusion, and refuse to work well for some time. Roosevelt presided over the confusion with a bland indifference to criticism and with a gaiety that especially infuriated his detractors. But in the end the pattern was set. The Presidency was made more effective.

In repeated storms of angry opposition and calculated ridicule, he tried until he found satisfactory devices. It became fashionable in later years to regard the NRA and the gold-buying adventure of 1933 as infantile mistakes; and boondoggling would not be dropped from Republican speeches for years to come. Republicans also had a few days of pleasure over a phrase in the report on administrative management prepared for him in 1937. It had spoken of the need for assistants "with a passion for anonymity." It seemed ridiculous to connect anonymity with any White House activity. Yet such helpers were exactly what was needed. Their successors are still useful in proportion to the self-effacement they achieve.

The Social Security system, the management of credit emissions and of taxation to maintain economic activity, together with other similar devices, were all Rooseveltian in origin, even if much modified as experience accumulated. No one has ridiculed them for a long time now. Not all of these were his personal inventions, but it was he who locked all of them into the structure of government. If it comes to that, it was not he, either, who invented the good-neighbor concept and spheres of interest as the basis for foreign policy. But he did fight the wearing hand-to-hand battles with the isolationists for the acceptance of these programs; and if his successors failed to implement the one and abandoned the other it would be seen in time that he had been right.

So, when he had long gone from the West Wing, he was still there, in somewhat the same sense that he was still at Hyde Park. There is this difference, of course: Springwood, its house, its library-museum, its fields and trees, are kept so that something of his personality can be felt long afterward by those who would like to understand him better; but the government's center must live and change, and not, on any account, be preserved intact. Upstairs in the White House the Lincoln bed is still pointed out; and associations with Jefferson, Wilson, and Truman are identified. So the West Wing was built by Theodore Roosevelt and put to intensive use by Franklin; the Oval Room, with all his naval prints, later became known for having Kennedy's rocking chair, was the scene of Johnson's tantrums and Nixon's cautious consultations.

Such associations have made the White House a conglomerate shrine for Americans. They sense the ghosts of many men—no women yet—chosen by themselves to carry the burdens of their time. All did what they had the strength and wisdom to do; and even the weakest are honored for efforts if not successes.

Between the East Wing and the West the mansion still asserts a steady dominance. It is there, even more than in the wings, that the Presidency is really alive. It has lost some of the sharp individuality it had in Roosevelt's time. It has been home to his successors less than it was to him. Then it was not so splendid, being well used, inconvenient, and becoming shabby. It was not even very white; there were pipes and wires showing; most of the Roosevelt living went on in what could only be described as a wide corridor upstairs. The Congress always found it easy to neglect the executive establishment. If the speeches by rural representatives denouncing Presidential extravagance were ever gathered together they would make an entire library. An Adams billiard table (bought by himself) became a "gambling device," and Monroe's "fancy French furniture" was evidence of foreign influence. Many Presidents and their wives had been battered into discomfort and inconvenience by a demagogue who found the White House an appealing symbol of pretension.

The Roosevelts were watched all right; and there was the usual criticism; but actually their tastes were simple and homely. It was not evident anywhere that any of the arts were important in their lives. It had not been at Hyde Park or at Warm Springs, and it was not in the White House. There was enough flowered chintz in that immense second-story corridor to have given a professional decorator hysterics. The pictures were the familiar White House portraits; but there were naval prints and photographs too. No Roosevelt was a musician, and the President's idea of a lively evening was a guitar player who could lead the company in familiar songs. But if there were no aesthetics of any account there was gaiety and pleasant talk.

It was the same house, much repaired, that Washington had planned and that Polk, Cleveland, and Uncle Ted had lived in. The Roosevelts had come to it in 1933 very much as though they were coming to a familiar and satisfactory home. It had been in one of its rooms that Cleveland had

said to small Franklin, accompanying his father on a visit to
the President, that it was to be hoped he would never have
the burdens of that office to carry. And it had been there that
the youngish Assistant Secretary of the Navy had been lectured occasionally by schoolmaster Wilson, who had not much
approved of him most of the time.

The traditions of the house lingered on as persistently as
the expanded responsibilities of those who worked in its
wings; but, when the Roosevelts moved in, ramps had to be
constructed for his wheelchair; those raucous chintzes appeared on the furniture; the naval prints and family photographs hid the walls where he worked; and his bedroom took
on an amazing resemblance to the bedroom at Springwood—
even the similar view to the southwest from the windows,
except that it was the Potomac in the distance instead of the
Hudson.

But, if not the physical arrangements, the habits of Eleanor
and Franklin did enrich the traditions of the house. Everyone
who was a familiar had his own recollections—such, for instance, as the relaxation of tea time. There cannot have been
many families by 1933 to whom tea at four and dinner at
eight-thirty were customary. These belonged to an age of big
houses and many servants; and such establishments had not
generally survived the changes of the century. The Roosevelts were survivors in such matters as well as in the commitment to noblesse that softened the age of opulent and less
disciplined living.

No one knew better than the Roosevelts that most Americans did not have an elaborate silver tea service in everyday
use, or such arrangements that the family could gather for
the four o'clock interlude. Often in spring and summer the
cart was wheeled out to the South Portico. The group there
made a storybook scene, mockingbirds in the magnolia, foun-
tain murmuring, and the trees quiet around the spacious
lawns, heavy with foliage in the afternoon sun.

But this was only one. There was the President himself in

a velvet jacket, at table in the family dining room, and only to be described as presiding. There was Eleanor knitting in the upper hall and talking, as her hands flew, about the most serious public issues. Washington society discussed with a certain shocked and reproving discretion how the whole house rocked with laughter as Franklin told a story or heard one from a visitor. But these were not Coolidges or Hardings; they were Hudson Valley Dutch, and the criticism was muted. Two tall people stood to greet a reception line as though it might be a privilege. They were in the people's house; but they belonged there.

Another innovation owed to Roosevelt was Shangri-La, the Camp in the Catoctin Mountains, taken over during the war from the Civilian Conservation Corps as a retreat from Washington pressures. It was not a country estate; it really was a camp in the forest; but every President afterward would find it indispensable. When helicopters became available it would be minutes away. For Roosevelt it was something more than an hour's drive. Eisenhower, characteristically, renamed it Camp David to take away the Roosevelt connotation; but it remains nevertheless what it was first called—Shangri-La. It serves the purpose of Chequers and Rambouillet.

There were many notations made about the family whose energy, personality, and acceptance of duty matched in every way the expectation of a nation passing through deeply troubled years; they were not awed by their duty. It was within their capabilities, and they would see to it as a matter of course.

While they were there it was entirely a Roosevelt Washington. Even the city itself began to grow up to its responsibilities, changing from a Southern town, segregation and all, to a metropolitan capital, one of the busiest and most spacious in the world. It was not yet inundated with immigrants from impoverished Southern farms; it was a little slow, rather tranquil, but stately. It would not stay that way, but no one thought much in 1933 of larger changes to come.

When Roosevelt was brought back from Warm Springs on his last journey and lay in state in the East Room, the American people, all of them, were in shock. Some wept. But others merely endured, dry eyed, the loss no substitution could ever make good. During their whole lives, this would be so. Many people, perhaps more in Washington than anywhere, even after many years, went on speaking of him as "the President." Successors were only substitutes for the real thing, either in the White House or in its wings. This lasted as long as his contemporaries lived, and there were reminders of it in later generations.

5. *The Country*

In April, 1945, when Roosevelt died, a sense of victory was already strong in the country. Except for the combat troops it had been the easiest of wars; early confusion had in time turned into satisfying accomplishment. Millions of men had become soldiers and had been transported to distant battlefields. The remaining workers had, however, amply supplied them with all their needs; more remarkable still, the civilian population had never been able to live so well. Producers were suddenly encouraged to find the best organization; workers who had cultivated the habit of giving as little as they could for as much as they could get had been motivated to give as much as they could for returns they felt were fair. The immense national capacity, for once fully engaged, had shown what could result from earnest effort.

Only a few times in the past had there been such elation as approaching victory brought in 1945. There had been similar ones following other wars; and there were many still living who could recall the national satisfaction after World War I; but it had never happened in other circumstances; and it had never lasted long. All such periods had been followed by letdowns. Going back to peacetime arrangements involved a return to the frictions and wastes of competition and bargaining for the sale of labor. This time too the evaporation of unity was swift.

The Great Depression of 1929 and after had been the direct, if somewhat delayed, result not of World War I but of the following peace. President Wilson had led what he fully believed to be a crusade, and it had been a credible belief. During crusades concern for self is put aside and reserves of energy are called out. Also privileges and rules give way to practicality. There had been an abrupt return, however, to old ways when that war had ended. The War Industries Board had been disbanded; the railroads had been returned to private owners; farmers had been left to dispose as best they could of swollen surpluses; and sullen workers had felt themselves abandoned by the agencies set up to protect their rights. By 1929, the stresses had accumulated until the whole economy was rent by a cataclysm; and that had been followed by paralysis.

Roosevelt, feeling his way, making many mistakes, but refusing to be bound by old rules, had gradually achieved a somewhat better situation. He had not been able to bring about many changes he felt ought to be made; but he had been able to correct numerous abuses. Workers were better able to claim a larger share in productivity, and some of that productivity was now set aside for the welfare of those who before had been dependent on a meager charity.

This was startling progress for a people who had always been convinced individualists; but it still did not supply any such motivation as had been felt so strongly when there had been one objective for all—victory for a way of life they believed in. Technological advances resulting from the wartime effort ought to have increased the national income. The product of each worker had been multiplied by the use of machines, of power, and of management skills; but, in peace, their use was resented because they seemed to reduce the number of jobs and because the resulting economies did not go to employees but to their bosses.

The most peculiar economic characteristic of the decade after that war was the continuous decline of costs accompanied by a sustained level of prices, so that, by 1929, real wages were no higher than before. Consequently, the accumulating goods made by improved methods could not be bought. There was a glut, and no one seemed to know how to relieve it. Hoover and his business friends were convinced that existing economic arrangements were sacred, and they held on until Roosevelt succeeded to the Presidency. The nation had by then been prostrated for nearly four years. It was ridiculous. The potential was there. It had been mobilized to win a war and had achieved miracles of production. The busy facilities of wartime were simply closed down. Chimneys of factories were smokeless, and their gates were locked. Men wandered in the streets looking for work no one wanted them to do.

Roosevelt had insisted that the paralysis was unnecessary; and he had spread purchasing power through relief and public work. So a new start was made. There was, however, a return to withholding, bargaining, suspicion, and competition. Again it was everyone for himself. The between-wars time was a disheartening interlude. Roosevelt was made President largely because of this; but the benefits he secured for the unemployed and the slow resumption of production were nothing to brag about. No one did very well, even though the miseries of the Hoover years were somewhat relieved. Something more was needed.

It was not until gradually, as the menace of totalitarianism in the world was realized, that an objective to be worked for again appeared. Hitler had become head of the German government simultaneously with Roosevelt's inauguration as

President in Washington; Mussolini was already the master
of Italy; and the Japanese dictatorship had passed the point
of possible return. Democracy was openly ridiculed; the world
had not been made safe for it in 1918, as Wilson had promised. The crusade would have to be undertaken yet again.

There was, to be sure, a stubborn reluctance. There were
many who felt that Wilson had been taken advantage of by
European politicians and that the same thing was likely to
happen again. There were others who felt that democracy
had become unworkable: its irresponsibilities, inefficiencies,
and corruptions were the result of systemic permissiveness;
the indiscipline of its workers contrasted with the order and
efficiency in the dictatorships. It might be better to learn
from the new order than to organize its destruction.

The excesses of Hitler, the pretensions of Mussolini, and
the professed intention of the Japanese to conquer all Asia
were pointed out over and over by Roosevelt. After war
began between the Allies and the dictators there was still
resistance to involvement. The Congress approved preparations for "defense" by the narrowest margins, and assistance
to the beleaguered British after the French collapse were
carried out by doubtful assumptions of executive power.

The Japanese at Pearl Harbor stilled American objectors,
and at once the same torrent of energy as had risen in 1918
rose again. It was then seen that the latent potential was still
there. Competition was abandoned, workers had confidence
in governmental protection, and technology was freed everywhere by being furnished with all the capital required for its
installations. The result could realistically be called miraculous. As in the last war, mobilization was accompanied by
rising output; the soldiers were well supplied, yet everyone
else lived better.

Roosevelt presided over this transformation of the economy; but he could pay little attention to it once it had begun
to roll. He was more concerned with the military victory.
Then, when that was assured, he became even more concen-

trated on the organization of the world for keeping the peace. The American power shown in the conflict, on land and sea and in the air, would make it possible this time, as it had not in 1918, to get agreement for an organization of the victors; and that organization would discipline all disrupters of international arrangements.

Concentration on the war and an amazing lift in living levels had concealed some problems sure to emerge when peace returned. How had so much been accomplished? How had American agriculture and industry fed most of Europe and furnished it with munitions, opened ways to supplying the Russians (the terrible Murmansk route and a line from the Persian Gulf to the Black Sea), raised a vast army and built a complete two-ocean navy, and yet increased the living levels of American workers?

It seemed impossible when it was recalled that no longer ago than 1933 farmers had been unable to sell their crops and had been struggling to keep their farms, that factories had been idle, and that financial institutions had been deep in bankruptcy. Could ten years have seen the national production multiplied by so much? The question obviously was: did war and preparation for war bring all this about? And would paralysis again appear when the war was over?

Americans had never given much thought to the future; and they gave no more to it as the war neared its end. Each farmer would have to do the best he could; and each business would have to find its own way to cope with the transition to peace. That was the way it had been after other wars; and it had always ended in depression. The period 1919–23 had been years of letdown for everyone. Industry had gradually recovered by using the technical improvements and new equipment acquired during the war. But, in succeeding years, there had been talk of "profitless prosperity." In the late 'twenties, during the Coolidge Presidency, there had been uncontrolled speculation in Wall Street, a financial bonanza for insiders; but their affluence had not reached farmers and workers, and, of course, the shortage of buying power had ended in the liquidity crisis of 1929, then in the crash.

During these years farmers, especially, had been squeezed. Hoover, as Food Administrator, had encouraged them to expand production. What he had done as Administrator he had refused to acknowledge as President; and one of Roosevelt's first problems had been to see that farmers got some relief. It was late. Many had already lost their farms and moved away. The Okies moving westward were only a better-known example of what was happening elsewhere. When the war ended there were thirty million farmers; ten years later there would be fifteen million; and in another decade, ten. The rest, with their families, would have moved mostly into city slums. And, as seemed incredible afterward, considering the consequences, this vast migration had gone on with no special attention from anyone, certainly not from the national government. The cities had simply become more and more crowded.

Roosevelt's agricultural measures had helped at first; but as always the more enterprising farmers knew how to take advantage of whatever benefits were offered, and the poorer ones did not. It was also a time of technological change. Power and machinery were not only displacing workers but also their horses and mules. Each acre was being made to produce more, and there was sharply reduced demand for what was produced.

The migration from the countryside was even more disturbing than the earlier waves of immigration from Europe. It was more tragic because these were Americans and always had been. Europeans had had modest expectations and were eager workers. These migrants were beaten people, starved out of their traditional employment, forced to find another living place; but there was no need for such as they. If they were supposed to have shared the common expectation of betterment, none of them were aware of it. In Harlem, in Chicago's and Philadelphia's south sides, in Los Angeles'

Watts, in Detroit and Cleveland and Dallas, they were a seething and hopeless mass; they had offspring by the dozens, as had been thought provident in a corn and cotton economy, but who in the cities were a burden.

Then there was maturing a technical and managerial revolution, spread now into every industry from the small beginnings of Frederick W. Taylor's scientific management. If there was a squeeze in agriculture there was a worse one in the factories. It was made easier for some by the arming during the New Deal of organized labor with laws and agencies to assist in collective bargaining. Unions, however, were fast becoming an elite, and a selfish one. They had always held that there was only a limited amount of work to be done, and they meant to have it for themselves and under such terms as their bargaining power could produce. Their exclusion of the migrants was defiant. They were holding to patent fictions of unfitness among outsiders; and they were developing an exclusiveness that matched anything industrialists had ever developed.

Added to these problems was the most serious of all those Roosevelt's successors would inherit. The American Government was obsolete; yet its bureaucrats were so well dug in, and those who benefited from its very obsolescence (because they found it so easy to manipulate) were so influential, that it was regarded as fantastic to suggest any serious reorganization. At the first mention of such a thing, traditional words poured from ready mouths. These included, with no reticence at all, democracy, liberty, justice, independence, free enterprise. Moreover, a slip of the framers now stood as a massive barrier. Amendments to the Constitution could only be initiated by a two-thirds vote in both houses of the Congress. There was the alternative of petition by three-quarters of the states, but it was even more unlikely ever to be invoked; and since any change would not only disturb the Congressmen but would discommode those who held the Congress well in their grip, none was likely to happen—that is, none that really affected the obsolescence.

Roosevelt himself, as soon as the worst fright of the panic years had passed, could no longer persuade the Congress to accept his recommendations. This became a fierce rejection of all his initiatives after the defeat he suffered in 1937, when, after a victorious election, he tried to persuade the Congress that the Supreme Court needed reform. He was in open conflict with the legislative branch from then on. It was a breach his successors would not be able to close—except Johnson for two short years; all the rest of the time, Congressional majorities were held by a stubborn opposition.

The Constitution had no reference to business or industry, to health or well-being, to cities or countryside, to international relationships or world problems. The Senate was as it had been from the first—a compromise, a continuing repudiation of the principle of equal representation; the House of Representatives was run by a clique of elders from safe (and reactionary) districts; and the Supreme Court had just about reached its long-time ambition to become a permanent constitutional convention.

The President was still called the "chief executive"; but execution had long since escaped from control and was exercised in a capricious and uninformed way. Roosevelt had been intent on being commander in chief for years and had left domestic affairs to others. The Presidency had been pluralized without having the change legitimized; there was no one really in charge; and government was more a number of poorly coordinated agencies than one center with purpose and policy.

When peace came, the accumulation of problems was overwhelming; and the means to cope with them were pitifully weak. The situation called for heroic measures and, indeed, for gigantic abilities such as those used to combat the depression and direct the war effort. What the country needed was to get Roosevelt back; what the country got was a county

politician raised to a senatorship by the most corrupt of the
remaining municipal machines and made Vice-President (displacing Henry A. Wallace) in 1944, because the campaign
managers feared defeat unless the party bosses were appeased.

6. *The World*

It might have been expected that the British, for instance,
would be resentful because Americans were so slow to agree
that Hitler's wild aggression was a threat to them as well as
other democracies. Between 1939 and 1941 they felt, and
sometimes said, that they were fighting battles they ought
not to fight alone. After France had collapsed only the small
kingdom in the North Sea had survived; the Swedes were
neutral; and even Ireland, holding to old grievances, refused
assistance. The British were still sturdily defiant, although a
well-known massing of invasion craft was taking place across
the Channel and not many in the United States really thought
England would be able to resist.

Of the few who thought it possible, Roosevelt was one. He
insisted, in spite of military objection, on depleting American
stocks to rearm the soldiers who had abandoned their own
arms on the Channel beaches. He insisted also that ways
must be found to furnish more as speedily as possible. There
were loud dissents from isolationists who said this was gambling with the nation's security. The country was more divided
than about any issue in memory; and it was not at all clear
that a majority inclined toward Britain's cause, much less
favored intervention.

Roosevelt may have been surprised, along with others, at the
gallant success of the Spitfire defense against the German

bombers; but, when the air battle had been won and the danger of invasion had been at least put off, he considered himself sufficiently justified to push again for participation.

It was then that he read Americans the elementary lessons in geopolitics that so many did not care to hear. Not for nothing had he studied Mahan as a schoolboy and served for nearly eight years as a navy administrator. Later, he had encouraged the lengthening of air routes across the oceans, and in other ways had insisted on preparations vital to security. That the underbelly of the United States might be ripped open by aerial invasion from a West Indian base seemed, when he said it, a fantastic exaggeration to sober inland folk. When they thought it over, they were not so sure. But when, at the same time, he spoke of producing fifty thousand planes a year in American factories, it was judged that he could hardly mean what he said. A President of the United States ought not to indulge in such fancies. The comments came close to ridicule. Yet, about this too, there were second thoughts. No further ahead than 1943, the skeptical nation's industries would turn out not fifty thousand but ninety thousand. The President had been right; but there were few to accept his estimate in 1939.

The British followed the President's nudging of Americans toward participation with the anxiety of a people whose survival was involved. Theirs was a lost cause unless the United States joined them; and none knew it so well as the man who had become Prime Minister in the darkest time and had steadily defied the Nazis. From his first day in office, Churchill had spoken of American assistance hopefully and assured his countrymen that their friend in the White House was doing all he could. When aid began to come he acknowledged the vast potential of the nation across the sea by deferring to its commander in chief.

Not all the British were happy to be thus subordinated any more than all Americans were reconciled to having responsibility thrust upon them; and there were those who thought

Churchill's humility no more than a cover for keeping the empire intact. But the two nations and the two leaders were joined by more than preference. Both geography and ideology linked them; and it was a combination the dictators could not withstand.

As the American effort reached its eventual gargantuan size and began to prevail, Roosevelt was still ahead of his countrymen. No one knew better than he the likelihood that victory would have an oversimple meaning to most people; once the enemy was defeated, Americans would most likely go stolidly back to their own affairs, disliking foreign adventure and having done all they had contracted to do. When the war neared an end, Roosevelt, exhausted and nearing death, had to find the energy for one more effort to counter this retreat into isolation. There must be established, with American underwriting, an organization for preventing further wars. The nations must be committed to assisting in the suppression of aggression whenever and wherever it appeared, and the Allies must be similarly committed; only when this was done could there be security.

Roosevelt thought of this assurance as resting on firm agreement among the five great powers—the Soviet Union, China, Britain, the United States, and, eventually, liberated France. But, as the "experts" drafted the plan without his close supervision, it began to resemble the defunct League. What had been simple became complex. Roosevelt had felt that the small nations, if allowed, would become troublemakers. Like the small states at the constitutional convention in 1787, they would, if they could, work themselves into positions not justified by their real power; and presently their politicians would be able to play off the great powers against one another. Roosevelt had no intention of creating another assembly capable of creating contentions but without any disposition to settle them; if this happened, American policy would be determined by others' interests. Such an organization would hardly live beyond its inauguration; and it would be utterly incapable of intervening in disputes among nations.

But the conception that agreement among the big four—or five—would preserve the peace was intolerable to the liberal believers in self-determination as well as to the ambitious politicians of the small nations. What resulted was a body well able and eager to start disputes but not to stop them.

So the rousing of the weary commander in chief to the establishing of an institution for keeping the peace was frustrated by the doctrinaires he had, while alive, meant to keep in subordination. When he died at Warm Springs in April of 1945, before the United Nations had come into being, it was as though the governor of the world's engine had been removed. The little people got their way. The old League, with all its weaknesses, was in effect re-established. Self-determination was again the principle of organization. Just as Vermont had as many senators as California, Ecuador had the same representation in the Assembly as the United States; and a few years later it was able to legislate. The Security Council was not what Roosevelt had projected—a place for the meeting of the great powers, for settlement of their differences, and for agreement to discipline unruly members.

This had not been the dominant principle at Yalta. There the controlling agglomerations of power were face to face. They found each other amenable to reason. Their mutual respect was based not only on knowledge of each other's strength, but on a sense of the responsibility each had demonstrated. This amounted to an allocation of spheres of interest. This arrangement had once been called a balancing of power. It had its reasons now; the United States and Russia each possessed a continent. Neither needed any resource monopolized by the other. To keep peace between themselves it was only necessary that each should recognize the other's area of interest. Obviously this ignored the missionary impulse latent in each to bring the world's people into ideological submission. But the activists were minorities, and the war had been a cooperative effort that might well last.

Churchill was present too. But he spoke from a declining imperial strength, now being constricted between two consolidated nationalities. His right to speak had rested on sea power; that was now giving way to an air power he did not control. British dominions were now overleapt every day by intercontinental planes, very rapidly improving, and capable of carrying absolute weapons. Churchill, with all his cleverness and eloquence, was reduced, between Roosevelt and Stalin, to a hopeful playing off of one against the other. They, being aware of this, regarded him as a man with obsolete interests whose intentions need not be respected. They were the genuine principals. The hard fact was that the British Empire was fragmented; also it was not British and what might repair the fragmentation was not recoverable.

Stalin and Roosevelt felt that they understood each other. Even politically, unlikely as that may seem at first, each was disposed to concede the other what was necessary to his position of leadership. Neither believed the other likely to depart from the reality of national self-interest, and so they could talk with what afterward seemed a most unlikely lack of restraint.

To them it was merely extending an existing situation. If the capitalists and communists each pretended to world dominion, the pretension had not necessarily run to secular rule; and so, when the statesmen got down to cases, it seemed only a minor annoyance. Such matters ought not to be allowed to divert attention from the hard realities of geopolitics. These tough realists would not allow such differences to torment the coming decade. Roosevelt wanted the United Nations to formalize this cooperation. He also wanted recognition that China and France must join the other three; they must because they were in the same kind of situation. There was the difficulty about France that she had unaccountably collapsed in a kind of national fright at the first show of

Germany's might. She had not earned a place in the Allies' counsels. About China there were as yet no such reservations even by Stalin, who knew well enough that Chiang Kai-shek was an anticommunist dictator. As for Germany, the proved troublemaker, there must be such an arrangement as would make further aggressions impossible. What better than to agree on a probationary period and set up a four-power supervisory force?

That this easy understanding would break down in the after-war bickering over a new government for Poland and other such issues neither principal evidently anticipated. It would not be difficult to meet and argue out any such differences, recognizing, finally, that strategic imperatives must be allowed their way. This, for Russia and the United States alike, was the development of their continental domains. There were no actual differences of interest.

At Yalta the two super-greats, Russia and the United States, carried a reluctant Britain into this arrangement and planned the final defeat of Japan.

The United Nations as proposed by Roosevelt was agreed to. Germany was to be made impotent by disarming; the Italians and Japanese were to be confined again to their own smaller spheres. Until, perhaps after a generation, the discipline imposed after defeat had civilized them, the enemy nations were to have no say in governing the world. The United Nations was to have an Assembly, but only for discussion; the permanent Council of great powers was to make decisions and exercise control.

When Roosevelt died at Warm Springs he was considering the speech to be made when the world organization came into actual being at San Francisco. He had already had his first difference with Stalin; but both were politicians, and they would find a common policy. The others did not really count. Britain was clearly shrunk now from imperial greatness to inferior dimensions, and China was in the confusion customary throughout its entire history.

That this conception depended on some fatal fallacies was not yet apparent. These had their origin not only in mis-judgment of the Russian and Chinese future; but in the lack of realization that, without Roosevelt's leadership, Americans would not accede to the conditions and would, in fact, fol-low a different course. Very deep in their ideology was self-determination. It went back to their own rebellion. It had actuated Wilson's insistence on a fractionalized Europe at Versailles. Roosevelt himself had insisted on independence for the Philippines in a hostile neighborhood; and he had refused interferences in the Caribbean when common sense called for them. Integrated world control was quite con-trary to the American—indeed, to his own—concept of inde-pendence for all peoples. He was, in fact, being inconsistent; but he had often been inconsistent before and had in the end adopted the more sensible course. His conception of world organization represented a triumph of practicality over inherited idealism.

What Roosevelt left to his successor was an arrangement for the peace to come that still had to be made operational and was unacceptable to his own progressives. The war was in the way of being won, but what would happen afterward was not likely to be consistent with the pattern he had in mind. He also left a people convinced by their exhibit of might that they were invincible. There had never been such self-confidence or, it has to be admitted, such self-satisfac-tion. And there had never been such a mistaken national no-tion of how it had all come about. The American intention was to go back to the internal arrangements of the late 'thirties, forgetting that the paralysis of the early 'thirties had been no more than partly overcome until the stimulus of war had come along. There was no Roosevelt to warn them, and this was an irresistible impulse.

Politicians very simply responded. They disestablished the disciplines and cooperative arrangements of wartime. They insisted on bringing home and dispersing the armies; and they refused to continue the assistance depended on by the Allies. Above all they would enter only with suspicion any contracts with the other powers—especially the communist ones. It was the general view that Russia might have had a mutual interest with the United States in defeating Germany but was not to be trusted in peacetime endeavors to keep the peace.

This fear of communist penetration was only slightly less because of having had a common cause. Throughout the interwar period it had been spreading. The Red-hunt during Wilson's last months in office led by Attorney General A. Mitchell Palmer had been a sinister expression of hatred having its source in the twin ideologies of Christianity and free enterprise. Both of these were repudiated by the Russians. Both were attacked not only within Russia but in other nations by revolutionary organizations fostered by Moscow. Communist parties had formidable support in France and Italy. In the United States the number was small, but there did exist a nucleus of professed revolutionaries directed from Moscow.

Such a frank intention to overthrow a government would be intolerable in any nation; but in one whose deepest professions were rejected and whose institutions were to be uprooted, the reaction was frantic. Its adherents must be exterminated. Wilson had been Presbyterian and a Progressive —that is, a believer in regulated capitalism—and his war had been fought to make democracy, not the spread of communism, safe for all peoples. Even when the war in Europe was over, an American army had gone to Siberia to bolster the enemies of communism within Russia. It had not helped the White Russians much; but it had shown where Americans stood.

After a generation of indoctrination in the evils of a communism whose tentacles reached out into every possible nucleus and which was governed by ferocious repudiation of all principle, Americans were not prepared by a brief association in war to accept these terrorists as friends. Whatever peace they agreed to would be one calculated to forward their cause. What was known as trust in the West would be regarded by communists as an opportunity for subverting the entire system.

Since the Roosevelt conception depended on internal confidence as well as self-interest, it would be accepted by Americans only with the most rigorous guarantees of good behavior. These the Russians were not prepared to give Truman. They were still communists, still had pretensions to empire, and would use every opportunity not only to safeguard their country but to cause dissension in others standing in the way—with the ultimate object of overthrowing democracy and capitalism. Only Roosevelt could have engineered the necessary softening and seen to their acceptance at home.

III
How It Was
Twenty-five Years Later

1. *Places and Presidents*

> . . . *in the decade of the '60s the Federal government*
> *spent $57 billion more than it took in taxes. . . . In that*
> *same ten-year period we witnessed the greatest growth*
> *of crime, the greatest increase in inflation, the greatest*
> *social unrest in America in 100 years. Never has a na-*
> *tion seemed to have had more and enjoyed it less.*
>
> RICHARD NIXON,
> State of the Union Address, January, 1970

Of all the places made familiar in one way or another by
Roosevelt's presence, Springwood at Hyde Park was least
changed in the years after his death. At that time it was already a library-museum; now it was a national shrine; but it
looked about the same except for some gates and paths
needed to accommodate visitors. From the highway a quarter
mile of road led to the parking area through an apple or-
chard; but the big house still stood as he had had it rebuilt,
its back to the slope leading down toward the river, looking

69

somewhat English but somewhat Dutch too. It might not have been found in either of those countries; its American character was unmistakable from the outside just as it was inside—comfortable but not really opulent or spacious or having any recognizable style. Inside there was a good deal of painted wood and the only marble to be seen surrounded the fireplaces on either side of the big added room to the south.

Roosevelt, his puckish humor at work, took some pains to see that the Vanderbilt estate a few miles north, was made a national monument too. It was not, he said, that anyone who had lived there was in any way worth remembering; it was just that the place represented such a contrast to the old Dutch places along the Hudson! It was lavishly French; everything within and without was marble, or something more expensive if it could be found. It was filled with European treasures; it was paneled, sculpted, carved, and cunningly shaped; but it was no more American than the vast Schwab chateau on Riverside Drive or the Fifth Avenue palaces of the gilded age. He thought it ought to be preserved so that later generations could see what extravagances the inheritors of vast untaxed fortunes had been capable of. He also enjoyed pointing out how uncomfortable it must have been to have lived up to all that splendor and how little pleasure all the activities of its owners must have yielded—this in contrast with Springwood.

The Warm Springs complex, unlike that at Hyde Park, had become unrecognizable. The hospital was much enlarged with funds from the annual March of Dimes; but it no longer treated many victims of polio. That disease had almost vanished; it had become something impossible for a new generation to appreciate. Every summer in the past there had been a lurking terror in parents' minds lest the annual epidemic lodge this year in their families, perhaps leaving a child crippled, if indeed he survived. Lifting such a fear was valued by those who could recall what it had been like; but there were few of those after a quarter-century. There was no more need to be grateful for its disappearance than for the extirpation of smallpox or the plague in a forgotten past.

An association of Georgians had been formed to make the Roosevelt cottage a shrine similar to that at Hyde Park. There were many reasons for recalling him there besides the rehabilitation center. When he had been Governor, and then President, he had come often to this remote and pleasant place on the slope of Pine Mountain. The house he had built was simple and small. Its rooms were ship-cabin size. In its galley, Daisy Bonner had cooked for only a few people; when there were more they had been sent down to the hospital dining room or taken to one of the barbecues or picnics that were always happening. There was a deck looking westward across the pines where the air was resinous when there was sun.

There was no more farm. That experiment had disappeared altogether. As a corner was turned on the way to Dowdell's Knob or further along the mountain ridge toward the valley where the Calloway Gardens were, a guide or an old inhabitant would say, perhaps, that the Roosevelt farm had been over there on the right; but there would be nothing to see.

The country roads where he had liked to drive his small automobiles were mostly hard-topped now, and a cloud of yellow dust no longer hid a following car as it once had that of the secret service men who had had to keep the President within view.

The way to the cottage in his day had been up a skimpily graveled lane from the institution below. Visitors now, coming to it from a regraded highway, found themselves in a small, piney picnic area. They walked to the Little White House from a new direction. They never caught sight of the institution; but they could visit an adjoining cottage given to the Association by a lady whose recollection went back to the time when Pine Mountain had been a summer retreat for escapees from Columbus' river-valley heat. It had been made into a museum and was filled with the curios visitors find so fascinating.

As for the other places associated with Roosevelt—the Albany mansion and the White House—neither was as it had been. The Lehman governorship had been a quiet one, relatively speaking, for the state. He had been a decent and adequate incumbent. In late years, however, Rockefeller had been a restless administrator. The square old mansion had been replaced by one suitable for the Empire State; and the bureaucracies now filled many new Albany buildings. A vast new system of higher education had its center there. So did the expanding welfare services, although an inquirer might well have thought New York City the capital instead of Albany, so much administration was done there.

In Washington there were changes too, although the new White House had the same outward appearance as the old one. In Truman's time that structure had seemed likely to collapse. It had been so many times patched, rewired, repiped, undermined, and added to that it creaked with its own weight. It had been entirely rebuilt. The Roosevelts had managed to give their living quarters, at least, a domestic atmosphere. It was now unsuited for family life and successors had spent more and more time elsewhere. They no longer had to drive first through the busy streets of central Washington. Helicopters took them to nearby airfields where Air Force One was always available—a great bird with special fittings—to take them elsewhere. Truman went to Key West, Eisenhower to Palm Springs or Augusta, Kennedy to Hyannisport or Palm Beach, Johnson to his ranch on the Pedernales in Southwest Texas, and Nixon to Biscayne Bay in Florida or San Clemente in California. They could go anywhere in a few comfortable hours—a striking contrast with the way Roosevelt had moved about on trains, taking days to reach the Pacific Coast and overnight even to reach Hyde Park.

All, however, found Roosevelt's Catoctin Mountains retreat convenient. It was not, of course, a real residence; its origin as a Conservation Corps camp was obvious in spite of its elaborate civilizing. American Presidents must have been the only heads of state in the world not provided with a country house; they were, besides, the only ones whose official residence was invaded every day by a horde of visitors. It was touted as the premier tourist attraction of the capital, and although the sight-seers were kept to the public rooms and the hours were limited, there was always an uneasy feeling that the downstairs rooms belonged to the shuffling hundreds of visitors. If this had bothered the Roosevelts they had not let it be known; but in their time the volume of traffic had not been so overwhelming; and during the war years there had been ample excuse for limiting it severely. In its new resplendence it had become an authentic showpiece of history; but it was no sort of place to live or to work.

The Presidency was made different by the development of responsibilities Roosevelt had been the first to assume: the welfare of all citizens; added protection for their rights and needs; expansion of leadership until every legislative proposal of any consequence originated in the White House —and this included the more meticulous budget; also assumption by the President of powers far exceeding those exercised in the pre-Rooseveltian times. Presidents now disposed the armed forces in support of foreign policy and even started and directed conflicts indistinguishable from war— as in Korea and Vietnam. The President had become a temporary Emperor-King with all the appurtenances of royalty—except privacy.

What historians would say of the quarter-century following Roosevelt's death, it seemed, was no more than that the nation had survived the gross mistakes and misdirections of his successors. Neither the sinister threat of nuclear war nor the risks of containment had resulted in the catastrophe so often predicted; but the cost of maintaining military forces necessary to the world-wide deployment had come to dominate the nation's economy. In Southeast Asia wars had been carried on whose only result was to leave the "protected" people with governments as dictatorial as they would have had anyway and far more corrupt. An army was still camped in Germany, not to keep the Germans from misbehaving, but to protect these former enemies from one-time American Allies, the Russians. It was not a credible defense; but it reassured the Europeans.

In the United States it would be noted that, in spite of the military burden, advances in productivity had enabled the levels of incomes to rise. Much of this had been illusory, since gains were steadily lost to inflation, and social costs had not been charged against the profits; but still people were better off. The most talked-of problem in 1970 was not the still-threatening danger of nuclear war but the looming possibility of being overwhelmed by pollution from industrial "advance." The chimneys everyone would have liked to see smoking in 1934 were now castigated for smoking too much.

Progress was a doubtful credit. There might turn out to be fatal elements in the apparent triumph of technology. It was not only in Vietnam that the nation was bogged down; the situation was even worse in the proliferated slums at home. Vietnam could be withdrawn from but not New York or Chicago.

2. *Disarray Abroad*

The decade is ending and there can be little argument that the 1960's was a time of turmoil, of bitter protest and brutal violence, of confusion and finally of near despair over the American destiny.

Time, December 19, 1969

From up there the world looked too small for all those divisions.

WILLIAM A. ANDERS,
commenting on his view of
earth, from half-way to the moon

During the twenty-five years since 1945, world order had not been achieved; nor, in fact, had any way been found to prevent resorts to war when small nations disagreed or when demagogues or generals threatened to displace each other. Among the great powers, capable of mass destruction, there existed only what was called deterrence, meaning that each was capable of retaliating if attacked and that each pretended, at least, a willingness to extinguish millions of people on the other side in order to prevent the humiliation of submission.

Of the five nations with nuclear weapons—the United States, the Soviet Union, Britain, France, and China—not all had deterrent capabilities; not yet, anyway. Britain's armament was no more than supplementary to that of the United States, that of France was rudimentary, and that of China was in process of development. The situation, in fact, was that the United States and Russia faced each other with ample weaponry to make good the threats offered in their verbal defiances of each other. It was a temporary situation, and its continuation balanced precariously on mutual distrust.

Item: There existed a genuine strategic standoff. Russia and the United States, on opposite sides of the world, could certainly destroy each other; but neither could do this without being itself destroyed in return. If one fired a first salvo it would decimate the enemy; but it would trigger an equally destructive blow at the aggressor's vitals. To attack was to accept casualties numbered in many millions. Immense sums were being spent by both, and their best technologists were making certain that the enemy could be assured of destruction if it attempted a pre-emptive strike. Therefore both uneasily maintained costly arsenals of genocidal weapons, tended with care, maintained at operating efficiency—using something like half the productive capacity of each—and completely immobilized.

The two superpowers were kept in this ridiculous posture by inability to make mutual accommodations. Meanwhile, however, as Americans were guarding Western Europe and Southeast Asia, and were quarreling openly among themselves about it, the Russians were edging into a superiority that might soon be sufficient for a first-strike success. If so, the time was not far off when the threat of annihilation could be used by the Russians to impose their will on the West. Quite soon, the Soviets hoped, they would be able to establish a defense against incoming missiles. Moscow would then become the world's capital, communism its religion, and state capitalism its economic system. Americans would have to accept disciplines on penalty of extinction. No one doubted that their imperialist ambitions, fortified with communism, would steel the Russians to the necessary massacre.

The United States until recently had had more and better weapons; but having more was not significant if Russia also had enough. The contest was carried on by a matching that had gone through many stages and had got to be a ghastly game. Each decided how far it could go in pushing national interests without provoking the other to attack. Americans, however, were faltering. They were questioning the immense cost of matching the Russian defense. Dissenters were demanding that resources so long used for military purposes be diverted to education, welfare, and environmental cleansing. This was a trouble the Soviets seemed not to have, and it seemed quite possible that before long they could count on a sacrifice, tolerable in their terms, that would destroy the capitalist society they had been taught to abhor and still leave them with a nucleus for making a new start.

The contest rose to war on some borders and approached it everywhere. The Russians were penetrating the Mediterranean, pursuing an old yearning to escape their ice-locked northern confinement. Two immense fleets, in those small seas, were maneuvering provocatively, often within sight, always within sound, of each other. In this too, the advantage was swinging to the Russians. Their navy was being built up, the Americans' was being reduced; and the United States had managed to alienate the Arabs, who welcomed the Russians as protectors against the Israelis, whose existence was guaranteed by the United States.

The differences between the United States and Russia, aside from ideology, seemed out of proportion to the risks being taken. The Mediterranean was the only area where contact was physical. It could roughly be said that each controlled a continent and that the interests of each in the other's continent were slight. If ever there was a situation calling for accommodation, this would seem to be it; but containment was the opposite of accommodation, and it was being pursued at vast expense and enormous risk.

On the borders in Southeast Asia the United States had challenged both penetrators and had succeeded in denying them, temporarily, half of Korea and half of Vietnam. That these were futile efforts was becoming clear; and American forces were in fact being withdrawn with nothing gained. Once involved, there had seemed no way out, it was now being found in the humiliation of retreat.

Item: In the Near East, bordering the Mediterranean, the Adriatic, and on into the Indian Ocean, each great power did have satellites. Those of the Russians were more understandable than those supported by the United States. They were either bordering countries or ones controlling the ports beyond the Bosporus; in those warm waters the Russians had for centuries meant to dominate.

The United States had inherited the British responsibility in that area, not for the reasons the British had had during the colonial era—to keep the way open to India—but as part of the containment policy—to keep communism within bounds. The two powers were facing each other there more dangerously than anywhere else. The Russian influence in the Arab world had been the mirror image of American and British support for Israel. That Jewish state, established on a narrow desert shore, had expelled Palestinian natives to make way for incoming Jews. These Palestinians, after some twenty years, were still living with their descendants in refugee camps. Israel was sustained by gifts from world Jewry and by the continuing favor of the United States. Two-and-a-half million Israelites were surrounded by a hundred million Arabs, who were dedicated to excising them from what they regarded as their territory.

What was more and more clearly in prospect was Russian control of the Mediterranean through Moslem allies. American bases were being closed, Russian ones were being established. How Western domination could be maintained it was impossible to see. Certainly Iran, Greece, and Turkey would not stop the Russian advance; and Israel was a liability. The United States had allowed its policy in that part of the world to be determined by a minuscule nation whose creation it had

supported because of its convenience to politicians seeking
Jewish votes; also perhaps because a Jewish state was a way
for British and Americans to escape guilt for years of discrimination at no inconvenience to themselves—only to the
Palestinians. A counter of vast importance in the future strategic bargain had been lost for a reason of no importance to
the national interest. The Israelis were a courageous and
admirable people, and support for them might end in an
American accommodation with the Russians, who were arming and advising their enemies; but the confrontation involved just such a dangerous one as Roosevelt had anticipated unless the great powers formed an alliance.

Item: In Europe, to the North, the maneuvering on the
borders had likewise become unmanageable. Only half of
Germany was allied with the West. The other half was the
most orthodox and intransigent of all the Russian satellites.
It was to prevent emigration to the West that a wall had
been built down the entire length of the border. It was
manned by savage guards. It had effectively prevented the
escape of unwilling communist captives.

Western Germany and other countries from Denmark to
Italy were members of a military alliance formed to oppose
further Soviet advance toward the West. It had been formed,
and continued to exist, as the forward bulwark of American
defense. All the member countries had regained a certain
economic prosperity through American assistance—beginning
with the Marshall Plan—but France, its central member, in
spite of colonial losses, retained Napoleonic delusions of
grandeur and refused to sacrifice any part of fancied hegemony to mutual management. De Gaulle, dominant in France
from 1958 to 1968, had insisted on an independent military
posture—including nuclear capability— not supported by his
country's strength; and France was rapidly surpassed in productivity by West Germany. He withdrew from the Euro-

pean alliance in 1966 and expelled his former allies from their French bases. He was gone by 1970; but his policy had contributed to German recovery, and it seemed more and more likely that once again that nation, perhaps reunited, would have to be reckoned the premier European power.

A Common Market organization had been formed with the purpose of establishing a Western Europe for economic purposes whose potentialities were at least as great as those of the United States. It lacked only the cooperation afforded by common government. On this, de Gaulle had scornfully turned his back, also refusing entry to Britain whose relation to the United States, he said, was that of a satellite. He also regarded a proposed European political community as an Anglo-Saxon conspiracy to dominate Europe. Now his successor faced the prospect of quite another domination.

Western Germany prospered most. There were not only the advantages of managerial skills and traditional workmanship but the prohibition, set up by the Allies, of military expenditure through a long recovery period. Without this burden and with assistance from the United States, the nation had become the most productive and orderly of the European nations—and again a potential source of aggressive expansion, at least to the Russian view.

Meanwhile Britain, former ally, bereft of colonies and with even the commonwealth virtually extinct, became a problem. Productivity failed to match the welfare expenditures demanded by a strong labor party; bankruptcy was so near that retreat from all old responsibilities was in rapid and disorderly progress now with the Tories in control.

What had to be said of this onetime center of world power, controller of the seas, protector of the peace, and senior among imperial nations, was that the British had quite suddenly become incapable of supporting themselves in the fashion they felt themselves entitled to. The United States, being anticolonial, had encouraged, even urged, the dissolution of the empire. The British economy had been exhausted and impoverished by winning a war that had enriched the defeated enemies. Britain had become a shrunken imperium, having spent her strength in world ventures and bequeathed her responsibilities to the United States.

The British aspiration to join the Common Market was opposed by a considerable minority who feared subjection to other customs and thought the unspoken American connection worth more in any crises that might be anticipated. It had happened before—twice in recent history—and the tie was very strong. The community being shaped on the continent, however, was very close, and it could hardly be ignored. The choice was a hard one, and the American descendants were distant even in a technological time.

Item: China had been alienated by a series of miscalculations. In the years before Pearl Harbor, Japan had undertaken to bring the whole of Southeast Asia within what was deceptively called a "co-prosperity sphere"—meaning that it would be developed with Japanese as overlords. This required, among other ventures, the conquest of China, which had been well under way when an inflated nationalism had led to the calculation that the United States, on her Eastern flank, would need to be immobilized. This accomplished, disorganized Asia could be brought into a system whose capital would be Tokyo.

The United States had been so hostile to this development that no accommodation seemed possible. The conquest was going well enough; but at a certain stage the Philippines, the Dutch East Indies, and French Indochina would necessarily be next, after China itself. This proved to be more than could be sustained; and Japan's defeat in World War II, after challenge to the United States, had left a chaotic situation throughout Southeast Asia; all the new nations were struggling hopelessly with insoluble economic problems. Worst of all, it had left China to be fought over by contenders with very different ideas of development. In this contest the United States had backed the losing one.

The immense effort in the Pacific had freed the small nations from the Japanese but had left them open to the later penetrations of the also freed Chinese. When China was committed to communism the "liberation" of these nations became an ideological mission joined in by the Russians. This presently became a contest between the missionaries. Communism being a thin cover for imperialism, its different interpretations were enlarged, and each called the other "deviationist."

The United States, having checked Japanese expansion, having seen the chosen side in China defeated and the communist winners become aggressive, compounded the mistakes already made by defending the nations on the south from penetration. Their own resistance for the most part was feeble; the United States was a far-off alien power with enormous logistical problems; and the communists had only to make thrusts from bordering provinces. It seemed hopeless to the victims.

During the years after the war, when these maneuvers were in progress, leaders in the United States appealed to several old traditions. One was opposition to the spread of communism, a totalitarian doctrine with a ruthless style repellent to democrats, and one, moreover, with the expressed intention of conquering the world. Americans involuntarily shuddered at the prospect.

Another firm ideal appealed to was the doctrine of self-determination. This had replaced, in American minds, the governing ideas of the empire era—that of spheres of influence. Just as all men must be equal, so must all nations. The definition of nation, however, was so indefinite that almost any ethnic or tribal group, however small, could claim its protection. The United Nations expanded permissively. There were, by 1970, one hundred and twenty-six members, some of them counting their citizens by thousands rather than millions; and all of them, again by American initiative, were now allowed to vote.

When these convictions brought Americans to the defense of the new nations on the communists' southern border, the first field of action was Korea; but the same impulse brought an expeditionary force into South Vietnam. There seemed for a while to be equally active threats to other Indo-Chinese nations and, worst of all, to populous India; but, since it was gradually realized that the defense of this enormous territory would be beyond any possible capability even of so rich a nation, the necessity for withdrawal had, reluctantly, to be discussed.

Colossal efforts had moved armies into South Korea and later into South Vietnam; but the military forces committed to this duty were not to make conquests; they were to assure protection from communist imperialism and then withdraw. Since protection proved to be impossible for geographic reasons if for no other and was confused by native guerrilla movements so extensive as to make it uncertain that the immense efforts would in the end result in anticommunist governments, retreat from the responsibility would have to be total. Nothing undertaken by Americans in the past had ever had such a result. Recriminations flew; blame was assessed; the nation was torn apart.

———

Item: Closer neighbors of the United States were disillusioned. All but one of the South American "republics" had become dictatorships, mostly military; representative institutions had not survived the troubles of recent years. Agriculture had improved, but not much; and there were massive movements away from farms; industrialization had been slow; population had gone on increasing; and the highest rate of increase had been among the poorest people. The small as well as large cities lost their unique character and became centers of spreading slums.

What had become of Roosevelt's Good Neighbor policy? Kennedy had given it a new name—the Alliance for Progress —and had tried to enlist the wealthy elite of each country in a joint effort; but the resistance had proved impossible to overcome. None of the hopes had materialized. Immense sums had been given for aid, but the needs so far exceeded the assistance that miseries multiplied; and the rich country to the north was blamed. Its businessmen were called exploiters, and their properties were so liable to expropriation that reluctance to go on investing was understandable. There was so much ill-will that, year by year, the Congress reduced appropriations for the various attempts to improve agriculture, education, and public works.

The allocation of blame had become so specific and so bitter that no prominent official dared visit South America. The few who had gone—one had been Vice-President Nixon —had been lucky to escape with their lives. Such hatred did not have to be deserved. It simply existed. If the United States had been equally poor, all would have suffered together. It was the contrast and the frustration that festered in Latin minds; but assisting the impoverished was not what the influential people wanted. They wanted prosperity on their own conditions, and they wanted their affluent neighbor to supply it. Both poor and rich were embittered.

The degeneration had gone so far that by 1970 no one had much hope of reversal.

Item: The continent of Africa could realistically be described as a shambles. Pursuing the dominant theory of self-determination, the empires (except Portugal, still holding on) had liquidated their colonial administrations—although many of the same businesses with large investments continued to exploit mines and other sources of raw material. There were numerous small nations, obviously not viable. Their people still held to tribal loyalties, and civil war was everywhere either potential or active. Their economies were as primitive as their civilizations. Their elites occasionally threw up a demagogue who had studied law in Europe; but the corruption of his regime was usually so flagrant that a military clique soon took over and held power until another overthrew it in turn. Since here too the population grew at a rate no advances in the economy could sustain and since there was little or no education, the pools of unemployable youths became larger and larger and more and more violent.

On the northern coasts, of course, were the Moslems, whose problems were the same but whose fanaticisms were different. The black nations below the Sahara resented their own poverty; but the Arabs were sustained by a special hate for the supporters of Israel. In neither region was modernization making enough progress to provide the approach to decent living promised over and over by their politicians.

Below the black countries the South Africans were as prosperous as any nation in Europe, made so by a disciplined and devoted citizenry; but they were deliberately excluding some three-quarters of the inhabitants who happened to be black. Their efforts to prevent being overwhelmed by the proliferation of colored neighbors were desperate but were obviously going to fail at some not very distant time. They would be engulfed by sheer numbers. Besides, they had gradually become international outlaws, and this was likely to interrupt trade if black minorities in Western countries could prevail.

Item: The third world—those people who had abstracted themselves from the European empires—were suffering helplessly from the ills more advanced peoples were at least combating. They had largely reverted to tribalism or to ethnic enclaves and thus had rejected the opportunities afforded by larger organization. They existed on sparse handouts from the more affluent economies of their former rulers. Practically all had been wrenched away from early attempts to operate democratic institutions. Dictatorships were universal.

Public health measures had modified the death rate but not the birth rate and had overcrowded primitively culti-vated lands. The surplus pouring into the cities found no employment; there were few public facilities; and even sani-tation and water supplies were lacking. The African slums were indistinguishable from those of South America. Obvi-ously there must be common causes.

These cities had an exaggerated likeness to those in the advanced countries. The crowding seemed to have reached a limit, yet there was in all those regions no adequate means for stopping the rot. Resources were lacking; there was little education; managerial talent did not exist. Even the assist-ance from without tended to dry up year by year as the larger nations tired of pouring aid into ungrateful communi-ties where no effort was made to cure the besetting ills. Mili-tary dictatorships were not much more stable than elected representatives. Officers quarreled among themselves, made temporary alliances, and soon overthrew anyone who was elevated to the Presidency.

There was no explosion in prospect with regeneration to follow. There was a slow inexorable deterioration, and neither the willingness nor the means for reversal were visible.

———

Item: The United Nations had fallen deeper and deeper into a kind of helpless state of inaction. Since the United States had moved to enlarge the powers of the Assembly and re-duce those of the Security Council, neither body had had any; the Assembly was controlled by minor nations inclined to embarrass the large ones; and the large ones carried out their negotiations in other places. The innocuous resolutions passed each year were respected by no one.

What had been intended as a meeting place for respon-sible nations, able to advance international law and keep the

peace, now swarmed with minor politicians from the dictatorships of the underdeveloped world. It had lost its meaning as an international institution. This, of course, was the
fault of those great powers responsible for its establishment.
They had not been united; they had been implacably competitive; and the United Nations had from the first been no
more than a forum for their mutual accusations. These had
finally become so tiresome that no one listened, and even
that usefulness disappeared, so far as they were concerned.
When they had some practical negotiation to pursue they
went to Helsinki, Vienna, or another place free from the diplomatic smogs of the United Nations.

This was so tragic an outcome of the movement for international organization, now generations old, that many suggestions were made for reorganization, for making a new
start; but none was able to enlist enough support from the
cold war antagonists to provide any hope of acceptance.

There was, for instance, the Clark-Sohn plan, put forward
by Grenville Clark and Louis Sohn and described in their
book *World Peace Through World Law* (Harvard University Press, 1966). The proposal would have provided for
weighted representation in the Assembly, giving the great
powers voting strength more nearly in accord with their
population and productivity. The Assembly then would have
elected an Executive Council, but in it China, India, the
United States, and Russia would have permanent members,
and four of the eight next largest nations would always be
represented. During the 'fifties there was much discussion of
this and of other proposals, but nothing was done; and, when
the nuclear confrontations were fully operative, the organization for international cooperation had no part in whatever
exchanges looking to coexistence that took place.

Item: During the quarter-century since 1945, then, there had
been a succession of catastrophes and continued estrange-

ments. Old arrangements were gone, new ones were unstable and unreliable. The monstrous bomb overhung the world; mass murders of unexampled depravity still tormented consciences; the old empires had disappeared and communist ones were being put together; the United States pursued the penetrations of other parts of the world incidental to the automatic expansions of technology; and it often caused the same reactions where it assumed control of enterprises. In reality the cold war was a Russian-American competition. Whatever effect it had on those within the respective spheres of interest was incidental. It must be said that the Russians were brutal and aggressive in a way the Americans would not have been allowed, by public opinion, to be. But it was a brutal world; and unless some civilized resistance appeared in the Soviet Union, the United States would continue to be the loser.

Besides all this, new economic and political theories were displacing older ones in America; there were very few sturdy farmers left, but there were millions of displaced persons and millions more, many of them youths, who could find no place in the new scheme of things.

Statesmen fumbled and faltered, and those in America, if anything, were worse than others. The nation was insecure as it had never been in the good days when oceans separated it from potential enemies; and obviously enormous spending on weaponry was not diminishing the perils of power.

The Center for the Study of Democratic Institutions discussed and revised the proposal for world government issued when R. M. Hutchins had been President of the University of Chicago; but it had minimal notice and no competition. No one could conceive that the world of 1970 might at any time soon give up its dissensions for orderly institutions.

3. *Disarray at Home*

Last week, acting under a code drawn up in 1968, members of the House partially disclosed some of their outside interests. Limited as it was, the information was startling. About two-thirds of 435 members of the House have substantial financial interests other than their salaries. No fewer than 92 are officers, directors or stockholders in banks or other financial institutions, while 87 have ties with law firms; 61 are stockholders in companies with major defense contracts. Ten Congressmen with direct connections to financial institutions sit on the House Banking and Currency Committee, six on the Ways and Means Committee; both committees pass on legislation that profoundly affects banking institutions across the country. If that is not a conflict of interest, what is?

Time, May 14, 1969

Our recent hearings . . . confirmed my worst suspicion about the gross inefficiency in public programs. . . . Neither the executive branch nor the Congress exercises effective control over the budget and the allocation of federal revenue.

SENATOR WILLIAM PROXMIRE (D., Wis.),
member, Congressional Joint
Committee on the Economic Report, 1969

If substantial and formerly confident citizens looked outward at the beginning of the new decade with apprehension, shuddering at what they saw, they had equal cause to shudder when they looked inward. There was a strange contradictory condition. The nation had never produced such a

volume of goods or offered so many services, and never had
had such a high average of personal incomes. So many of
its people had never before been freed for learning, experiment, cultivation of the civilized arts, and for the use of
recreational facilities. Nor had so many been mobile, made
so by automobiles, the highway system, and an air route
network. Yet never had so many been hostile to their own
government and its traditional processes, so suspicious of
their officials' integrity, so convinced that they were not
really represented and that government was not for them
but for someone else.

As for business, the cynicism was unlimited. People believed themselves merely the objects of exploitation. Workers
had lost the sense of loyalty they had had in simpler days
to the enterprises they served. Their employers had become
enemies from whom they extracted as much as they could
get in return for as little as they could give; and this showed
up in shoddy products and sullen service.

Citizens were reasonably free, well nourished—and, in un-
counted numbers, were desperately unhappy. Patriotism declined; even for the prosperous a feeling of guilt spoiled
pleasures; the accoutrements of living were accepted with
indifference; everything seemed too complicated and the
sources of their displeasure too remote to be changed. A sim-
mering discontent erupted occasionally in violence; indeed
violence was resorted to as a technique in pursuit of many
causes, and not only by black militants and student activists.
Law and order was a professed ideal; but the law was selec-
tive and order was for those who, imitating their elders and
betters, resorted to violence.

Item: Technology had acquired a momentum of its own.
Each operating concern—governmental or private—maintained, or retained, a research and development organization
whose activities were directed to the specific advancement

of its own program. Defenders of this separation could cite classical economic theory going back to Adam Smith. What was relied on was the underlying, if usually tacit, assumption that any discoveries or advances in efficiency would yield a benefit not only to one individual or organization but to the whole. A prospering business was regarded as a social credit. It ought to be encouraged since it gave employment and provided goods. The trouble was that not enough was done to make what was good for one good for all. Nevertheless the theory was believed in implicitly by small as well as big businessmen, by unionists as well as employers, by farmers as well as bankers. All knew, however, that something was lacking. As the nation grew larger and richer it seemed to have less and less cohesion, more antagonism and less co-operation, more dissent and less loyalty.

From individual enterprises, however exclusive, there were, nevertheless, certain fallouts—unexpected effects—and these did reach others in unpredictable ways and to unpredictable extents. That they were resented as often as they were welcomed was disturbing. To be consistent, those who were free to do as they liked ought to accord others a similar freedom; but when others' rights impinged on theirs, these rights were not easily granted. The collisions never seemed to result in the establishment of limits or to show convincingly that such limits were a condition of successful pluralism.

There was the same inherent paradox in this as in additive conclusions of all kinds. Many parts did not make a whole. They simply made many parts. They would only make a whole if they were accepted, fitted together, made to complement each other, and put to organic uses. This, however, required a kind of effort alien to orthodox economics and politics. In the books it said that adjustments were automatic, made so by the operations of the market. Diverse undertakings were not expected to bring themselves together; it was regarded as reprehensible for them to try. They must adjust to a price reached in free competition; but what was produced in this competition was no one's affair but the producers'. Still clinging to additive theory, businessmen, unions, and government had joined in establishing everywhere it was possible invulnerable agreements, rules, and regulations. The effect of these was to make it impossible for the market to influence one particular area. Prices were set by manufacturers, wages were embodied in contracts, rates were fixed by public commissions. None could be changed by anything but a bitter struggle, and resistances were fierce and effective.

There were, however, certain persistent coordinative tendencies in the nature of the process. Competition in business, carried far enough, eliminated itself by destroying the weaker producers and leaving only a few stronger ones; these could then conveniently arrange among themselves such matters as how much they would produce and what they would demand as prices. So, for a century, the more efficient or more effective enterprises had been growing, buying out competitors, or merging with them until the few hundred largest had substantial control of the whole economy. Since there was an over-all growth, the size of some had become colossal. This tendency accelerated as managerial skills improved, and it was made suddenly more effective in the 'sixties by applications of power to calculating machines. It was easier to run a nationwide organization now than it had been to run a single factory or store in McKinley's day.

The propensity of operating organisms to centralize was recognized much as sin was recognized. It existed, but it was immoral, a weakness to be checked. Concentration was contrary to official policy; it always had been since the "trusts" were first recognized as oppressors. Instead of persuading wholeness and order to develop toward a natural conclusion, government, reflecting popular theory, continued to view organicism with alarm and to regard growth as evidence of illegitimacy.

An active division of the Department of Justice was devoted to breaking up or, when it could, preventing, concentration. Others—private undertakings—largely escaped in spite of disfavor. The escape was owed to the ambivalence in law-makers' and regulators' minds. They approved of business but not of the results of business. Besides, the businesses had more and better lawyers working for them—far more and far better—than worked for the regulators bent on making competition effective. These were the most prestigious members of the profession, and, since two-thirds of the regulators belonged to the profession too, the influence of the lawyer-lobbyists was immense. If antitrust was official policy, easing up was the real policy. Big business was seldom seriously hurt.

Since all orthodox theorists consistently opposed enlargement of enterprises and since the enlargement nevertheless was allowed to go on, such conglomerations could neither be legitimized, nor prevented from growing. They were simply deplored and sometimes harassed. The situation, after decades of this ambivalence, was curiously contradictory. There existed a few hundred commercial behemoths whose activities were unrelated to each other or to any public plan or purpose. There was a kind of anarchy among the giants that was in complete contrast to the order each imposed upon its internal organs.

So the nation's economic policy became more and more self-defeating. As the situation became more futile, orthodox disapproval increased. This, however, had no effect on business. Since it was under constant suspicion anyway, it might as well behave with complete indifference to the public interest—whatever that was. The providing of goods and services was only incidental to such other aims as making money, increasing dividends, and protecting the positions of officials and unionized workers. It became normal to exploit customers and degrade products. Advertising was finally an acknowledged skin-game; it lived on deception, somewhat deflated by general skepticism; and the harm done was mostly the degradation of the whole system. It made no sense.

A theory so contrary to reality was bound to weaken everyone's faith in what he and others were doing. From a people charged with hope and energy, Americans were becoming withholders and disbelievers. If in their working lives they were giving as little as possible to get as much as possible—and feeling guilty about it—in their public lives they were complaining and sometimes indignant; but they did very little to encourage movements for reform. The truth was that they did not believe in the only reform with any effective potential. They had created an interlocked, rigid, highly sophisticated system without any plan for its governance and with a frightening internal cutthroat competition whose victims were consumers. It made all calculations of any general nature quite impossible.

Item: The economy was beset by inflation. The purchasing power of the dollar, measured by the prices consumers had to pay, fell every year but an exceptional few between 1945 and 1970. This continued depreciation was the cause of infinite disturbance. Every industry, every union, and, indeed, every individual must try to maintain a favorable relative position in the economic scale or even to improve it; and the means used were primitive. Clothing and food prices advanced, medical costs rose, and housing became more costly; workers then demanded adjustments in their pay scales as contracts were renewed, and these were resisted by employers. Acrimonious bargaining often ended in costly strikes; these invariably resulted in pay rises; but even if those immediately involved were benefited, it was only temporarily, since prices rose again to diminish the purchasing power of the higher wages. This, however, was not the result of an automatically operating market. It was the result of bargaining among those associates in the country with the most cohesive organizations. The market followed, it did not determine.

There were increasing numbers of citizens with fixed incomes, especially pensioners, who, since they were not able to bargain with anyone, saw their purchasing power steadily diminish. They were less and less able to live in the decency they had been led to expect. The government, for instance, continually urged the buying of savings bonds; but in many years the interest did not equal the depreciation from inflation. It was a swindle.

The worst result of this nonmanagement of the economy was the turmoil it caused. Everyone must continually try to get the best of someone else. Increases of income were often necessary just to go on living; fighting for existence was a savage business. There was no possibility of reaching stability, and all institutions were undermined by the stealthy filching of real incomes by rising prices that went on and on until, in 1970, the rise was the worst since 1951; and that had been the worst since recovery from depression was being fought for in the 'thirties.

The measures taken to curb inflation were mistaken; they tended to delay any return to the normal relationships necessary for a cure. Extreme measures were advertised as necessary for "cooling off the economy." This meant reducing production—if it meant anything—but how restricting the amounts of goods being bargained for would make the price of each less it was impossible to explain. Nevertheless, this was the orthodox remedy, and it was pursued with vigor. It could only result in still more bidding for goods, in unemployment, and in a check to expansion.

Item: There was pervasive disillusion about political processes. This may have been added to by unhappiness with the economic system and inept attempts to manage it by politicians; but discontent centered on what the disaffected called "irrelevancy." The Congress simply did not work; it was obstructive and dilatory. Disappointed and indignant citizens could get no attention. This frustration led to distrust in the system itself and, on occasion, to vociferously voiced dissent.

Cynicism concerning officialdom was universal. Federal, state, and city bureaucracies were equally suspect, and executives, governors, mayors, even the President, shared the blame for a performance that grew worse and worse. In spite of inordinate and increasing taxes public services were inadequate; the post office was unable to handle the mail; regulatory agencies appeared to assist those they were supposed to regulate; public lands were overgrazed; parks and recreation areas were uncared for; highways did not get built; airports were unsafe and overcrowded; railways abandoned passengers to what one financier had called "rolling slums"; educational facilities lagged; welfare workers treated the unfortunate as though they had caused the situations they found themselves in.

The conviction was widespread that somehow the existing institutions not only did not produce results but that they never would. Candidates for office so often seemed unsatisfactory that elections did not much matter. This was made worse by the suspicion that from top to bottom elective offices were, in effect, bought. To be elected, a candidate had to be very wealthy himself or have even wealthier associates; and the vast sums spent, it was shrewdly concluded, were not spent for no return. Revelations about this were revolting to voters. They were not so innocent as to suppose they really had representatives.

There was also the deeper cynicism of all those who watched campaigns being conducted—or helped to conduct them. Candidates were merchandized in exactly the same way as toothpaste or beer—by techniques so impersonal it was impossible to see behind the speech-writers' phrases and the make-up men's cosmetics. Those who won were not real people; they were synthetic creatures. Moreover, when in office, they were managed in the same way by public relations experts who controlled them at every turn.

It had been different in Roosevelt's time. When he had spoken on the radio, what he had to say concerned his efforts to improve what he knew was a bad situation. Listeners were not cozened and deceived. He sometimes said frankly that what was being done was experimental; but he always said that if it failed to work he would admit it and try something else. He often urged causes, but they were not for some private benefit. He was political, professionally, but those he appealed to were asked for support so that something could be done that they ought to believe in as he did.

In these later times the merchandizing of successful candidates had to go on, and it was paid for by the taxpayers instead of the supporters who had gambled on putting up a better front than the opposition. To displace an officeholder it was necessary to match unlimited public television facilities with those paid for by hopeful opponents, and the astronomical sums involved required the making of lavish promises —none likely to result in any public benefit.

This feeling about politics was not new; but the cynicism was much deeper; and it had much fact to support it, so much that the erosion of confidence in elected governments was frightening. People were being deceived; but they knew it, just as they knew that a particular toothpaste recommended by fantastic advertising expenditures was no better than that next to it on the retailers' shelves.

This wide knowledge of fakery had so undermined confidence in public institutions that if some sort of return to plain speaking and simple honesty did not soon come about there would be a general giving up to the public relations men and abandoning of any pretense that democratic institutions any longer really existed. Reform was spoken of by intellectuals in a wistful way; but they too were individualists. They were losing their belief that majorities ought to prevail. There were excuses for dissenting action, and sometimes for violence; and elaborate defenses of minority rule could be read in academic journals. The minority, of course, was not to be the existing establishment; but how those in power were to be displaced was another matter—if by a coup, it would not be the intellectuals who would succeed to power. They seemed not to know this; or perhaps their indignation had supplanted the reason they claimed to defend.

———————

Item: Younger people tended to withdraw in large numbers —simply to separate themselves from a society they regarded as lost in its illusions, its separateness, and its self-seeking. Few young men or women joined any more in singing "Beulah Land," whose verse ran that he—or she—looked away across the sea "where mansions are prepared for me; and viewed the shining glory shore, my heaven, my home for evermore." This tendency too was not new. A proportion of at least two generations had been unwilling to enter the contest for advancement on the terms fixed for them by their elders. Such an investment of time and effort did not seem worthwhile to them, especially since the time was so much lengthened, and the effort so much intensified, for acquiring the skills needed to arrive among the managerial or technological elite of so valueless a society.

Anyway, the best results from long discipline would be a success many did not respect and did not want for themselves. It was measured mostly in money and power; and what was done with these, when they were acquired, was considered to be largely indecent. They could not be recruited for business careers; and some among them suspected that other employments—science, public service, technology —would be put to uses determined by the businessmen who were the least respected of the elite. Many who had all the requisite skills joined those dropouts who had not bothered to acquire any at all.

These were not the whole of a generation; they were indeed a minority, just how small no one could say. Many assumptions about this were based on slight evidence; those who wished to emphasize dissent and disapproval tended to enlarge the number of troubled young, and those who preferred minimized the number, finding them only an infinitesimal few. It was incontestable that there were some, however, and some of the best. No society could afford such losses from the more creative members of its future generation.

There was as wide a range of proposed remedies as of estimates of numbers. The universities were special objects of suspicion. Their authorities were charged with making the campuses breeding grounds for disloyal and disruptive revolutionaries; but the radicals denounced them as being training places for entry into the abhorred establishment. Research done there, it was said, was directed to ends no young person of conscience could tolerate. There was no doubt that dissidents hung around and disrupted the routines. Some even wandered off to listless lives; they could because their baffled families supported them. Parental love was unfairly tested by sons and daughters who were, as they said, "turned off" by what was held out to them as rewards.

This malaise, if by no means universal, was certainly too prevalent to be ignored. It alarmed the more thoughtful among the working elders who knew of its existence but could not penetrate its causes. Especially they could not accept the conclusion that it resulted from the pursuit of objectives never before questioned. By application they had made a world of affluence and of opportunity; mankind had always worked for release from the tyranny of labor; they had nearly accomplished it. Far more product resulted from much less effort than had ever been true before. Nature had been harnessed and organizational skills devised. The Industrial Revolution, in the making for two hundred years, was in its culminating phase. There was talk of abolishing work —at least as a forced condition of survival. What would it be worth if a new generation should reject its rewards and refuse to undergo the disciplines it required? Parents were aggrieved; but they despaired of recovering the respect of their lost descendants; and with the loss went the meaning of lifetimes spent in earnest endeavor.

These children really were quite lost—not only to their families but to themeslves. They tried some strange resorts. They flocked to causes—usually protesting against something. They often called the object of protest "the power structure." When one cause no longer aroused enthusiasm—often because they rejected responsibility for devising reforms—they turned to another. It was like styles in beards and clothing; they changed overnight. In the few years preceding 1970 there had been mass demonstrations for civil liberties, for control of the universities, for stopping the war in Vietnam— and, in 1970, there was a rising anger over despoliation of the environment.

Most of the protesters seemed to be at the mercy of small core-groups of activists who preached crusades and whose intention was mindlessly destructive. Furious screamers were able to enlist repeatedly hordes of demonstrators who marched through miles of city streets carrying placards and chanting slogans. It had become an occupation, floating, of course, on the prevalent affluence. Every gathering was reached by modern transportation. It was all paid for by those at whom it was aimed. And those who paid grieved, but there was a slowly gathering anger too; and it carried Nixon into the White House. He owed his election, he said, to the "silent majority," which believed in old values; and it seemed that "permissiveness" had finally reached its limit. There was danger now of violent suppression.

It was a certain prospect, statisticians said, that the 'seventies would see a forty-four per cent rise in the numbers of Americans between the ages of twenty-five and thirty-four. Among them there would be those who had become disillusioned and disaffected in the 'sixties. What they might do— or not do—their elders shuddered to think. If they simply had the intention of destroying established institutions, they, at least, would not join in sophisticated searches for improvement. Civilization might just run down, much of its youth withdrawn from the disciplines necessary to the operation of highly technologized systems.

The Congress, looking for favor from a large new electorate, approved a law dropping the voting age to eighteen. This appeasement by the politicians was one they might find frustrating if it neither compelled compliance nor attracted participation; and if it skewed public policies toward permissiveness it would make matters worse.

Item: American civilization had absentmindedly become urban, or at least urbanized. The census of 1970 showed more suburbanites than inner city people; but that would be rectified by metropolitan governments and insistence on integration. The important fact was that the fifteen million farmers of 1960 had dropped to ten million in 1970. The era of homestead farming was over. There were rural backwaters remaining, but there were undertakings, earnestly pursued, meant to bring them into the common pattern. Appalachia, stretching from Pennsylvania to Alabama on either side of the mountains, was the most conspicuous of these; but there were others, almost as extensive, in other regions. Few family farms continued to yield even a meager living, and their operators had drifted away, usually to some city.

Statistics were not really descriptive. Actually the countryside was emptying itself into the urban areas. The exodus left decaying hamlets and homes, and decaying people as well. Small farms had been consolidated into larger ones—powered machinery made this more profitable; and the operators of these seldom lived any longer in farmhouses; they had moved to town and were commuting to their fields. Powered machines, improved roads, electricity, telephones, and sophisticated management made agriculture just another enterprise.

A farmer saw his acres as a manager saw his factory—only when it was necessary during working hours.

Displaced rural families added to the city's own increasing population, crowded further the center precincts, and made a welfare problem of massive proportions. A farmer in the city was as helpless as a city worker on a farm. He found only marginal employment, and his family, growing up in the slums, joined the detached generation from the more fortunate neighborhoods in attacking the agencies improvised to find futures for the one and to mitigate the hard conditions of the other. Solutions were impersonal and inadequate. They might have been the beginning of better things if time had been given; but time was not given; the avalanche of problems was immediate and overwhelming.

Item: The cities, as a consequence, had become unsafe, uncomfortable, and, indeed, difficult to manage at all. They had no defenses against massive immigration, and no resources— or at any rate none that were adequate—for meeting the problems of uncontrolled enlargement. As immigrants crowded into an inner core already packed with earlier comers, ancient buildings bulged with unhappy people, many of them in actual misery. There was some public housing, but its construction was so slow that yearly increases of people were far greater than any year's new additions of places to live.

The cities, besides, could not maintain their services; buildings were inspected and condemned, but, if they were closed, their renters had no place to go. Schools were so slowly replaced that children often spent their days in rackety rooms used for fifty or more years. Unemployed men and dropout youths were constantly in trouble and easily gathered a mob of sympathizers if disciplined by the police. It was inevitable that the enforcers of order should be regarded as enemies; and there was often something undistinguishable from warfare in the streets.

The slums pushed outward, engulfing neighborhoods formerly belonging to more fortunate citizens, who abandoned them for a suburbia still independent of the city. The regions beyond the city's formal limits allowed their affluent taxpayers to escape the city's burdens. They commuted, since their businesses were still in the city. This was doubtless a hardship, and the separation of work and living was inefficient; but the families of the commuters did prefer the roomier communities with the amenities their incomes entitled them to. They forgot, or tried to forget, the problems they had left behind.

It seemed to harassed officials that all their difficulties grew worse and the resources they had to work with grew more meager. Municipalities were chartered by states not disposed to yield more home rule than was forced on them, and extension of the cities' limits was made difficult not only by legislative prohibitions but often because the metropolitan area had spread into adjoining states. Most federal funds came through state bureaucracies and were naturally passed on grudgingly and with maximum harassment.

The making of annual budgets had become more and more a futile exercise. The programs for education, health, hospitals, recreations, sanitation—the hundreds of services expected of municipal government—had to be brought within incomes wholly inadequate. The weighing of education against health or street maintenance against parks had to be done; each had to do with funds taking them further each year into decline; but there were no guides. The saying from the rural past that the wheel with the loudest squeal got the most grease applied here. But if the wagon could not last long without attention all around, greasing one wheel was not a satisfactory solution. For the first time in American history strikes of public employees became common. Teachers, sanitation workers, even police and firemen, competed for scarce funds, protesting low pay and obsolete equipment.

There was only reluctant recognition that the cities' prob-

lems resulted from nationwide movements, unsolved problems, and indifference. Migration, pollution of air and water,
clogged transportation and communications—none had local
causes; but there was no adequate recognition of this; and
so the cities, objects of so much reforming zeal in a past generation, became embattled refuges for immigrants and in-
hospitable places for their older inhabitants.

What was to be said of a favorable nature about urban
troubles was that those who came to crowd them and cause
the problems came because they would be better off in urban
than in rural slums. There was at least welfare; and the
services were comparatively generous. City authorities were
all trying very hard to keep services adequate and to meet
the demands made on their inadequate departments. It was
noticeable that even the most vociferous protesters had no
inclination to go back to where they had come from.

One of the worst troubles was racial tension, and the worst
riotous eruptions occurred in black neighborhoods. But blacks
could vote, and they could protest. It might possibly turn
out after some time that urban mixing had been the most
effective integrating agent ever known. By 1970 there were
several black mayors of large cities; but they were finding
that urban troubles were only in small part racial. Their
causes were not even internal. They had to be sought in
national neglect.

———————

Item: What was good and helpful for American citizens
seemed continually to be canceled out by what was bad and
potentially disastrous. All too often these contradictions were
linked. Medical discoveries contributed to increased survival
and so increased the numbers of those beyond the age of
work and eligible for old age benefits. These threatened to
outrun the resources of trust funds gathered from special
taxes unless these were increased beyond the imagining of a
few years in the past; and pensions seemed to melt as in-

flation persisted. Most of a growing number of the elderly lived in degraded circumstances. Their poverty made them seem an ugly nuisance to the young. There were more of them than there were of the blacks, who at least attracted liberal sympathy, something the elderly somehow did not get.

Highways and automobiles made smog much more than a nuisance. The pesticides that eliminated malaria and protected crops poisoned the land, leached into the rivers and eventually made fish in the sea inedible. These conditions were remediable; but they had hardly been considered at all before, in the 1960's, Rachael Carson published a book called *Silent Spring*. After that, protection of the environment became a universal concern; but conservation promised further troubles. It would increase costs, disturb readjustments, and upset calculations about the supply of food and fibre. Even the smokeless nuclear power plants were suddenly discovered to be thermal threats; their boiling water reactors poured discharges into rivers or lakes and waterways, altering balance in natural ecosystems.

Land, water, and air comprised a grand organism capable, without man's intervention, of completing reconstitutive cycles without loss in the chain of life. Growth and decay working together eventually reached equilibrium. Man's interference, now that his population had grown with much less control by pestilence and starvation for half a century, was substantial. His wastes threatened to interrupt life-renewing cycles unless some drastic changes were made without delay. Already the degeneration had gone so far that the techniques of renewal would require massive expenditures. Since the ultimate penalties would not occur until most people alive would be gone, there was question whether the necessary sacrifices for posterity would actually be made.

This was a general problem; but there seemed to be little interest in it anywhere in the third world. In Asia, Africa, and Latin America, where proliferation of population was greatest, and where the limits of nutritional deprivation had already been reached, the problem was not only out of control but out of consideration. Whatever was done in the United States or Europe was only a fraction of what must be done by a still mostly indifferent world.

It had to be noted too that the universal use of credit tended to pile up dangerous debts and created periodical liquidity crises. Preservation of private enterprise and maintenance of a competitive economy provided the conditions for monopoly; and governments everywhere became more and more vulnerable to management by the privileged for private purposes.

Each change appeared without planning and, so, without counting the cost of its effects. There were ways, but not sufficient ones, of sharing gains; the technique of power applications and improved management resulted in increased supplies of goods and services; but the number of the alienated multiplied, and, since no conclusion had been reached about their lives, and incomes were not equalized, they became protesters against the system, and sometimes violent ones. They were joined by unhappy consumers who progressively lost purchasing power because of inflation. Together they made dissatisfaction a chronic condition, worsened by the knowledge that a better life could be had if only the disorder could be straightened out.

Item: It had for generations been a source of pride that American productivity had outrun that of any other nation; but the appreciation of good things was suddenly embittered for Americans as they moved about with new facility. Somehow the skills so richly productive had been made futile because of their narrow dedication. The costs had not been calculated. Not only had the community been defiled by wastes, but the product had not reached many unfortunates. In 1970 it had to be acknowledged that millions of people were ill nourished; that even more were ill housed; that too many children spent their days in tumble-down schools. Within sight of suburban luxury there were living conditions no better than those in the world's most backward countries. It was an inescapable and constant reproach to all the affluent who also possessed a conscience.

Perhaps the oldest tradition of life in the new world was equality; but not even equal *opportunity* had been achieved; and equal access to goods and services, even when productive facilities were fully used, had not been attained.

There still existed many deprivations; and since all the means existed for their elimination there was no tenable excuse. The knowledge that this was so could not be ignored. The nation had not met its principal obligation. All men may have been *created* free and equal, but the plain fact was that in affluent America the creation had been smothered.

Item: One significant statistic appeared in the last year before the 'seventies began. The productivity per man hour of American workers decreased. This had never happened before. Was the source of affluence running dry? Since Roosevelt's time it had risen regularly, the rate during that twenty-five years averaging 3.2 per cent yearly. In this year it declined 5 per cent. This explained, if consumers were listening, why there were power failures, transportation delays, telephone breakdowns, postal paralysis, and sullen services of all kinds. The incentive for making a larger contribution to the general good was evidently no longer felt as it once had been. If this was so, then it was a measure of the mistakes, the dissensions, and the indifference of past years. All these were human failures; nature was generous; power had been substituted for labor; new inventions had multiplied; food was in surplus. They simply were not being used fairly and effectively. Those who were using nature's gifts were losing interest in using them better.

Item: The Constitution of the United States, devised during the steamy summer of 1787 in Philadelphia, remained substantially as it had been when consigned by a majority of its framers to chancy ratification. Immense social changes had since occurred. A ninety per cent agricultural population had become ninety per cent urban. Thirteen seaboard states become forty-nine continental ones and Hawaii, some distance out in the Pacific. There was, as well, one associate state in the South Atlantic—Puerto Rico. A self-sufficient rural economy had been transformed into a factory and commercial system. Tracks through the forests and across the prairies had become multilane highways. Horse transport had given way to motor vehicles that crossed state boundaries unknowing. A few elementary schools, mostly private, had become a vast public educational apparatus.

The Constitution, however, remained essentially unchanged. It had been amended twenty-six times; but none of the amendments affected the structure of government. There were still separated powers so that authority should not finally lodge anywhere to harass citizens or so that forward movement should be precipitate; the states, although thirty-seven were not parties to the original contract, were formally still sovereign, and the central government had only those powers conceded to it in the document; there was a bill of rights but none of duties; the legislature represented localities (states or districts), and the upper house had two members from every state, however small; only the President was elected by all the people and thus stood alone for national interests against the legislature's consistent concern with local matters.

All this meant that in an age of continental commerce, rapidly spreading across the seas, there still remained a central government devised for the minimal purposes of defense but having had consigned to it, without serious reconsideration, the oversight of vast enterprises and the accompanying burdens of adjustment as these enterprises ploughed their way into the future. The Constitution had not mentioned politics, had not anticipated industry, had taken no notice of education, transportation, communications, public health, or poverty. It had assumed a nation of small farmers who had now diminished almost to the vanishing point.

Worst of all, it had consigned the making of amendments to the legislatures—federal and state. As a consequence, changes had become almost impossible, especially if they appeared to touch law-makers' prerogatives in any way. Among the many anachronisms, the legislatures were the worst, of course, since they had perfect defenses against interference. They simply would not act, and they could not be made to act.

With the basic law thus frozen, the bursting enlargement of the whole society from within found its necessary accommodations as best it could. There were some creations not even faintly suggested by the Constitution—such, for instance, as the regulatory agencies; but the principal source of law became the Supreme Court's extrapolations. The Court was not representative; and it was hampered by the inability to decide unless cases had come to it from previous tedious procedures. It was, besides, only one of three separate powers. Nevertheless it had worked toward supremacy—that is, the ability to say what the others (the President and the Congress) might or might not do. This satisfied the legal profession; but it did not serve to modernize a government that must somehow make itself master of the environment, acting for citizens caught up in the multifarious changes brought about by scientific discovery and the following technology.

4. *The Credit Side Abroad*

Tacitly, but fairly unmistakably, during the 1960s the two superpowers . . . have reconfirmed their unwritten agreement not to go to war with each other.

The Economist, January, 1970

Roosevelt's contemporaries and even his immediate successors were now retreating into the shadows, writing memoirs and explaining to a younger generation how inevitable it had been that so much had gone wrong. There was remarkable agreement that *they* were not to be blamed. Like Hoover's explanation that the Great Depression had been caused by "blows from abroad," the dishevelment of 1970 was said to have been caused by a communist conspiracy to disrupt the "free world"; and it was pridefully claimed that necessary measures to combat the effort had been taken and had succeeded.

It was, of course, true that the Russians had refused to cooperate in establishing international arrangements on terms disadvantageous to themselves. It was true also that China had simply left the company of nations and caused enormous troubles on her borders as she became aggressively expansive. These occurrences, however, had causes, and the causes must have involved negotiations. Since the United States had been the principal victor in the war ended in 1945, and the most powerful when it was over, the world's troubles must have arisen from situations American politicians had participated in bringing about and ought to have done something to avoid. To deny their responsibility was to charge them with incredible carelessness and inexcusable failure to use the vast power at their disposal for enforcing the peace.

There had been a whole decade when the Russians had been without the nuclear armament necessary to bargaining from strength. It had been during that time that the Baruch proposals had been put forward and been rejected, whereupon the effort had been given up, to be succeeded by a protracted slanging match. While this had been going on the Russians had caught up and could then bargain as equals. The opportunity for generosity had been lost.

Was it all the fault of the Russians? One sort of answer to this is an assessment of what would have had to be conceded in order to have got Russian agreement. The Russians had got without negotiation most of what it was desired to withhold from them. Coexistence, an essential of survival, continued only in the poised mutual threat of a ballistic missile duel. But dangerous as it was, it had sufficed to keep avowed enemies from actual attack on one another.

There had been a time during Eisenhower's Presidency when Dulles, his Secretary of State, had spoken of "liberating" the nations of Eastern Europe; he had also spoken of "unleashing" Chiang Kai-shek, who had retreated with a fragment of government to Taiwan, while the communists kept the mainland. Dulles' dreams proved to be evanescent. By 1970 Russia was holding Eastern Europe in fief, and half of Germany, held in the communist grip, was the source of fulminating hatred. Then too there were the humiliations in Asia—Korea and Vietnam, most conspicuously; but the rest of the former French empire being lost as well to Western influence. These, together with the alienation of nearly all the Moslem world, and the disillusion in South America, made credits in foreign policy hard to find.

What were pointed to proudly as outstanding accomplishments by those who had been involved in these proceedings were, most conspicuously, the Truman Doctrine, the Marshall Plan, and the North Atlantic Treaty Organization. The first had kept Greece and Turkey from becoming communist, the second had assisted immensely in the rapid resuscitation of

Western Europe, and the third was supposed to have kept communist armies from marching to the English Channel.

It was true that neither Greece nor Turkey now had a communist government under Russian domination; but it was also true that neither had a democratic one. The choice between a military dictatorship and a communist regime was not one with highly visible advantages on either side.

It was also true that France, Italy, the low countries, and the western half of Germany were again productive and able to support themselves; but the most conspicuously advanced of all was the Germany so many men and so much treasure had been expended in defeating. None of the others could match her remarkable recovery, and some were less well off than at any time in recent history. Britain and France, before the war proud, imperial, and rich, were now reduced to small and barely viable nations. France was self-sufficient if old and tattered glories were renounced; but Britain must expect to exist on a much reduced scale. Neither had yet adjusted to the restrictions they must accept, and their electorates were insistent on consuming more than they produced.

As for the third accomplishment, NATO, it had been paid for by the United States, mostly, even when West Germany had become one of the most affluent economies in the world. It was doubtful whether its fifteen or twenty divisions, even before the French defected during the 'sixties, could have stopped the attack of a hundred Russian divisions, backed up by their satellites and supplied not across an ocean but by an immediate hinterland. What seemed more likely in retrospect, as has been suggested, was that the limits of practical advance had been reached and that the Russian objective of security had been attained. The buffer was wide enough and sufficiently under domination to make another invasion from the West practically impossible.

All this was a strange result not only of a costly war but of an even more costly postwar interlude extending through a quarter-century. Critics added to the calculation that Japan, whose treacherous forces had attacked Pearl Harbor and had caused an emotional reaction seldom equaled in American experience, was again dominant in Asia. This time it was not necessary for Japanese forces to invade and subdue. Americans were doing for them in the 'sixties what the same Americans had prevented them from doing in the 'forties.

Sheltered by the American military, and with no armament to support, Japanese affluence had become phenomenal. The nation possessed the third most productive industrial complex in the world and was prepared again to displace all others in dominating Asian commerce. Even if ground forces should be withdrawn from Vietnam and Korea, the sixth fleet would prevent interference with Japanese commerce. Still, it could be said that the reconquest was being gone about in a more acceptable way. The military clique was destroyed. The invaders of Southeast Asia were now purchasing agents and salesmen. This, at least, was an improvement over the harsh oppression of armies.

It was only too plain that credits claimed by statesmen for their achievements during the quarter-century after the war rested on the resuscitation of enemies regarded once as threats not only to international order but to civilization as well. It was ironic that those men who had fought from '41 to '45 across Africa and Western Europe and across the Pacific to Japan should have made their sacrifices to benefit the enemy; and it would have been hard to explain to the rows of dead in the military cemeteries how they had served their country by giving their lives for such results. Had Japanese and German hearts been changed? Evidently that was assumed; and the assumption became vocal concerning Germany, when, in 1961, President Kennedy proclaimed from a rostrum in Berlin *"Ich bin ein Berliner."* Presumably he spoke with official authority; but did he speak for the soldiers buried in vast European cemeteries with their endless rows of headstones?

That explanation would have had to rest—did rest in oratory over those graves—on the containment of communism.

Germany was now a barrier; and forces were united precisely as Hitler had tried to unite them against Russia. The Allies had defeated Germany, Japan, and Italy; but victor and vanquished alike were now devoted to the defeat of Russia and China. The Russians and Chinese, however, seemed to be prospering as well as the Germans and Italians. They had found a formula for imperialism. However cynical and betraying, it appeared to fascinate their victims. Their obvious aim was to extinguish inferior identities and turn all eyes to Moscow and Peking; but their appeal was often, during the preliminaries, to a nationalism stifled by the older imperialists, and somehow the promise of independence seemed credible. At the same time it was made to seem unbelievable that Americans could be in Korea and Vietnam for any but imperialist reasons. The communists were received with joy by peoples about to lose every last vestige of autonomy and with it whatever freedom their liberators felt to be dangerous.

What would have happened if, in 1950, the United States had stayed off the Asian mainland; and what if Russians had been conceded a position in German postwar disciplining that would have soothed their fears of another invasion?

South Korea would have been joined with North Korea in a communist government; but what she had now was a military dictatorship and was under constant threat from the North. This was bad enough for the Koreans, but it was costing Americans many millions a year in subsidies and the need to support fifty thousand protective troops. Germany would have had a compromise regime, not democratic, certainly, but not hard-line communist either. The nation was now split, half democracy and half communist—the most intransigent and dictatorial of all Russia's satellites.

Claims that communism has been contained are hardly credible. Unless the United States continued to maintain an establishment amounting to much more than half its total expenditures the policy would collapse; and there was real question whether it was not beyond the nation's capability.

The expanding Russian empire seemed certain to include the Mediterranean; the Chinese would very likely take Taiwan and perhaps most of Indochina. The question whether it would be worth to the United States what it would cost to prevent this was, in 1970, being asked with more penetrating skepticism than had been heard since Truman and Dulles first declared war on Russia and proclaimed the support of Southeast Asia to be a Christian missionary enterprise. The neglect of domestic needs was a cause of bitter resentment.

The credits abroad were few indeed. But the missiles had not flown to their targets across the oceans. Perhaps this made up for all the rest.

5. *The Credit Side at Home*

. . . While our system works very well to produce auto-mobiles and electronic communications and roads and highways, it doesn't supply us with surface transporta-tion, it doesn't supply us with acceptable housing, it doesn't supply us with agreeable urban communities. . . . It seems to me we had better assume not structural workability but structural unworkability. This will force us to look much more deeply at the requisite changes, to be much warmer in our response to the discussion of planning, for example . . .

J. K. GALBRAITH,
in *The Center Magazine*, January, 1970

All was not well twenty-five years after Roosevelt died; but all was not as bad either as pessimists claimed. Somehow during the quarter-century none of the catastrophes most dreaded had happened. Moreover a people who had been forced to live with the possibility of instantaneous extinction had not only survived but had gone on to scientific and technological achievements of vast consequence. There had been such increases in supplies of food and fiber that the Malthusians had been proved wrong again, as they had again and again in the past. Population had doubled, but the production of food had much more than doubled. Predictions of mass starvation were not new, they had been made in every generation; but the predictors had been especially confident during the 'forties and 'fifties. Emergence into the last years of the century found people better nourished and clothed than ever in the past, a success that disappointed the prophets of doom and constituted a remarkable credit for producers. All was not well; but much was certainly better.

The new generation was in a belated frenzy about the befouled environment and the exhaustion of resources. The contributors to progress were mostly managers and technologists who were—honestly—practically illiterate; in consequence their defenses when charged with wholesale pollution were feeble and consigned to institutional advertising; and this was regarded with skepticism not only by their critics but by almost everyone else. There was much talk of credibility in politics; and there did go on the usual irritated dialogue between the purveyor of goods and services and the users of them.

Behind the producers the massed ranks of physicists, chemists, and advertisers were regarded as little better than fakirs. They were no match for the extremely vocal intellectuals; but even these did not seriously contend that there existed no connection whatever between productivity and the good life. They tended to disparage it, but their disparagement made excellent use of all the facilities for communication and none went without automobiles and the other products of technology. In a New York meeting of the Center Club, Michael Harrington was chided by a questioner for being concerned rather with the quantity than the quality of life. Professor Galbraith, who was present, spoke up. "I am prepared," he said, "to accept all the wounding blows at my profession that are legitimate and honest—and there are a great many; but I'm damned if I will accept those that are ridiculous."

Harrington himself responded with a more temperate reproof:

> I have just, God help me—gone through the experience of reading Hegel's *Logic* in German. Nobody should be subjected to that; but as a result of the punishment, I am at the moment very conscious that quantities become qualities; that is to say, the spiritual life begins only after you have settled the material life. Hungry men are concerned about their stomachs. I think it is very important not to separate those two aspects of human existence. I think that what all of us have been talking about for a long time is how to order those quantitative material priorities, precisely to allow the individual the possibility to pursue in whatever odd way he wants his own spiritual priorities. I think we would make a mistake were we to set the one against the other.*

This from Harrington was likely to lose him such credibility as he had among the disenchanted; but he had always been alien to those who thought the nation not worth saving. Also he was too industrious for their taste. The importance of his conclusion, however, was considerable. Not that it was novel; many of his elders had believed all along that progress consisted mostly in the enlargement of opportunities to consume.

Efficient production was America's genius, if it had one; and it had resulted in libraries, laboratories, schools, hospitals, and recreation facilities as well as in the automobiles, the washing machines, the refrigerators, and all that array of prepared comestibles to be seen in the supermarkets. Household maintenance, the daily tasks of those who lived on

* *The Center Magazine*, 83, January, 1970

the old homesteads and in the villages—woodcutting, canning, laundering, tending the horses and chickens, endless cooking, keeping the kerosene lamps and stoves in order— all these had disappeared. With them had gone an eternal slavery to chores. There was time now for other occupations. Besides, the hours of work in industry had steadily decreased and factories were palatial compared with those of the time before such conditions were subject to bargaining.

There were some harsh criticisms of what was done with the time saved. It was pointed out what ineffable rubbish the TV networks, dominated by advertisers, provided all day and into the evening. Critics said they mostly seduced witless viewers who would have been better employed doing those household chores they no longer had to do, or even working longer hours at their employments. It was even doubted whether those millions of automobiles people rode around in were such an improvement over earlier means of transportation, a doubt whose realism would have been more credible if staying at home had had the appurtenances of the self-sufficient homesteads now gone forever. Suburban electric trains had disappeared; so had the urban trolleys; and most houses in new developments had no footwalks on their streets —something their predecessors would have been astounded to learn, recalling with what labor wooden walks had emancipated villagers from the mud of winter and the dust of summer.

Television had begun to be practical by 1945, and radio had been familiar for some years before that. The proliferation of these communication devices was no more than an expansion of earlier beginnings; but the expansion had had a curious effect. It had supplied much the same amusement as the old movie palaces; but it had also distributed information in condensed form. This might not please those who felt that it restricted discussion and participation—people simply sat for hours taking it in—but it could not be denied that millions knew what only hundreds had known in 1945 about happenings in the world. It came to them from newscasters who were interrupted a dozen times an hour by pleas for products of exaggerated usefulness; but it did come; and it must be admitted that the commentators were remarkably independent of the sponsors who cheapened and vulgarized the programs billed as entertainment. They were among the best-known personalities in America and were more trusted, far, than the politicians who would like to use them but found it difficult. Like that of Presidents, the better of them, the newcasters' support came from the people, something ultimately irresistible in a democracy. Even the businessmen who owned the stations and networks recognized this and had to be cautious about trying to curb or deflect too obviously the swells of opinion that sometimes swept across the country.

Roosevelt had learned communications techniques as the media had developed. No President since had matched his skill in its use; and it had been he who had insisted on the establishment of a commission to protect the public's title to the airwaves. His successors, however, had not insisted that the protection should be maintained; there was a curious inhibition at work; and no way had been found to overcome it. If television was to cost viewers nothing and advertisers were expected to pay for it, there must be some return; that return was permission to persuade, and this unfortunately ran over into the domination of programming. The industry built on this foundation was enormous in size, worse than mediocre in performance, and positively sinister in its potentials.

Roosevelt had seen how necessary it was, if economic pluralism was to be maintained and the adoption of state socialism avoided, that there should be public agencies to fix rules and enforce them. This was the condition of decent services in a highly organized system with independent businesses. Its utility depended on the vigilance and integrity of the public's regulators. He was frustrated from the beginning by weaker legislation than was needed, whereas it should have been even stronger than he had urged, if it was expected to be disciplinary. Its weakness was directly owed to Congressional subservience when lobbyists made demands, the worst defect in the governmental complex.

It did not stop there. However adequate the law, its effectiveness depended on its forceful administration. Roosevelt's appointments to the Communications Commission—and to such others as that to oversee power development and the security exchanges—were at least meant to be individuals devoted to the public interest, although some even of these proved to be untrustworthy. His successors allowed the personnel of the regulatory agencies—old as well as new—to be dictated in many instances by the industry to be supervised. From Roosevelt's time, these agencies never approached the fulfillment of their purpose.

This was one reason for the growing anarchy in the economic system. There was no central discipline, to say nothing of planning. Except for treaties made among themselves by the industrial giants when it suited their interests, there was no control. The elaborate regulatory agencies simply did not have the necessary power, or, if they had it, did not put it to good use. They might better not have been there, since there was some public belief that regulation was in effect.

Each industry, those nominally regulated as public utilities as well as those not regulated because they were regarded as private, became more efficient as engineering improved and management learned the techniques of large-scale management; but there must have been interstitial wastes of half their potential from lack of planning and coordination. Devotion to the arts of deception had become a highly respected occupation, an enormous one, and had taken the place of loyalty to old principles of workmanship, integrity, and honest service. "Caveat emptor" had become basic to business. "Caveat purveyor" was ridiculed.

Estimating that productivity was no more than half what

it might have been, however, that half still made an impressive record in the twenty-five years after 1945. At the end, there existed a surplus of nearly everything people wanted, even though there were almost twice as many people. Ordinary workmen—if such could still be spoken of—went to their employment in automobiles. They started out in the morning from homes indistinguishable from those formerly thought of as belonging to an upper, or at least a middle, class. If they lived in the big cities they used the same transportation and possessed the same amenities at home as their employers— television, powered devices for housekeeping, and furniture limited only by their tastes. It was an immense accomplishment.

There had to be deducted the miseries of those who had missed, somehow, the expanding prosperity and had been neglected—the eleven per cent still living in real poverty, still having menial jobs, and, of course, not sharing the affluence of unionized labor. Even these, however, were not so helpless as they had been in the 'thirties. There were welfare benefits and hosts of social workers to distribute them. Even if there were slums, there were no Hoovervilles in odd corners of the cities. It was a measure of the achievement that recipients of public aid were perpetually annoyed by its insufficiency and by the stiff rules for eligibility. There had been talk of guaranteed support for everyone below a minimum level of income, and something was obviously about to come of it.

The persisting enclaves of poverty in the countryside and the slum areas in the city were regarded as shameful failures. Even the most conservative politicians promised their elimination. But this was what Roosevelt had said in 1934 was a national necessity and had begun to do something about. It ought long ago to have been accomplished; but that the poor had been reduced by more than a half was at least something.

There was another credit quite different from those measured by quantitative gains. It was disturbing, and sometimes even frightening, but it clearly had not happened, and could not have happened, some decades in the past. This was the vocality of those who, for one or another reason, felt themselves discriminated against. Inequality had become intolerable. It was indignantly protested. Threats and frequent, if localized, outbursts of violence where reminders that what the poor could see as a possibility they felt justified in demanding; and inequality became more and more difficult to defend.

Looked back on after another half-century the period would be almost as notable for the advance of colored people as for the technological advances that had made it possible. They were still a majority, a vast majority, in the slums. Immigrants from the segregated South were almost as segregated in the Northern cities, largely because whites, whose economic situation improved, moved away from them. This, of course, tended to perpetuate itself, as it had in the past for other immigrants. Urban schools fell into racial patterns, and breaking them up was not easy, but, of course, something had to be done, and bitter controversies arose over attempts to integrate schools when housing remained segregated; this was the failure, but a multiplicity of obstacles held back the most earnest attacks.

Truman could claim enormous credit for integration in the armed forces; Johnson, after the Eisenhower interlude, had sponsored many laws, when he had had briefly a pliant Congress, removing political and economic inequalities. He had a Negro Cabinet member and had appointed another to the Supreme Court. By 1970 there were a half-dozen black mayors, some in cities as large as Cleveland and Newark. It might be slow, but it was progress. Americans had to live together.

There were many among the colored—black, brown, yellow, and red—who were bitterly resentful of remaining discriminations; and they had not yet been admitted in numbers to many old exclusive white privileges—such as trade unions. The migration from the South to Northern cities had been so rapid, there had been so little preparation for it, and slums now were so largely black, that all the frustrations and disadvantages so familiar to the Irish, the Polish, and the Jews were worse, even if not different in kind.

It was often hard to see that things were better when they seemed so much worse. But living in Harlem was better than trying to exist on a sharecropper's allotment in the Mississippi Delta; and the way out and upward was after all easier.

Best of all there was the general recognition that equality was a right. To be black was not to be inferior, it was merely to have skin of a different color. To deny that in 1970 was to admit to a discredited prejudice. No one held it in public, however much it might lurk in the shadows of old habit.

So a democracy advances, and especially when it has the capability of producing what its citizens demand and distributing it with decent concern. It had to be said that neither the intentions nor the performance were what Roosevelt had hoped for—the performance was, in fact, much, much less. Nevertheless Michael Harrington had called attention to something important in the intimate involvement of quantities with qualities. Why he found for the first time in Hegel what American philosophers had said much more lucidly, he did not explain; but the source did not matter. What did matter was the admission that the American contribution to civilization was not nearly so useless as was claimed by its critics.

The sheer quantity of research facilities and the devotion of those who worked with them were offering revolutionary gains—or perhaps they should be called challenges. The mechanisms of life were being experimented with in hundreds of laboratories. There was confident talk of "thousand year men" and of clones. There was no doubt about raising the levels of capability; and the stretch-out of individual existence was about to occur, perhaps, in the order of twenty-five per cent. All this was causing questions about where human kind might find itself in a few decades. Was it prepared to reconstitute itself? The model was not agreed on; but the capability was definitely within sight. And it definitely flowed from affluence.

The richness of what lay ahead was immeasurable; but, as Roosevelt had known so well, it might not materialize, or might prove catastrophic rather than miraculous, if self-interest was not curbed, if love of country should be lost, if the pluralistic society could not devise the connective tissue and the directive mechanisms it must have to be a whole, not just a conglomeration of parts, and if humankind could not join in nature's ecosystem.

Among the adjustments man on earth had been struggling with over the quarter-century was the knowledge being so rapidly disclosed of the vastness of space and the intricate organization of particles. A solar system had been absorbed as reality in a few hundred years; a galaxy in a few decades; but what should a limited imagination do with the fact of many trillions of galaxies. They were certainly there in all their majestic indifference. Each of these countless stars and their planets was finite and had a relation with each other; and this vast system, going on and on, had amazing likenesses to the infinitesimal particle system beginning actually to be seen, not just guessed at.

Wonder was not the only sensation. These strange new reaches of knowledge demanded that something be done, that an accord be established. Men could only proceed with their affairs, now that they knew, as though they did not know. An inquiring youth, fifty years ago, might talk with Thomas Hunt Morgan about genes; he might talk too with Harlow Shapley about the stars. The stretching of his mind would be an effort, but his whole universe of reference would be merely enlarged, not made obsolete. He might make an effort to understand Einstein but would probably be baffled. What he would get from these impacts on his store of received ideas would be a recognition of the need for enlargement, for adjusting his thinking to the possibility of the unknown.

He might be more baffled by quantum theory than any of the other new confrontations. This seemed to disturb, what neither astronomy nor biology had, his sense of order. The objects out there in space and those within the cells of life seemed to have laws, and laws were comforting; but if there was a disorder about the nature of things, everything seemed to crumble away into hopeless chaos. He could only tell himself that even quantum jumps would finally be discovered to have laws too, just as mutations of living things did.

Men were learning about and grappling with all these and other disclosures during the time they were trying to establish order after a World War, a Great Depression, then another World War. One thing they ought to have known and clung to was that this was no time in man's history for the antagonisms, the dangers, the costs of what came to be called the cold war.

Some sympathy from future historians will be in order for the generations who had to make these incredible adjustments. No such swift overwhelming of received knowledge had ever happened before to torment those who were entrusted with the maintenance of order. Surely, however, the credit for all this plunging into the unknown, and drawing from it possibilities undreamed of by their fathers, ought not to be withheld. It will still be hard to explain why in such a time men like Roosevelt's successors should have been chosen to preside over the scientific and technological revolution; but the revolution was not prevented from going on. Perhaps the permission was inadvertent; but they did, after some fumbling, dispose of Joseph McCarthy and of a dozen others like him; and, even if they were better suited to have been county supervisors than Presidents—Kennedy excepted —they allowed their faith in progress and in democracy a controlling place in domestic if not foreign policy.

IV
What He Wanted

Hopkins said he could see what Roosevelt did; sometimes he even knew what was about to happen; but from where it had come, and what part it was of a pattern, he could only guess. What he had come to believe, however, was that something tremendous was there and was being worked out. One thing he knew: It would be done.
(From Tugwell's notes on a conversation with Harry Hopkins in the old naval hospital in Washington during Hopkins' last illness)

1. *National Security*

What Lincoln brought to the Civil War, what Franklin Roosevelt brought to the Great Depression and the second world war, were, above all, an intense imaginative understanding of the nature of the crisis, perceived in the full sweep of history, with a bold instinct for innovation and a determination to mobilize and apply social intelligence and a compassionate sense of human tragedy. It was this embracing vision that gave particular policies their meaning and strengthened and inspired the American people to rise to their obligations and opportunities. Today, alas, our national leadership hardly seems aware of the fact we are in a crisis; in fact, it hardly appears to know what is going on in America and the world. It is feeble and frightened, intellectually mediocre, devoid of elevation and understanding, fearful of experiment, with-

*out a sense of the past or a sense of the future. This is
one reason why our crisis of confidence is so acute. It is
as if James Buchanan were fighting the Civil War or
Herbert Hoover the Great Depression.*
                          ARTHUR M. SCHLESINGER, JR.,
                              in *Newsweek,* July 6, 1970

It is a gross understatement to remark, in view of an easily
catalogued list of terrifying situations, that mistakes were
made and that undertakings went wrong. Mistakes? Many
were deliberate policies in pursuit of disastrous objectives.
Most were not mistakes; they were sacrifices to an ideology
quite indifferent to calculations of national interest.

Roosevelt had justification for believing, in the spring of
his death, that the nation, having come within sight of victory, would be able to carry the *élan* of the war into the
peace. He had prepared the way for international order, most
domestic irritations had been vented, levels of living had
risen, and the Social Security system was fully accepted; but
he was not complacent; much remained to be done.

For instance there was something very wrong with government. He had had occasion just recently to castigate the Congress for subservience to special interests; not for a long time
had it recognized its duty to the public. He was so disgusted,
and expressed it so plainly, that Alben Barkely, the Senate
majority leader, threatened to resign. Institutional, even constitutional changes, however, were not, he felt, impossible;
and, as for the same special interests who seemed to think
they owned the Congress, he had disciplinary intentions. He
looked forward to changes that would enable them to discipline each other in pursuit of mutual interests; in fact a
return to NRA was expectable.

The end of the war would free immense energies. They
had only to be engaged for domestic objectives as they had
been for foreign ones—the new enemies being poverty, in-
security, displacement, and latent dissension.

What went wrong? Roosevelt had hardly gone when malice and fear came uppermost in the minds of national policymakers, Truman's to begin with. As soon as he stopped being commander in chief in a hot war against Germany and Japan he became commander in chief in a cold war against Russia. The former ally who was suddenly an enemy was given no allowances; recognition of the free world's authority must be acknowledged; if it was not, the Russians must be driven in upon themselves and isolated from more civilized peoples. They were presumptuous challengers, and they must be "contained." If it should be necessary to confront them and have it out, they would meet their match—and this soon became missile to missile, rather than gun to gun.

This possibility of serious confrontation came as a surprise to Truman's sympathizers—including his recent colleagues in the legislative branch—who thought the scientists from whom legislators were hearing were simply being disloyal when they insisted that the secrets of atomic weaponry could not be kept; that indeed the Russians must already have them. Nuclear knowledge could not be monopolized; but most politicians would not believe it.

Thereafter, regardless of its manifest futility, the arms race would be liberally funded. Within a very short time it was proved that the scientists had been right; the Russians not only had nuclear capability, they were soon firing missiles across Pacific ranges where the American navy had been thought to have a monopoly. This brought about a renewed xenophobia. Everything was sacrificed to keep superiority.

To projects for domestic advancement only token resources were apportioned; they could wait. Vast fleets were built to prowl the seas; new bombers filled the skies; armies were kept in readiness; and elaborate radar defenses were improvised. The countryside fell into neglect; the cities rotted; the occupations of war kept workers from those of peace. No serious attempt to assess mutual interests was made.

There was at hand everything necessary for recasting the whole encasement of men and for reordering their relations with one another. There were skills, rich stores of materials, and unlimited sources of energy; but there existed a simplistic conviction that communism was ruinous and must be combatted at any cost wherever it appeared; and, of course, a similar conviction in Russia about capitalism.

There is no doubt that the Russians were equally intransigent. They believed, or professed to believe, that they were threatened by pre-emptive attacks; and neither side, fear and pride dominant, made such approaches as reason dictated for two powers, each with vast and sufficient resources and neither with cause to covet what the other had. There seemed to be no end to this; there was no break in the stern, even violent, attitudes on either side.

All this would be seen in time to be waste. The most immense potentialities for progress in all the history of mankind waited to be opened; but everything was sacrificed to a war that could not happen.

Twenty-five years was time enough to discover these realities; technological progress, given the momentum attained during the war, was phenomenal; each scientific breakthrough burst into a constellation of potentially useful consequences; the number of those who could have used this time and these resources for better purposes was more than adequate; but nothing would be clearer after a quarter-century than that genocidal weapons had at once created a situation precluding their use and that going on with their manufacture and deployment had been folly.

In assessing how much of the concentration on such policies was the result of events moving out of the past into an inevitable future, and how much could have been averted or modified by probable Rooseveltian strategies, there may be no certainties, but there can be something more than guesses. These can be supported with some credibility by what is known of his hopes and intentions both for his own people and for others.

If it is taken this way—as what Roosevelt would have wanted—it is relevant to ask what *were* his beliefs; what *were* his pledges; what *were* his talents; what *was* his expectation of being given leave to go on?

James Reston said something worth repeating just at the end of 1969 (December 26, in his newspaper column):

> Were the young men and women right that the new problems destroyed the old values? Not in middle-aged terms but in their own? The dream of the best of them—for a new philosophy and a new world of peace and justice and equality, and a new personal world of meaning and serenity—would this really be achieved by denying the old values of religious faith and fidelity and austerity in personal love, and by mocking, not only the old hypocrisies, but the old verities?

He thought not, and ended by remarking that "the problems of life go on, and the '70's may need even more faith, and even more trust in human relations than the '60's."

It can be put down as the most undeniable of all the possible assertions about Roosevelt's view of the future that his verities were these same old ones. He would say that Americans' troubles do not come from the source the young men Reston spoke of would assign. The impasse was reached because those values were *not* honored, at least in such ways as would make them effective. This is one difference between Roosevelt and his successors that may be spotted at once. They had the same intentions, but they were faithful to them in very different ways, ways so different that the ends themselves were distorted.

More precisely it may be said that the large were confused with the small; the accustomed were assumed to be the essential; the open were confused with the closed. It was a disservice to have designated part of the world as "free" in contrast with a part that was "not free." The Soviet Union was meant, of course, to be excluded when the free world was spoken of. It was not mentioned that in Czarist Russia there had been even less freedom, or that, if anything, communism had been a gain in that respect. As for expansionism, it was forgotten that Russians had always meant, if they could, to reach the warm water ports to the south; this had been a first principle of national strategy during the centuries when sea power was paramount and not having it a fatal weakness. Had the *Drang nach Osten* of the Germans also been forgotten? It was essentially the same ambition that had persisted through Russian history: to open the Dardanelles and be free to use the Mediterranean.

There was no reason why, in new arrangements for the peace, the Russians should have been excluded from these waters, and no reason why the Moslems should have been allowed to play the familiar game of setting one great power against the other. The United States did not need to assume the British responsibility for blocking Russia at the Dardanelles. It had been an imperial necessity, but was no longer; and what did the United States have to gain? The Mediterranean could not be made an American lake. It was important for world commerce; but it could well have been shared. If it had, the Suez Canal might have been kept open, and warfare along its banks might never have occurred.

The insuperable obstacle was that neither Russia nor the United States accepted the new reality that control of the air had superseded control of the sea as the means to power; the corollary that, technically, the air required to be shared, naturally was not accepted either. The skies could not be monopolized; and there were no recognizable boundaries. The doctrine of exclusive air space was impossible to enforce except as to landing places; and the invention of long-range jets, then of satellites, made it obsolete even while its enforcement was being expensively undertaken. It was lingering in the past—statesmen joined generals after the war in blindness about the technology of the future—that was responsible for hundreds of thousands of casualties in jungle and brush wars. To confine communism within invisible fences, incredible sacrifices were made—all tragically futile. The result, at best, was the division of Germany, Korea, and Vietnam in order to save half of each from the communists. Abandonment of geographic and economic sense to achieve these results would be looked on almost at once as examples of stupidity inexcusable in statesmen. The quite legitimate question whether, for their people, either the South Korean or the South Vietnamese governments were better than their northern counterparts was never asked; but both were dictatorships, and both were run by a privileged military elite. How much, actually, was there to choose?

Nothing answered to the test of reason in Europe but a United States of Europe reaching to the old Polish border; and nothing answered to that test in Southeast Asia but putting together again the new nations of the old Indo-China. It passes understanding that Americans could have hoped to make viable by force half of Korea and half of Vietnam, open to invasion from the North and with a long and unmarked sanctuary to the west. Yet such an effort was assigned to the military forces; and it was allowed to absorb half or more of the American national budget for the best part of a decade. This was an allocation of resources defensible only if disaster should be imminent; the budget was continually in deficit.

To make matters complete, there soon appeared second and third generations of weapons; intercontinental ballistic missiles were armed with nuclear warheads; and presently each missile carried numbers of such weapons. Within a few years the East-West confrontation could be seen to have been revolutionized even by the blindest eyes. The navies as well as the armies were overleapt. The artillery of World War II (until the final phase when the German V-2 bombs became operational) had a range of no more than a few miles. The missiles stretched it to thousands. Russians now covered Chicago and St. Louis as well as the buried missile

silos in midcontinent; and Americans were prepared to eliminate the nuclear centers in Siberia as well as Stalingrad,
Kazan, and Moscow.

The President of the United States as commander in chief
never stirred without being tailed by an officer with the key
to the release of intercontinental missiles; and it was certain
that some one in Russia was similarly on call.

Since neither superpower could achieve more than deterrence, this mutual arming finally reached the limit of absurdity. The weapons could never be used but must always
exist as a sterile retaliatory threat; but all mankind lived in
the shadow of the monstrous possibilities of technical error
or mistaken release. Fear that this would happen or that the
responsible individual might be stricken with paranoia (as
one American Secretary of Defense had been) must lurk in
the back of every citizen's mind.

Yet, until the 'seventies began, there was no serious attempt to reach agreed behavior in the standoff. There was
only the mutual threat trusted by each to be sufficient.

It cannot be conceived that Roosevelt would have allowed
such a situation to develop. He was traditionally a navy man;
but he had startled the nation in 1940 with a speech warning
inland cities that attack from the air was their greatest
danger and must be met not by building more ships but by
producing an incredible fifty thousand planes at once. He
had modernized the lessons he had learned as a schoolboy
from reading Mahan on seapower.

The new navy, built after Pearl Harbor, had been victorious at Midway and had gone on finally to sink the whole
Japanese fleet. It had abandoned guns for plane-launchers
from carrier decks. Battles were conducted not by ships can-
nonading each other but by the sighting of enemies by radar
and bombing them from the air. A British admiral went down
with the *Prince of Wales* off Singapore in 1940 protesting
that his ship was invulnerable from the air. This was the
end of the battleship. Roosevelt's active nostalgia did not

interfere with his perception that an end had come to an era and that another was beginning.

Others, however, refused to be convinced. In 1970 the seventh fleet, a magnificent anachronism, patrolled Asian waters to keep open the narrow passages leading to the Indian Ocean. The equally splendid sixth fleet cruised the Mediterranean to protect the underbelly of Europe, to shelter Israel, and presumably to frustrate the extension of Russian influence in the Near East. If that was its purpose it was failing. The Dardanelles were open, and Turkey was following the Arab nations into the Russian orbit. The Russian fleet matched that of the Americans. The two, playing a childish game of interference with each other's maneuvers, created perilous potentialities; but there were no negotiations for their reduction or for accommodation.

The Russians were acquiring bases along the southern coast of the Mediterranean, and the old Allies were being expelled as enemies of the Arabs. Russian fleets would be at home there as the sixth fleet was on the northern coast in France, Italy, and Greece. But what relevance had either if missile bases as well as port facilities should be established?

What could be more obvious than that the way to have avoided this was by arrangement between the Russians and the Americans? One element of this would have been not to have encouraged Israel to plant herself like a thorn in the side of the Arab nations but instead to have negotiated for coexistence. It would have been better, obviously, to have made a mutual pact for sharing the Mid-East waters. Why not? What the Russians wanted was access to the warm seas. The Europeans did want Arabian oil; but the Arabians also wanted to sell it. There was the complication of oil companies' profitable businesses, but the Red Sea was a distant area for the American flag to pursue the dollar. Besides, the dollars were actually mostly pounds, francs, or kroner. The United States did not need the oil, and assurance of oil companies' profits was a doubtful national objective.

The solid determination to make the Mediterranean an American naval monopoly, and to encourage further affronts to the Arabs, was the more foolish because it deliberately sacrificed the Moslem revulsion from communism. The unnatural alliance between Arabs and Russians was an entirely unnecessary occurrence. It was one of John Foster Dulles' worse attacks of moral energy that led the Arabs to seek Russian assistance. As a final gesture he petulantly withdrew the agreement to build the Aswan Dam. This project was a symbol of Egyptian ambition. Its abandonment signaled a hostility the Russians had no difficulty at all in exploiting. They went on and did the construction. With Moslem allies, they were thereafter firmly fixed in the Eastern Mediterranean and would gradually extend themselves toward both East and West. The commitment to Israel was one the United States, if for no more than geographic reasons, could not maintain.

This illustrated something considered by Roosevelt to be elementary—that allies are better than occupying forces. The conclusion subsidiary to this is obvious: nations, like people, should never undertake more than they can do. World hegemony is not only impossibly expensive, it is not even possible if there are other more or less equal powers in possession of some parts of it. It is prudent to measure how much is of genuine interest to one or the others. The quixotic notion that communism could be contained involved shutting Russia within fences she would not and need not recognize. It was one thing to help Europe, for instance; it was quite another to undertake the defense not only of Israel, but of Greece and Turkey.

Roosevelt meant the occupation of Germany to be a disciplinary arrangement. That the former enemy should almost at once have become a fiercely defended ally was a provocation to the other partners in victory.

After 1945, distances no longer guaranteed security. The seas could not be relied on as they had once been. Two allies in the war—Russia and China—were alienated; and Britain and France no longer counted greatly in the balance of power. While the American nuclear monopoly lasted—only some ten years—it provided a dissolving advantage. The logic of containment and of temporary capability clearly called for a preventive attack on enemies it was firmly believed were intending world conquest. Why was it not undertaken?

The answer to this is obvious. It would have been outrageous to do so. An accounting to mankind or to history for such an act would have been impossible to sustain. Genocide —the indiscriminate slaughter of populations—was so repugnant that, although it might end communism, it would never be forgiven. There were those who advocated it; but they were not seriously listened to. This was a weakness because, when the monopoly disappeared, the fears of Russian expansion would remain and would dominate foreign policy; but by 1970 nuclear superiority had vanished, and arrangements for coexistence had to be undertaken that might better have been made in the beginning, when American nonaggressive protestations would have been more credible.

If there was one thing about Roosevelt more evident than anything else it was his realism. He directed the obliteration of Hitler, Mussolini, and the Japanese military clique because it had to be done; they might well have conquered the earth and imposed upon its people their joint imperialist rule, holding the lesser populations in submission. But his active sense would not have allowed him to join in Russian containment. It was unnecessary, and, besides, it was impossible. It required a crusade without the slightest possibility of victory.

His successors acted from fright. They took seriously the communists' pretensions to world conquest; but Roosevelt would have seen that Russian expansion must exhaust itself not far beyond the borders it would reach anyway by 1970— that is, on the line across Europe and at the openings into the Mediterranean. Their drive to go further could not have succeeded if they had not been provided with allies by American mistakes. As it was, their attempt to dominate China failed, and their hegemony in Eastern Europe was no longer sustained by unthinking loyalty to Moscow as the Mecca of communism; but American assistance had no part in establishing these limits. Efforts to contain were exhausted by the futile defense of Berlin, by support of Israel, by wars in Southeast Asia, and by the cost of immense naval and air fleets. In the end so much had been spent on these that internal decay had made itself frighteningly apparent even to the survivors of the containment generation.

The United States was not made insecure by enemies but by the folly of its statesmen. Roosevelt would not have been one of these. Security must rest on a strong and loyal nation; it cannot rest on a weakened and divided one.

2. Well-Being

When Roosevelt reminded his increasingly affluent countrymen that one-third of their fellow Americans were still ill-nourished, ill-clad, and ill-housed, he was accusing them of an indifference he meant to shatter. Here was an injustice they could not excuse; there was no lack of resources; they were simply being used for the benefit of two-thirds; the others were excluded. Good Christians professed to be their brothers' keepers; but actually they were neglectful. This was not because the more fortunate were bad people; they simply did not realize that it was no longer possible to rely on the principle that each man looked after his own and that the few exceptions would be taken care of by local charities. Poverty had become a national problem. He did not conceal that there was a price, a high price, attached; but, he reminded them, the social costs of neglect would be much higher.

A man who wanted to work but could not find a job could not support his family; he could not support it either if he happened to be disabled or too aged to work any longer. Being unemployed was not necessarily his fault; his job may have disappeared; he may have been displaced by a machine, by a new invention, or by some other change beyond his control; or he may have been forced to move to a place where what he knew how to do was not wanted. Anyway, allowing children to suffer for their parents' maladjustments was to punish them for something they had not done. It was worse; it was to make certain that the citizenry of later years would be incompetent and disaffected.

He made these arguments over and over; and presently he began to prevail. The Congress was often antagonistic for reasons of its own—there was insensitivity, there was preoccupation with other matters, there was concern for localities; and then too it was naturally obstructive. At any rate what was done was not enough. Nevertheless the country was started on the way to responsible mutual care through government. He meant to see the policy grow and expand until no one had to go hungry, or cold, or without a place to live.

If someone had suggested to him that some thirty years later another President would find it necessary to launch a "war on poverty" he would have thought it incredible. He himself had begun with the temporary measures made possible by the panic in 1933 and the temporary consent he could win for extraordinary measures. The Federal Emergency Relief Administration, later to become the familiar Works Progress Administration, the Public Works Administration, and, a little later, the Resettlement Administration, made beginnings. Then there was assistance for farmers and homeowners who were about to be dispossessed.

All these would have been unthinkable in 1928, before the

Depression set in. Almost at once, Roosevelt had progressed (in 1934) to the launching of the Social Security system. This last, with its various programs, was meant finally to be the agency entrusted with the permanent ending of poverty. It was to provide for the aged, the disabled, the unemployed, for mothers with unsupported families, and for orphaned children. The traditional poor-houses of rural America were to be put out of business. He did not have the illusion that all individuals could be made productive or that some of them were not naturally shiftless, but he did mean to lessen the consequences of even these failings for their dependents, who were not to blame.

His successors, to put it bluntly, did not enlarge what he had started. They did not stop it; but the system was starved, kept at levels so low as to be far less than the need. Also, because its administration was largely left to the states, it was very unevenly managed, with comparative decency in most Northern states and penuriously throughout the South —where much of the displacement problem had originated. Racial discrimination complicated this, sometimes sabotaged it. Southern officials simply found it impossible to bring blacks up toward equality. They were used to subservience; and they found independence intolerable. The levels of benefit were kept very low indeed all along the Gulf and were only somewhat more adequate in the border states.

The administration was so ungenerous and the funds so limited that there was, indeed, a need only less critical in 1964 than there had been in 1935. By 1970, in spite of Johnson's brief and frustrated "war" in the 'sixties, it had taken on ugly characteristics. Assistance was so disgracefully stingy that there were still proliferating slums and still hungry children. It was made worse by the knowledge that the insufficiencies were not attributable to lack of resources but rather to repeated decisions that meeting the responsibilities of world power—and especially of containing communism— were more important than the realization of economic equality at home. Both could not be paid for except by intolerable inflation that would take away much of whatever was provided. Even with the levels that were maintained, deficits and inflation were continuous.

More was involved in the demands of foreign policy than the outlays for expeditionary forces in Europe and Asia, high as these were. There were the other costs of containment. American armament had to be more destructive than that of the Russians, so increasingly elaborate weapons systems were repeatedly developed and, almost before their installation, were abandoned. This happened to the early warning system facing Russia across the Arctic. It happened to the buried silos containing missiles that became a surplus item put up for sale almost before they were operational. This was much like the experience of France with a Maginot line before the Germans outflanked it in a few days of 1940. It was true of the immense strategic air command that kept giant bombers in the air for unexplained years after their usefulness had vanished. Their ceaseless patrols gave way only belatedly to the reality of intercontinental missiles. Meanwhile, like other obsolete weapons systems, their costs approached the fantastic.

The constant improvement of nuclear weaponry not only required the construction and abandonment of intricate installations but also absorbed scientific, technological, and managerial talent that ought to have been at work on domestic improvements—for instance, the cultivation and distribution of food, the improvement of power resources, the creation of transportation systems, the rehabilitation of cities and the provision of housing. All these, except the provision of food—there had been near miracles in agriculture—were registering shortages in 1970. There were not enough communications, highways were crowded and unsafe, city slums were spreading, schools were antiquated, water supplies were unsafe—the catalogue of things undone that might have been done was long.

What could be done to increase the food supply was demonstrated during the 'sixties by privately financed effort in the Philippines, and Mexico, where research developed strains of rice so superior to the ones in use that productivity could be increased without delay by several times. Impressive gains had been made at home by Department of Agriculture scientists; but what they served to show was how much more could have been done if such efforts had been more generously supported. Actually there were surpluses; they had to be reduced by shipments abroad. Clearly no one needed to starve; nevertheless starvation was uncovered by investigations in 1970; and there were millions of families who still were to be described by Roosevelt's earlier words: they were ill-nourished, ill-clothed, and ill-housed.

Roosevelt had meant people to have food; he had meant them also to live decently otherwise, in homes they could take pride in and with no fear of being put out into the street by the traditional bailiffs. He had meant more. He had meant to see their environments reconstructed, the slums razed, the cities spread out and made a constellation of centers with greenbelts interconnected and mutually supporting. In 1936 he got approval for all this. He got it from the electorate by such overwhelming majorities as had not been known since Jeffersonian times. It had become customary for Presidents to be granted second terms; they got them, however, by conscienceless use of party machines; these had been nurtured by patronage and favor-giving; and their majorities were invariably reduced. Roosevelt's victory was a different kind. It came from that coalition of the disadvantaged who instinctively understood that he was assisting a better world to emerge from the old one. In his first election he had not so much won for himself as profited by Hoover's unpopularity; in his next, the result amounted to a popular uprising. His supporters then expected, as they had a right to do, that he would go on to fulfill the promise of his first term. Now returning prosperity would absorb the unemployed; now poverty would be cured; now the nation's physical equipment would be made adequate; now the land and its people would be rehabilitated; now there would be freedom from old fears.

That did not happen. His victories, because of the curious hostility of legislators, in the American system, to the chief executive, did not win him Congressional influence. He had more enemies than supporters. His party had a majority; but their resistance to Presidential leadership was strengthened because it was he who had carried them into office.

There were other reasons why those who were elected in 1936 opposed Roosevelt. Many were Southerners who objected strenuously to independence for farm workers and sharechoppers; some represented employers whose fears had been aroused by the legalization of unions; others resented the closer regulation of bankers and speculators; still others resisted exclusion from public resources. Legislators' loyalty was owed to their particular supporters—campaign contributors, local bosses, lobbyists—who had favors to give. The President represented a public to whom the legislators owed no debt.

It was then that Roosevelt turned to the Court for approval of the New Deal measures already passed. It was too late for some; they had been declared unconstitutional; but he imagined he might after all win approval by mustering the vast public support manifested in the election. If he did, however, and the validation was refused, he would be no better off than before. Finally he proposed a reorganization of the Court; and, in this, enemy forces found a cause they could exploit. It was said that he was attempting to destroy a sacred institution; and to the two-thirds of the legislators who were lawyers his scheme seemed unforgivable effrontery. Many of them—those who had fully recovered from the panic of a few years earlier—applauded the Court's refusal to approve the New Deal measures. Important members were

from safe Southern districts; and these, together with the
naturally antagonistic Republicans, set up an alliance that
effectually resisted Presidential urging.

In fact, conservative Democrats had organized a Liberty
League in the campaign of 1936 and had tried their best to
convince the country that they must not re-elect a dangerous
radical, who, if he kept on, would destroy the most precious
institutions of the Republic—beginning with the Constitution! They did not much influence that election; but they did
form a hard core of resistance to change.

The proposals for reorganizing the Court in 1937 seemed
to confirm the fears of conservatives. Certainly many more
were brought into the opposition than had joined it before
the election. Roosevelt's majority had been so overwhelming
that it had included among its numbers many Democrats
who were presumed by their constituents to be his supporters, but who actually would work to check him if they could.
Besides, resting on the popular approval just registered, he
was careless in the maneuvering of that spring; and he was
defeated. Not only the Court plan was lost but also the power
he had hoped to re-establish over the Congress. The country
was confused. There was so much conservative hysteria that
even staunch Rooseveltians developed doubts. One success
for his enemies encouraged other resistances. He could no
longer ask for legislation and get it. He could no longer even
get the funds he requested for the measures already approved; some agencies were refused appropriations altogether. There was question for a while whether Social Security might not be repealed. This, however, was too much;
the swelling protest at any such suggestion awed even the
most determined opponent. This, at least, would survive the
succeeding years of stalemate.

Before the election of 1940, when Roosevelt decided to
ignore the custom of quitting after a second term, he had
reordered his forces and gathered the coalition spoken of by
Scammon. This in itself was a political feat requiring sophis-

tication and the use of all his professional talents; it was, however, so well calculated a change that it seemed, afterward, to have come about almost by itself.

In his first campaign, in 1932, the South and the Midwest had united in an agreement to oust Hoover. The South was solidly Democratic; but the Midwest was almost as solidly Republican, although it had often exhibited a kind of rural radicalism; before the new century had begun, and when adjustments were being made after the Civil War, the Populists had made life hard for both the old parties in the prairie states. They were farmer dissidents who ranted about the "barons in Wall Street" and the "money power," and who felt themselves ill-treated by the new industrialists in general, and the railroads in particular, who charged too much for taking their produce to Eastern markets.

Especially, however, both Westerners and Southerners hated the financiers who held their mortgages. The interest on these was extracted without mercy and, if not paid, led to foreclosure. The grievance persisted as settlements moved westward across the prairies; it turned into Progressivism and split the Republican party in 1912, when Theodore Roosevelt headed the Bull Moose movement. Progressives returned to the Republican party after T.R. was defeated; but they were uneasy and often intractable. This Roosevelt appealed to them much as the older Roosevelt had done. He promised a better time for farmers. He did not ask them to become Democrats, only to vote for him. This they did in 1932 and, less enthusiastically, in 1936, having become better off by then and not really liking their inadvertent Democratic association.

By 1940, they had defected; and the South was none too loyal, not liking the New Deal much since it tended to make the colored folks more independent. Southerners were not yet ready to leave the party they had belonged to since the nation's beginning; but they were dead set against the threat federal welfare offered to their special institution.

A new coalition was forming. The city bosses and the labor leaders were joining forces to support a program both regarded as theirs. A good deal had been done for city dwellers, especially the poorest ones, mostly those who had migrated from farming country. Relief and work-relief had made the difference between the starvation of the Depression years and the sure, if minimal, incomes of the welfare system. This might not be much, but it was something. As for labor, it was newly enfranchised; collective bargaining was legalized; unions were burgeoning; and generations of virtual warfare with employers were ending in victory for labor. This was Roosevelt's doing, and labor was willing to repay him with votes.

In 1932 Roosevelt's most ardent enemies had been the city bosses. They were Al Smith's supporters; he was one of them, straight out of Tammany Hall in New York. When he lost the nomination to Roosevelt they were sullen and uncooperative during the campaign. By 1940, however, a new generation of bosses was beginning to appear, ones who could accommodate to the welfare workers. The hold of ward leaders on the slum dwellers had been undermined; the boss was no longer asked for a scuttle of coal, a small loan, or help in getting a job. He now had to be a genuinely political leader and more beholden to the party organization.

The workers, now organized and meeting employers face to face in equal bargaining, meant to keep the President in power who had wrought the revolution in their circumstances. They set up political adjuncts to union organizations, collected funds, did industrious service, and, as the older leaders defected, took their places with enormous satisfaction.

Between them, the city bosses and the union representatives gave Roosevelt his third victory against the bitter opposition of the conservative party elders. Garner, the old Texas war horse, was displaced as the Vice-Presidential candidate by Henry Wallace, the Progressive from Iowa; and even Farley, so closely identified with Roosevelt since Albany days, left the party chairmanship and joined the opposition. He could not accept, he said, the third-term innovation. Actually he held to a partisanship now fading from politics. His people were the machine bosses, now being replaced by a younger generation. Some of the older men held on by going along with the new dispensation, as Farley would not. Ed Flynn in New York, for instance, took over the chairmanship of the party and ran a very effective campaign. Farley simply disappeared from public life.

Roosevelt had now swung things around so that what he wanted for the nation was exactly what his new supporters also wanted. The nation was on the way to a change so well anchored in public interest that indifference would never return. The Congress, however, had changed very little; it was there that he was checked.

Then both Hitler and the Japanese warlords had to be dealt with. Roosevelt had watched Germany with growing concern ever since Hitler had become Chancellor—coincidentally with his own accession to the Presidency. He seemed to Roosevelt to offer from the first an indecent threat, with his talk of Nordic supremacy, his totalitarian regime, and his aggressive rearmament. Before long, Roosevelt's fears were supported by events; and he became convinced that whatever sacrifices had to be made would be worth it if the world could be rid of the Nazi menace. He had been certain for a long time too that the Japanese were working up to a confrontation in their determination to subjugate all of Asia. These looming necessities would require a vast national gathering of energy. It would be necessary to rearm; but this would have to be prepared for by making clear to the people how serious the threat might be. They were preoccupied with recovery and the resumption of progress, and naturally so; it would not be easy. Besides, he had no intention of abandoning his plans for domestic reform and rehabilitation. These might have to be modified or even put aside for the moment; but they could be come back to when whatever necessary had been done to cleanse the earth of totalitarianism. Dr. Win-the-War would give way then for the return of Dr. New Deal.

3. *Good Husbandry*

When Harold Ickes died in retirement, Walter Lippmann said of him that he had been "a proprietor in the nation's estate." Ickes had been Secretary of the Interior and so directly responsible for many resources—replaceable and irreplaceable; but the remark would have been equally appropriate if it had been made about Roosevelt. His reason for choosing so dedicated a conservationist had been precisely because of Ickes' reputation among Progressives for this sense of proprietorship.

It was a dedication understood very well by Roosevelt, whose father had taught him firmly that ownership of land carried a responsibility for its care. It must always be put to its best uses and must each year be made more productive than it had been the year before. Everything must increase; nothing must run down. James had taken his small son by the hand on expeditions about the estate to show him what was meant. The details of management were explained—the crops, the woodland, the animals, the orchards. In all weathers the boy had watched what went on and had had a part in it. Before the day of automobiles he had had a pony—and taken care of it himself. He had seen milk produced, butter made; he had seen hay come in from the fields to feed the cattle and the manure saved and spread to increase fertility. All of this had become a part of his life.

Springwood was an estate, of course, more than a farm.

Its operations would not stop if they did not pay; but it was better not to run deficits. The family had a house in New York City but it was used less and less as the years passed, and the boy liked it much better in the country. They traveled too, having numerous friends in England who lived on similar estates and had the same sort of properties. What it meant to own, and care for what was owned, became something accepted and right. Like his religion, young Roosevelt never questioned his responsibility. His relation to the place that became his mother's when his father died, and gradually became his own, is not to be described as love, exactly; more, what is—or used to be—conveyed by the word "proprietorship." It was where a person belonged, so it was home too. In Robert Frost's words, it did not have to be deserved; but it was better to deserve it than just to accept its benefits.

His attitude in later life toward the nation's land and waters, as well as the people of his constituencies, is better understood if this about him is kept in mind. He thought of the country as being made up of families who should all have the duties and cares that went with home ownership. What had been going on, and grew much worse during the Depression, was a taking away from people of their home places and giving them in return only temporary lodgings belonging to someone else. This was what happened to millions in the South displaced by agricultural machinery. It happened also to the dust-bowl farmers. It was made worse because they could find refuge only in strange environments where just getting along required a kind of expertness in survival they did not have, and, above all, where they had no land to look after and to support them.

Never in American history had so many displaced people been forced to migrate and live temporarily in city slums or roadside camps. How could they think of themselves as responsible citizens interested in government and concerned with national problems? It was absurd to think of them as full and contributing citizens. Roosevelt wanted them to be settled and, if they had no land, at least to have jobs; then they would take part in the country's affairs. They would think of it as theirs.

He never really accepted cities; he said, as a young legislator, that they did something distressing to those who lived in them. They detached citizens from duties they ought to have and separated them from the harmonies of nature. For years he had the hope that a countryward migration would take place, reversing that to the cities. It ought to be possible to provide homesteads, small ones, of course, where unhappy and badly adjusted city people could get back their accustomed relationships, find new respect, and become self-supporting. It was an impractical dream, considering the massive displacements then going on, but as Governor and as President he tried to implement it. When his subsistence homesteads proved to be failures, he tried other ways of accomplishing something of the sort. One of his early projects was an enlarged farm credit organization, quickly followed by a Federal Home Loan Bank. These were meant to keep people from being put off their farms and out of their homes and having to join the appalling number of renters and drifters.

This conviction about people and their responsibilities carried over into his relief policies. His constant urging to Hopkins, who was in charge, was to find work projects rather than to provide money; he believed there was a deep instinct involved in it. This had to do with self-respect and doing for those who were dependent. He not only wanted every citizen to earn his way but also to have a say in what that way would be. Some of the unemployed were actually put to work building homes. Hopkins did it in the cities on a small scale; it was done by the Public Works Administration tentatively; and it was undertaken by Suburban Resettlement; but none got very far, being opposed by embattled realtors and by the building trades unions as well, both supported by the press. There were more results from the guaranteed mortgage plans of the successive Federal Housing Administrations. In these the bankers and realtors could share; and union labor was employed. The trouble was, as with so much during the depression, that the problems grew faster than the most massive moves to meet them. The Congress was horrified at every successive proposal and yielded appropriations so reluctantly that there were no more than token results. The degeneration Roosevelt had feared went on. If he had lived beyond the war, he would certainly have returned to the resettlement effort. Before 1970 it might have transformed the countryside and made the cities more livable.

Then there was Social Security. This proposal, announced in 1933, when the Depression was just beginning to be relieved by emergency measures, was a surprise to everyone; but it had been in his mind for a long time and had evolved out of the same conviction that some attachment must be restored. He was well aware that it had had such an effect in Britain and Germany; and he saw no reason why the United States should not follow their example. He thought of the system as giving the elderly a reward for having worked all their years and others protection from the risks of their working lives. It would not be something given; it would be insurance, not charity; it would be deserved because of service of one or another sort. People could be sure that in sickness or when they were old they would have incomes. There would be freedom from the petty tyrannies of loan companies, no need to sell votes or to depend on charity. They could have homes and not be afraid of losing them.

As to the use of the public estate, he meant to enlarge and improve it in several ways. As population grew there was need for more reachable open spaces and more recreation areas. During his Presidency many new parks were established, especially in the East, where until then there had been very few; forests were expanded, and the Civilian Conservation Corps was set up with the double purpose of taking idle young men out of the cities and putting them to work, and of improving the forests and grasslands.

Combined with this was the program for retiring from use land submarginal for agriculture and putting it to other uses. People were living—some poorly, some desperately—on worn-out farms that never again would be productive. Often they had used up all their resources and could not even move. To get a better farm was impossible since there was no money and no credit. If, however, the government bought their farms and loaned them the funds to provide themselves with better ones, they could be brought again into a hopeful working life. The unproductive land thus purchased could be consolidated into forests and recreation reserves. Millions of acres of cut-over timber, eroded hillsides, and worn-out farmlands were bought, and the people there given the opportunity to start again in better circumstances. States and cities accepted the freed land for parks; and they were put in shape by the Civilian Conservation Corps.

As for the cities being overwhelmed by the displaced rural people who could not be returned to agriculture, there ought to be satellite towns of a size somewhere between the metropolis and the village. The suburban division of the Resettlement Administration had sixty of these in preparation in 1935, but by 1937 the only three actually granted funds for construction were so savagely attacked by the real estate interests, through the press they controlled by advertising, that the Congress refused more money. The three were never finished, and no more were built. But it was an idea Roosevelt never gave up, and, finally, it could be seen being returned to in a hundred places in 1970. This was much too late to prevent serious degeneration. By that time cities were beset by problems that ought never to have become acute and were being freely described as unmanageable.

All of these ways of improving the land and the condition of its families ought to have been returned to after the war and in such a size and shape as would amount to renewal. This was what he meant to do; agricultural evolution would have been controlled, and displaced farmers and workers would have been provided for; there would have been satellite towns with protective greenbelts; public lands would have been improved; and the problems of overcrowding and of pollution would have had attention. This was an entirely possible program if the suddenly adopted policy of containment had not absorbed all available funds.

Year by year after the war the situation should have been improved; instead, year by year it deteriorated. By 1970 the most careless citizen was made aware of the mistakes and miscalculations he had allowed his leaders to make. If he was old enough he recalled the surge of hope and patriotic endeavor felt everywhere when Roosevelt took over from Hoover. If he was younger he wondered what might have happened if that kind of leadership had been available when victory over the totalitarians had been won and the opportunities of peace had opened up. The energies and resources available would have been more than adequate.

4. *Justice*

They were still calling it "the Roosevelt Court" when, in 1969, Warren Burger was appointed to the Chief Justiceship of the United States in place of Earl Warren, who had just resigned; thereafter it began to be called the Nixon Court. It had been a controversial twenty-five years; it had begun in differences between Hughes, as Chief Justice, and Roosevelt, as President, over the rejection, as unconstitutional, of the National Recovery Act and other New Deal projects, followed by Roosevelt's subsequent attempt in 1937 to "pack" the court with appointments of his own. He lost the battle, it might be said, but won the war; resignations soon gave him the opportunities foreclosed in 1937, and he was able to establish a liberal majority. It approved every measure he could persuade the Congress to pass; and it lasted for twenty-five years, the one consistently liberal enclave in a government devoted uncertainly, but too often, to suppression at home and aggression abroad.

Adolf Berle went so far as to call the Warren Court of the 1960s "a revolutionary committee," but, although this charge came from a respected Professor of Law, the characterization was disapproved of with practical unanimity by his fellow academicians. They regarded the Court's expansion of its own powers as no more than proper implementation of the Constitution. Particularly the amendments constituting the Bill of Rights were discovered to have meanings undreamed of since 1787.

There was hardly a time during the whole period when the Court was not being thus praised or attacked and often both at the same time. Its detractors were certain it was undermining the foundations of American life; journeying across the South, a traveler would repeatedly see billboards urging with bold brevity: IMPEACH EARL WARREN. Endless law review articles were written to prove that the Court was only making the Constitution effective at last; even more endless speeches asserted that the Justices were substituting themselves for the legislature and that they were ignoring the principle of separated powers. They seemed revolutionary to some but not to others; but the question whether the Court had exceeded its constitutional warrant and had become another legislative body was not contested. It had; but the further question whether it should be restricted was not so clear; nor was it clear how it might be done.

At one time the controversy centered in permissive decisions on pornography and obscenity; at another, censorship was practically outlawed; presently a "separate but equal"

criterion for segregated schools was reversed, outraging an
already annoyed majority in the South. Educational integration was now decreed; and this was even more irritating. On
this, and some other issues, the Court relied on the equal
protection clause of the fourteenth amendment, bringing it
to the support of the earlier amendments in the so-called Bill
of Rights. There was serious polarization between liberals
and conservatives, just as Roosevelt had expected; and the
way had not been prepared by Presidential leadership. Even
in 1970 it was Nixon's policy to conciliate the conservatives
and to deplore the harassment of those who held back from
the establishment of equality.

It was certainly true that the judiciary seemed to regard
itself as warranted in disposing all the powers of government.
Issues were decided not only in principle but were directed
to be corrected in specific ways. In controversial instances
such as segregation, federal judges, calling on the Justice
Department for an army of marshals, saw to it that submission to their decrees was complete, even setting time limits
for compliance. The position of the Court—its claim to supremacy—became an issue transcending the particular instances.
It was pointed out that a different majority might have taken
an opposite stance, and there was an increasing objection to
judicial settlement of controversial matters more properly
belonging to politics.

The Warren Court had not decided all such questions;
and it was feared that similar decisions would follow. One
of the most annoying to conservatives had been the require-
ment that state legislative districts should be reapportioned.
Redistricting was not only directed, but the percentage of
permissible departure from absolute equality of representation was prescribed. This had furious repercussions in the
Senate, and it seemed for a time quite possible that jurisdic-
tion over such questions might be restricted. The Senators
were conscious, naturally, that their body was the most notorious example of malrepresentation it was possible to imagine

—it was hard to explain why a compromise in 1787, calculated to appease the smaller states, should still persist in the late twentieth century, giving Rhode Island and Texas, Vermont and California equal representation in the upper legislative house. In view of this the well-seated legislators of the states felt themselves unfairly discriminated against. Anyway, they distrusted city people; the old rural values were being lost. Nevertheless the decree stood.

Then the Court offended those who were charged with the administration of criminal justice by firming rules for the protection of those suspected or charged with offenses. The police, already losing in their effort to cope with a rising wave of crime, were restricted in making arrests on suspicion, in questioning without restraint, and generally in taking the measures they regarded as essential to the control of criminals. Streets were no longer safe, and whole neighborhoods were at the mercy of apparently unchecked hoodlums.

The causes were numerous, beginning with rural migration to the cities; and this went back to excessive birth rates among the poor, expulsion of workers from agricultural occupations, the unemployability of the displaced, and the unwillingness of the Congress to authorize planned resettlement. To have discovered, after more than a century and a half, that suspected criminals were being deprived of their constitutional rights was regarded as ridiculous. Crime went on increasing as its causes intensified; but after the Court's decisions the law enforcement authorities were able to pass the blame on to the Justices.

Another issue was equally disturbing. The separation of church and state implied in the few words of the first amendment having to do with "establishment of religion" was used by the Court to prohibit prayers—or even any reference to deity—in public schools. It was pointed out by outraged orators that American coins affirmed a trust in God and that this was as close to identification with deity as prayer in school, and there was uproar throughout the Christian community;

the Congress was very nearly persuaded to restrict the Court on this issue too.

Altogether, the Roosevelt Court, using the Bill of Rights, together with convenient passages from the thirteenth and fourteenth amendments, intended for the protection of freed slaves, managed to offend conservatives of every conviction and especially by repudiating the Protestant ethic of stern punishment for sinners.

Curiously enough none of this unusual and rather sudden judicial law-making extended to economic arrangements. A majority of the justices were liberals. This meant that they would go far to protect individual rights in changing circumstances. It did not mean that they understood or meant to approve the organizational changes going on in commerce and industry as a result of growth, invention, and managerial advances. On the contrary they were clearly hostile to large-scale organization and meant to follow more intensively the Brandeis line of aggressive attacks on bigness. Business was bad in proportion to its size, Brandeis had said, and, whenever possible, expansion must be repressed. This had been the theory depended on for overthrowing several New Deal measures; and it was still dominant not only in the Justices' minds but in those of the liberal community generally. Its relation to Populist theory was obvious.

The conformance of these judicial tendencies with Roosevelt's intentions for the future is not difficult to assay. He would have been pleased by the expansion of the Bill of Rights, even doubtful extrapolations of its words, such as the Court's "symbolic" free speech; but it will be recalled that the early differences leading to his court-packing effort arose from cases having to do with industrial reorganization looking to the encouragement of consolidation, concentration, and self-government in the interest of increased production and industrial peace. If he had lived he might well have had another confrontation with the Court on this issue, he proposing a policy of concentration and control—a revival, in principle, of NRA—and they clinging to orthodox *laissez faire*.

It has been hinted, however, that there is something else to be said about the Court's actions in this period. It had measurably advanced what by now seemed a persisting movement toward judicial supremacy. In one notable case, having to do with the seizure of steel mills to ensure continued production when work was stopped by an unsettled strike, it had asserted its right to tell the President what he could or could not do in an emergency; and, in another, having to do with the discipline of a member, it had asserted the same power to tell the Congress what its duties were. In a government of presumably separate and interdependent powers this was a tour de force. If it stood, interdependence and even the separation of powers no longer really existed. That is to say, neither Presidents nor Congress could define their own powers and act accordingly; they must look to the Justices for their authority.

The separation principle was so fundamental to the Constitution and was so effective in preventing any branch from gaining absolute power that the framers, having established this, had seen no need for protecting individuals from arrogant officialdom. It was doubters, after the document was submitted for ratification, who insisted on the additional protection of the first ten amendments. To have a structural principle so softened as to be nearly destroyed by Court decree was something the other branches could not afford to accept; and it would have been thought to be something constitutional lawyers would have viewed with the gravest concern.

It happened that the case affecting the Presidency* was decided in the Truman Administration. Unfortunately it did not concern a clearly defensible use of Presidential powers. In any case Truman was so awed by the Court that he gave in without protest. The case affecting the Congress was not

* Youngstown Sheet and Tube Co. vs. Sawyer, 343 U.S. 579 (1952)

very defensible either, and it was not effectively protested.°
So the Court not only survived untouched, but emerged
strengthened. Thus something begun by Chief Justice Marshall (in Madison vs. Marbury) was far advanced by the
Roosevelt Court. Judicial supremacy was, in fact, established
—or so the Justices may well have assumed.

It is as apparent as any such conclusion can ever be that
Roosevelt would not have accepted the Court's presumption
about his powers as President any more than he would have
accepted its view of economic organization. It was an issue
of this sort that had begun his trouble with the Court in the
period 1935–37. The Justices had challenged him. He had
struck back with the court-packing law. He failed to get it
adopted; but it was ample notice that the Presidency was
not willing to wait for judicial approval when emergencies
arose. What Roosevelt wanted was a government able to
act, and act promptly; one willing to accept the most productive economic organization; but careful to protect rights, and
committed to equality of opportunities and benefits.

He would have felt that the Court was dangerously ob-
structing progress toward economic efficiency, exaggerating
rights over duties, and making the government powerless in
emergencies. He would not have accepted any of this without
a struggle.

It was argued by defenders of the Court—and this included
practically all of the legal profession—that this assumption
of power by the Court was good for a number of reasons.
Among them, two were most often advanced: that Courts
were more likely to be trustworthy than Presidents, and that
only the Court, interpreting the Constitution, could prevent
disastrous decline into obsolescence.

The first was hardly demonstrable on the record; the second did make the Court, as Chief Justice Burger said, "a continuing constitutional convention." There was hardly any

° Powell vs. McCormack, 395 U.S. 486 (1969)

mention, however, of one obvious way out of both difficulties: amendment of the amending clause of the Constitution so that changes might take place more readily. The Presidency might then be adapted to modern responsibilities; and the Court might be kept from legislating. Something of this sort must have been in Roosevelt's mind. He was not reaching for more power, only for movement and adaptation to circumstances.

5. *Tranquility*

If tranquility is understood as it was meant in the preamble to the Constitution, along with other words and phrases, it becomes the most expressive word in that passage of the document. It is certain that all were carefully chosen by Gouverneur Morris and his colleagues on the Committee on Style. It did not come last either.

> We, the people, in order to form a more perfect union, establish justice, *insure domestic tranquility*, provide for the common defense, promote the general welfare and secure the blessings of liberty to ourselves and our posterity, do ordain and establish this Constitution.

Of all these intentions, tranquility, as meant by the framers, was most in jeopardy twenty-five years after Roosevelt's death. There was even question whether it was any longer as high on the list of American preferences as it had been on his.

As Roosevelt saw it, the state it described followed from responsive government, family security, equal justice, fair sharing, and a productive economy. It could not exist without protection from a remote and elitist government any more than from the vagaries of speculators, exploiters, and common criminals. Roosevelt often wondered, speaking to associates, how the American people had managed to restrain themselves during the hardships of the Depression. It was, in fact, a time of singular peace. He thought it must be because what had happened seemed to be an act of nature, not of any individuals. If factories were closed, their owners were not blamed; if debts could not be met, it was not the fault of creditors. He was quite certain, however, that if ways out were found and opposition arose, there would be trouble. The pressures were tremendous, and the pent-up distresses must be explosive.

During the Depression, nearly all, and certainly the worst, hardships had been borne by the unemployed workers and their families; at least their sufferings were more ravaging than any businessman's loss of profits or property. This would inevitably induce violent behavior when desperation gave way to a glimmer of hope. Hungry and homeless people can hardly respect institutions that allow them to be uselessly deprived of income; children cannot become well-behaved adults if they have been raised in slums. It cannot be expected that people will accept quietly exclusion from the good life others visibly enjoy.

Roosevelt wanted to end this exclusion, wanted people to have opportunities and to feel that they lived in an open and fair society where they had a chance to assume the responsibilities all men expect and ought to carry. During all his time in the White House there were no seriously violent protests directed at employers, landlords, or civil officials. The exception most often noted by historians was furnished by— of all people—farmers in the Midwest who, during the Depression, used force to prevent foreclosures or to protest ruinous prices for their products; but the masses of unemployed who had already undergone frightful privations for several years almost never demonstrated or threatened to seize by force the food and clothing they could not get otherwise. These necessities could be seen in store windows, and their families might be close to starving—but they stood it stolidly as something nothing could be done about. This very passivity was moving.

It became fashionable in later years to characterize American society as a violent one; and in time there would be plenty of evidence to support the description; but there was a disconcerting quietude in the 'thirties. It was not because he feared outbreaks of this sort that Roosevelt sponsored relief measures; he believed that, if people were told that all the resources available were being used to alleviate the deplorable conditions they were living in, and if the promises seemed credible, they would accept disciplines and endure the waiting. It was certain, however, that patience would come to an end finally; privations would not be suffered without protest when they seemed unnecessary.

So when he became President, Roosevelt moved instantly to make government the source of temporary relief and public work; but also he moved to assure the skeptical and alienated that government could and would do better than it had been doing to set things going again. Recovery from depression was not impossible; and this was a first priority. Beyond that, depressions ought to be made impossible in future—at least ones so destructive and prolonged as the one being gone through then. Only if a promise of this sort was made could some sense of belonging, some reason for contributing, be encouraged and the tranquility spoken of in the Constitution be ensured.

Tranquility had been among the framers' objectives because it had been so conspicuously lacking in their time. They were men of property, and riotous mobs were much feared. The cities then were not large, but their streets were unsafe, and householders went in fear of their lives. Besides, the rebellion had set neighbor against neighbor. The exodus of loyalists had been accompanied by bitterness and often injustice. The mutinous colonists had for long periods had their largest towns occupied by British soldiers, and the colonists had made their lives miserable. In the war's aftermath there was violence just as there had been before its beginning. The Liberty Boys of the rebellion are still spoken of by British commentators not as patriots but as murderous hoodlums. They made as much difficulty for authorities when peace was concluded as they had for the occupying British. There were hard times, and there was resentment. Such respectable people as made up the membership of the convention were vulnerable to violence, and one of the objectives of their new government would be to establish order.

When the dissensions leading up to the Civil War tore the country apart again, there were innumerable resorts to violence. They occurred everywhere. Until the race riots of the 1960's the worst disturbances in American history were precipitated in New York City by the drafting into the army of immigrants who had little or no interest in the issues. But, if these were large-scale incidents, later struggles between workers and employers were only less extensive, and they went on intermittently from the 1880's until the Roosevelt devices to insure industrial peace came into effect. Collective bargaining, conciliation agencies, and especially the acceptance by government of responsibility for welfare brought about an era of comparative reasonableness.

Depression had seemed to smother protesters' spirits when factories closed; but demands were made again when recovery began. By then, however, to strike was no longer to rebel against government. There had been, in the workers' long struggle, incidents that seemed incredible afterward, when collective bargaining was legitimized. Homestead, Pullman, Centralia, Gastonia—a long list of symbolic names represented to the working class the scenes of struggle for rights they could attain in no other way than by resisting with force the force used by their employers to compel their submission.

Roosevelt meant to stop this war; and he did. His conception was that if the tranquility of the Constitution meant anything it was that Americans should be persuaded to live with each other under a system of agreed rules. This in turn required prevention of the injustices that gave rise to rebellion. It had to be made certain that rights could be had without resort to violence.

Roosevelt's associates heard him say, many times, how proud he was that during his difficult four years in the governorship he had never called on the National Guard for the restoration of order. He carried a similar ambition into the White House. During his first months there, an incident occurred with all the potential trouble experienced by Hoover when the Bonus Marchers descended on Washington in 1932. The veterans, it will be recalled, felt that payments promised them ought to be forthcoming more promptly. A few began a march in the Far West that, by the time it reached Washington, had grown to thousands. To Hoover—fearful anyway that hungry people had stood all they could—it looked like an invasion; and, when the marchers established a camp on the Anacostia flats and began to make demands, he reacted by calling on General MacArthur—assisted by Major Eisenhower and Captain Patton—to expel them. Their tents were burned, they were driven into the streets and then out of the city. It was all merciless and unnecessary.

When a similar veterans' invasion occurred in Roosevelt's early days in the White House, he sent assistants out to treat with them, furnished coffee and sandwiches, tried to find out their specific grievances, and generally treated them with courtesy. If what was asked could not be granted, something was found that could be done; and, if not satisfied, the protesters at least knew that they had been listened to and respected. The right of petition is an old prerogative very deep in the democratic regard. Roosevelt knew that to deny it was to ask for the trouble its rejection would bring.

Workers and unhappy veterans were no longer sources of

violence in 1970. The workers had rights and veterans had
pensions (as well as other such privileges as free education
and hospitalization); also the bootleggers, responsible for
so much crime while prohibition was in effect, had been put
out of business by repeal; but the nation, nevertheless, was
in the most disturbed state since the Civil War. Drug addiction had become prevalent; and pushers were worse than
the bootleggers had been. Crime was epidemic in the cities.
Much of it was highly organized and seemed immune to
repressive efforts; but even more sinister was the number
of youths who grew bolder and bolder in their depredations.
Holdups, burglaries, invasions of banks and stores, abuse of
school teachers, and even rapes and murders increased yearly
by incredible percentages.

The causes were not obscure. The slums were the most
prolific source, and the slums had been brought to their
present state by the migrants who crowded in on the already
hopeless poor. Dropouts from school formed street gangs
and roamed widely into less crowded neighborhoods. They
snatched purses, stole other valuables, and sometimes left
their victims beaten or even dead. It was easy to escape, since
police no longer walked beats and only passed occasionally
in well-maked vehicles; not only that, it was usually found
that escapes were made possible by the easy theft of automobiles. Since addiction to drugs was costly and since habit-
ual users became desperate when deprived, their resort to
robbery ignored all risks.

The situation had become so frightening that law and
order was debated in the campaign of 1968, which was largely
won on that issue. The Democrats were blamed for the over-
protection of criminals and the Supreme Court for making it
harder to catch and convict wrongdoers. Ethnic minorities,
who supported the Democratic Party, furnished most of the
criminals; the Republicans promised to restore discipline
and make life and property safe for the majority.

Attorney General Mitchell seemed to be convinced that

the cure for crime was its suppression; and he was reluctant to admit that the obvious causes required attention. The criminal emerged from slums, and slums ought long ago to have been eradicated—and might have been if Roosevelt had lived. After the war he would certainly have turned to a massive satellite city program and to a renewal of planned resettlement. He would have insisted on recognition that general and not local causes were at work and would have assumed responsibility.

During the New Deal there had been not only the Civilian Conservation Corps to absorb most of those who were the potential criminals in 1934, but immediately after, the National Youth Administration had started a varied program to improve schools and see to it that young people were able to stay in them. If, directly after the war, these programs had been renewed, the crime rates of the late 'sixties would have been no higher than they had been in the 'thirties—and they might have been lower.

Lack of attention to the internal problems of migration, crowding, education, welfare, and improvement of the environment would be the explanation historians would assign for increasing disturbances. They would have to note that tranquility had been a long way from being a characteristic of the United States a century and three-quarters after the framers had made it the second item in the preamble to their Constitution. It had been a particular concern of Roosevelt's, and nothing can be more likely than that if he had lived he would have seen that what was necessary for prevention would have been done—just, for instance, as he had caused to be established the institutions necessary to industrial peace.

V

How It Went Wrong

Truman
Eisenhower
Kennedy
Johnson
Nixon

1. *A Short Dissertation on Vice-Presidents*

In spite of the numerous resulting misfits, Vice-Presidential candidates have continued to be chosen for irrelevant reasons to succeed Presidents if they should die. Eight times Vice-Presidents have become President in this way. They were John Tyler, Millard Fillmore, Andrew Johnson, Chester A. Arthur, Theodore Roosevelt, Calvin Coolidge, Harry S Truman, and Lyndon B. Johnson. Four of these were subsequently elected to the office for terms of their own. These were Roosevelt, Coolidge, Truman, and Lyndon Johnson. The rest had no further political future.

The whole is not a distinguished company; and for this there is a very good reason. Not one of them was chosen because he would make a good President. Most were selected by an already nominated candidate because in his opinion they would add political strength to his own candidacy. For example, Lincoln needed a border-state candidate in 1864, when the Civil War was at a critical stage, and Andrew Johnson was a Tennessee loyalist. Garfield from Ohio needed Arthur from New York because the latter controlled a powerful political machine. Roosevelt needed Truman in 1944 for a similar reason—he belonged to the Pendergast crowd in Kansas City, and Chairman Hannegan said that the election was doubtful without the support of the city bosses. Kennedy, a New Englander, needed Johnson, a Southerner; and Eisenhower needed Nixon because he was a reactionary from California and was reputed to be a savage political gut-fighter.

In the twenty-five years after Roosevelt's death, only Eisenhower, among the five Presidents, had neither been, nor tried to become, Vice-President. Truman and Johnson succeeded to office because of death; Nixon had been Eisenhower's Vice-President; and Kennedy had made a strong bid for the nomination that Estes Kefauver of Tennessee got instead.

The chance that someone chosen for the usual reason will become a weak President is more than a risk; it approaches certainty. At least, of the whole number, only Theodore Roosevelt, who succeeded McKinley, is regarded as distinguished, and several—among them Tyler, Andrew Johnson, Arthur, Fillmore, and Coolidge were just short of disastrous. The latest two, Truman and Johnson, made mistakes in strategy of colossal proportions.

— Vice-Presidents, since they are not chosen to be Presidents, cannot be expected to be satisfactory ones. It is incomprehensible, in view of the numerous occasions when they nevertheless have succeeded to office, that something has not been done to assure higher competence. This would require bringing the political system into the area of constitutional government. It has no place there now, and its operations are not governed by federal laws.

Nominations are made, and campaigns are run, as private arrangements among politicians. The party with the most money has an advantage inconsistent with democratic principles. The stakes are high, and candidates are chosen to please large contributors, who then sell their choices to the people as they are accustomed to sell goods and services. Vice-Presidential candidates to them are minor commodities, carefully calculated to make it easier to sell the whole package. A shudder ran through the country when Nixon and his backers chose Spiro Agnew to run with him. It was no secret that it was done to win support for Nixon among ethnic groups and in the South. Agnew was unknown outside of Maryland, only recently had been a county official, and had no more idea of foreign affairs—or indeed national ones— than the most ordinary citizen. His performance in office showed very quickly that he belonged to the long line of those chosen for other reasons than a judgment that he would be a satisfactory President.

and on Generals

Most Americans are surprised when told that ten Presidents have been generals and that two more held that rank without having had field service. The list: Washington, Jackson, William Henry Harrison, Taylor, Pierce, Grant, Hayes, Garfield, Benjamin Harrison, and Eisenhower. Add Andrew Johnson and Arthur as having had the rank because of being appointed to wartime positions.

To complete the account, four generals were defeated as candidates: Scott, McClellan, Frémont, and Hancock.

Perhaps fortunately, no admiral has ever been nominated.

It will be seen that among the generals only two were career officers, if Washington and Jackson are omitted. Jackson was a politician; his generalship was incidental; and Washington was more a planter than a military man. So the two "real" generals were Grant and Eisenhower. Grant rode into office as victor in the Civil War, Eisenhower as Supreme Commander in World War II. The records of both would recommend disqualification for military men of their training. Most of the other general-Presidents were actually something else—lawyers, usually, who attained brevet rank in national emergency when an army had to be created in a hurry. But these two were soldiers and elected as such.

This is spoken of here because in eight of the twenty-five years after 1945, Eisenhower occupied the Presidency and has to be accounted as responsible for much of the degeneration during that period. For instance, being an amateur statesman, he trusted Dulles and allowed him to dominate the formulation of foreign policy, and, knowing only the army, he let the other departments pretty much go their own way. As for the regulatory agencies, the simple notion that men who knew the business best would control it best, confirmed an already visible trend during Truman's time—the agencies tended to favor the interests they were supposed to control.

Professionalism in the armed forces is obviously not a good preparation for the Presidency.

and Senators as Well

The danger that a senator will achieve a major party nomination has immensely increased in recent years. In fact all the Presidents in succession to Roosevelt, except Eisenhower, had served in the Senate, some for long periods. Of these Truman and Johnson were most typical. Kennedy never worked hard at his legislative duties and never became a member of what is usually described as the inner circle, as Truman and Johnson did. One was chairman of an important committee during the war, and the other was majority leader. One had been in the Senate for ten years, the other for twelve. Between them, as Presidents, they account for more than half the period between 1945 and 1970.

There was a time when governorships, especially of large states, were the favorite places to look for Presidential candidates. Cleveland, Coolidge, and both Roosevelts were governors; but F. D. Roosevelt may prove to have been the last. Governors no longer command national attention. Senators do. They can always attract television attention by conducting a sensational investigation or denouncing an ill-doer; and they are much in demand as speakers. Some of them more than double their incomes in this way, as well as fattening their campaign funds.

They have an exposure not matched by any public figure except the President himself. Part of this advantage is that they need not put forward any alternative to the performances, public or private, that they choose to denounce. Practically all acceptable legislation originates in the White House. The Senators need only assume a critical or supporting position—after they see how things are going.

That supervising a group of investigators and appearing at hearings, together with an active career as a paid lecturer, are not adequate preparations for the Presidency ought to be obvious. An argument can even be made that it is quite the reverse—that this training incapacitates an individual for the tough and demanding duties of the office. If Truman, Kennedy, and Johnson are offered in evidence as contrasted with Roosevelt, it can be seen what is meant. None had an adequate grasp of domestic problems or foreign affairs, yet all appeared to be confident decision-makers. Their assurance led to errors hardly matched for consequence in all American history.

2. *Truman, Taking Over*

*I believe that it must be the policy of the United States
to support free peoples who are resisting attempted subjugation by armed minorities or by outside pressures.*
                        HARRY S TRUMAN,
              message to Congress proposing aid
                to Greece and Turkey (later called the
                  Truman Doctrine), March 12, 1947

*A man with Dean Acheson's background is full of fas-
cinating stories—such as the one he has now told about
Harry Truman and the late physicist J. Robert Oppenheimer, father of the atom bomb. "Oppie was one of the
most naive people I knew," said Truman's Secretary of
State, now 76, in a* New York Times *interview. "How he
reached his age and knew as little about the outside
world as he did, I don't know—though he was extremely
cultivated and read widely in many languages. I accompanied Oppie into Truman's office once. Oppie was
wringing his hands and said, 'I have blood on my hands.'
'Don't ever bring that damn fool in here again,' Truman
told me afterward. 'He didn't set that bomb off. I did.
This kind of sniveling makes me sick.' It made me
slightly sick as well."*
                                  Newsweek, *October 20, 1969*

The occasions have not been many when it could be said
that everyone in the United States shared one overwhelming
emotion. The nation was so various in its geography; so many
of its people were nostalgic for other homelands; there were
such divisions among rich and poor; there was such trouble
between workers and those they worked for; the interests of
farmers and city people were so irreconcilable; young people

seemed so unwilling to accept the values and disciplines of their elders; and racial irritations were so persistent in spite of all efforts at reconciliation: this down to, say, 1930.

Even after World War I, there had been lingering rancors left by the rebellion and the arrangements made for bringing the Southern states back into the Union. Four generations, more or less, had passed with surprisingly little accomplished in reconciling sectional differences—until Roosevelt. There were Northerners in the Congress who said bitterly that he at last had allowed the South to win the Civil War.

Money made in the North was taxed and flowed freely southward through New Deal agencies. Southerners were in complete control of the Congress; and Roosevelt's Cabinet had several. It was true that Roosevelt's "home" in Georgia had given him a chance to see the low state of the Georgia farmers and townspeople. Erosion, the boll weevil, and six-cent cotton having left them prostrate, they were every bit as resentful as their ancestors in the 1850's; not much more, however, than the farmers of the Midwest who were getting thirty cents a bushel for their wheat and practically giving away their corn. There was common cause here; and Roosevelt knew how to turn it to his own purposes.

In a very short time there was a notable softening of old antagonisms. The contrasts and sectional conflicts were too durable for complete cure without drastic change; nevertheless he set out to insist on such beginnings as could be made. This caused resentment among those who had more interest in their own concerns than in national ones.

Irritations about the ways funds were used during the New Deal came to the surface in Roosevelt's successive campaigns, and it was gradually seen to be more a complaint about appropriations for relief than about their use for any particular purposes. The large-income receivers found it hard to accept the necessity for paying the real costs of doing business. They were as annoyed about "boondoggling" and "welfare bums" as they were about helping farmers. They did not complain about the massive rescue operations for banks and insurance companies; it was only the unemployed who ought to earn their way, and, if they could not, were considered to be shiftless and improvident.

Roosevelt was soon denounced as an enemy of his "class." Its members were few; but their dislike for New Deal policies was never modified. When it felt free to do so, the Congress, responding to lobbyists, amended laws, softened regulations, and quietly cut appropriations. This sort of sabotage became easier as the war approached. Roosevelt's pleas for defense measures made it possible for Congressmen to demand in exchange an easing up on their wealthier supporters. One after another New Deal agencies were starved into ineffectiveness or actually abolished. Some of this was not too harmful since defense spending proved a perfect cure for unemployment. The appropriations went to contractors who took their profits as they paid wages so that they were more agreeable about spending. Roosevelt's image changed somewhat; but the conservatives never forgot his sins and never gave in to his liberalizing notions.

When the news spread that Roosevelt was dead, a sense of something ending drew Americans together as nothing had done in years. An object of loyalty had been lost. Other Presidents had made themselves symbols of national unity. It is the natural condition of the Presidency, in fact, and unless something is done to alienate large numbers of supporters it remains invulnerable. It still seems remarkable that grief for Harding could have caused an emotional outburst; he had been in office only a little more than two years, and his vices had been more publicized than his virtues even during his life. That strange mourning had shown what place all Presidents are accorded in people's regard. Desire for a central figure of trust is almost independent of performance; but not quite; it can be lost—as Hoover lost it, for instance.

Harding was the last before Roosevelt to have died in office. Others for whom there had been a general fondness—

Coolidge, for instance, and Wilson—had lived on into retirement and had passed into death well after surrendering their claims to centrality. McKinley's going had caused a genuine grief; but the nation had not yet become the explosive ethnic conglomeration of more recent years; it had been neither so crowded nor so divided.

Roosevelt's going out of people's lives left a vacuum. Even the well-identified Roosevelt-haters felt lost. The "economic royalists" of his second inaugural were doubtless relieved; but, besides these, those who felt no grief were mostly those whose positions had been diminished—such ambitious men as the coterie of partisans in the Congress he had recently denounced in such a blaze of wrath for their devotion to private rather than public interests. To have said to the legislators, as he did in a message, that they had lost interest in the needy and become servants of the greedy, was to use unprecedented words from a President to members of his own party. But even if they had resigned from respect for his leadership, they too were used to dealing with it and would now have to find new affiliations. They were familiar with Roosevelt's presence. They would require time to escape from the wary habit of looking out for what he might do next.

Operations rooms all over the nation were paralyzed. All movement stopped. There was an emptiness, bare and bleak. The war went on, but fortunately it was in its final phase.

Mixed with the prevalent sense of loss, there was another emotion: a good number discovered what they had not been aware of before in any active way; their accustomedness had passed into a phase so well adjusted to that it resembled love. The tenor voice from their radio receivers, and more lately the worn but confident face on news screens in the theaters, had been more a part of their lives than had those of the politicians closer to them in distance. He had managed to supplant these local fellows; and not all of them realized what had happened.

This was true, as well, of labor. The collective bargaining fought for by unions for generations had become legal; but John L. Lewis, William Green, or Philip Murray had only prevailed because Roosevelt had made it possible, and the workers knew it very well. Lewis, particularly, was ambitious and resented this. He tried unsuccessfully to break away; even, with characteristic presumptuousness, threatened to become a candidate himself. That this was considered ridiculous infuriated him all the more. He may have turned away a few votes but not enough to count. How could a miner vote Republican? The others accepted their secondary status and actually people in the cities' most crowded parts, together with union labor, became the most steadfast of Roosevelt's political army.

It was this tour de force that gave the two parties their contrasting character. The Democrats were committed to the oppressed, to the masses in city and country, to working men and women. Since there were many more of them than there were of the "upper class," they prevailed in elections. They supported Roosevelt through four campaigns. Would they have supported him through another? It is at least possible, although prosperity did rather quickly turn voters into Republicans.

Returning prosperity had taken many of the farmers in the Midwest back to their traditional Republicanism; and many workers no longer relied on relief. These and others did tend to forget the gratitude they had felt a few years before; so Roosevelt's majorities in 1940 and 1944 had been smaller than that overwhelming one in 1936, when the New Deal had been really new and on trial. He himself might have had narrowed victories in future—supposing he had lost his political agility. It was never safe, however, to assume that Roosevelt had lost his campaign cunning; and it was certain that his intentions were unchanged.

The war, however, had intervened; and for those who came after, there would be new problems as well as a demand for answers to old ones. The workers and farmers had seen their sons drafted and sent across the seas and then had watched their battles. While the soldiers were away those at home had been under a certain discipline, never accepted gracefully; their living levels had risen, even during the war, but there had been restrictions on wages and prices; there had also been rationing.

There had been some exposures of profiteering, enough to cause suspicion that there probably had been a good deal more. Not only that, the Congress seemed to lose all sense of order and decency in the last year of the war. Responding to lobbyists' pressures, they gave favors, refused to continue civilian disciplines, and generally behaved so outrageously as to provoke Roosevelt's famous reproof.

There had been what Roosevelt spoke of as his "fat cats" in the wartime administration. He had needed them to set up the complicated machinery of mobilization and then to operate the vast logistics of overseas operations. He knew and they knew that their jobs were specific and within his control. He knew how to use them and how far to trust them; and they were never expected to yield him more than the loyalty they owed the commander in chief. They were there, in office, however, when he died; and Truman needed them more than Roosevelt had. Besides he had some provincial awe of their wealth and their ability to run large enterprises. It took him years to find out that *they* were using *him*. It was a failing that almost cost him his re-election; and it was his inability to manage without them that caused power to slip from his control. Meanwhile, they persuaded him to make decisions they would not even have suggested to Roosevelt—ones that fitted their views and preferences.

Coming to the White House to take his oath, Truman presented the picture of a man overwhelmed with what was expected of him—humble but determined. It was a false impression. He had a simplistic mind. There were decisions to make, and since he was President he would act like one. He had got there by methods he believed in, and he would expect others to assume his capability and give him support.

He had inherited the office, but he had not inherited what it required of its incumbents. There was some rallying around, along with a struggle for sharing his power; but there was also a good deal of insurgency. Some old Roosevelt hands were still present. Ickes in Interior, Morgenthau in the Treasury, Perkins in Labor, and Wickard in Agriculture were well-seated in their Departments; others were somewhere around: Henry Wallace, Averell Harriman, even Harry Hopkins, and, of course, Sam Rosenman. Naturally, even if they meant to be helpful, it was hard to take orders they thought mistaken from the mediocre product of the Pendergast machine in Kansas City. It was not long before all were gone and had been replaced by Truman's selections: Krug (Interior), Snyder (Treasury), Anderson (Agriculture) and Schwellenback (Labor). All were generally regarded as several grades below their predecessors.

The replacements in the White House itself were even worse. With the exception of Ross (Press) and Clifford (Counsel), they were disastrous. Several ended up in disgrace or even in jail.

A county politician had become President. His White House staff was deplorable; in the departments he had men of much the same quality. In Defense and in State, however, he had in Forrestal, and presently Byrnes, quite different sorts. Forrestal was already paranoid about communists. They pursued him in his imagination until they drove him to suicide. Byrnes was committed to containment, a policy developed to an active strategy when Acheson replaced him in 1948. Besides he had no respect for Truman and set out to make his own policies. He was not long in office. Even when General Marshall was turned to as Secretary of State, his capabilities were those of an austere professional soldier. He saw the advantage of helping Europe, but his inability to cope with the China problem would have long consequences.

Since the Truman succession to Roosevelt must be set down as a national disaster, one being paid for still a quarter-century later, Roosevelt must share the responsibility. Truman's nomination in 1944 to be his Vice-President was inadvertent. He was not paying attention; and it is true that Hannegan, his campaign manager, told him in all seriousness that the renomination of Henry Wallace would jeopardize the election. Wallace was considered to be impractical, even mystical, and his affiliation with the party one of convenience. His whole family had been Republicans; and Iowa Republicans were the most devoted kind.

Worse than this Wallace had alienated the senators over whom he had presided as Vice-President. They looked with horror on the possibility that so erratic and unpredictable a man might become President. The Democratic strength could not be mustered, as it must be in this election, unless Wallace was replaced.

Even if this estimate was as accurate as Hannegan insisted, there were other alternatives; and Roosevelt should have examined them more closely. Just then, however, he was deep in the concerns of the war and the peace to come. Understandably, perhaps, he felt that he must not be diverted by the usual demands of a campaign. At any rate he did much as he had done in 1940—refused to make the selection himself. There is reason to believe that he gave not only Wallace but Byrnes reason to believe that his support would be forthcoming. He also, a number of times, rather tentatively mentioned Justice William O. Douglas as a possibility.

When finally, in July, shortly before the convention, he sat down with the party politicians (Hannegan, Frank Walker, Ed Flynn, and a few others) he met with unanimous opposition to Wallace; and other names mentioned seemed to have substantial opposition. This was even true of Byrnes, who felt his claim to the succession ought to be recognized: he had been practically Assistant President for some time

past. Byrnes, however, was a Southerner and would have
had to overcome a prohibition that had lasted since the Civil
War.

The professionals wanted Truman and would not agree to
any other suggestion. Roosevelt can only be said to have
given way without actually saying so, leaving the selection
to the convention. Hannegan's problem then was that Truman had, for some reason, pledged himself to Byrnes, and
he would not believe, without being told directly, that he
was favored over Byrnes and Wallace, to both of whom there
seemed to be some kind of commitment. By convention time,
Roosevelt was in San Diego inspecting war installations. By
telephone he finally had to indicate that Truman was needed.

That this was an abdication of responsibility can hardly
be denied. He had no knowledge of Truman except that he
had been chairman of a committee on the conduct of the
war with potentialities of the kind of trouble a similar committee had made for Lincoln. He had kept it firmly within
bounds, and its operations had been helpful rather than
damaging. Otherwise he had been an undistinguished senator, one of the inner circle, saying little but doing his party
chores faithfully. He had never given up his affiliation with
the Pendergast machine; but this, instead of making him
suspect, gave him credit with the professionals who counted
at the convention.

To have abandoned Wallace in favor of Truman was, for
Roosevelt, to abandon also his liberal friends; but their steadfastness had sometimes been doubtful. What seemed to him
essential, evidently, was that the election should be won,
and, for that, Truman seemed to have the fewest liabilities.

The real question here is whether this was an accurate
appraisal. There is also the question whether the apparent
alternatives would have been better. Accepting that Wallace
might have made winning uncertain, Douglas could not have
been nominated by that convention unless Roosevelt had
urged it; and this would have immobilized the whole party

machinery—so Hannegan insisted and the other professionals agreed. The others were equally difficult to center on.

The choice has to be weighed against the possibility of defeat and even the probability that Wallace might not have carried enough weight to have prevailed in the difficult times ahead. As for Byrnes, he would have made the same mistakes as Truman; in fact, those immediately following Roosevelt's death were participated in by him.

Left at that, it is far from satisfactory; but a leader of such stature has seldom if ever had a satisfactory successor; and it may be that Truman, who seems now to have been the worst possible choice, was really the only alternative. Democracy has such inherent risks; and they cannot always be escaped.

That they are enormous it is all too evident.

3. *First Mistake: The Bomb*

. . . before the atom bomb was used, I would have said, yes, I was sure we could keep the peace with Russia. Now I don't know . . . people are frightened and disturbed all over. Everyone feels insecure again.

DWIGHT D. EISENHOWER,
speaking in Moscow, 1945.
From Bernstein and Matusow,
The Truman Administration

The dropping of the bomb stopped the war, saved millions of lives . . . .
Let there be no mistake about it. I regarded the bomb as a military weapon and never had any doubt that it should be used. . . .

*The atomic bomb was no "great decision" . . . not any
decision that you had to worry about . . .*
                              TRUMAN, *Memoirs*, vol. I

No President ever began with more good wishes than Truman. As he undertook his unaccustomed duties, there was
a general realization that he had a very special problem. To
succeed such a man as Roosevelt, so long in office, so beloved
and so trusted, and especially for one who was relatively
unknown and inexperienced, was to undertake something so
difficult that all possible allowances must be made and all
possible support given. Truman had been Vice-President for
only a few months, and it was no secret that he had had no
part in wartime decision-making and only the slightest brief-
ing on national affairs or on arrangements for the coming
peace. Germany, however, was defeated; and Japan, whose
armies were spread throughout Southeast Asia, was being
closed in on and had no chance of defending the home
islands successfully; it was a question of time.
    Truman's first duty would be to join in the arrangements
for bringing order to Germany and, indeed, to Europe. His
next would be to finish with Japan and then to preside over
the return to peace at home. The establishment used by
Roosevelt to carry on the war was heavily weighted with
executives who had been counted on to enlist the whole
business community and support the military efficiently.
They ran the complex war machinery, calling on the productive facilities of the whole nation, and attended to the deployment of forces in the distant theatres. They were not of
his political sort, not liberals in his sense, not democrats, not
listeners to dissent, not leaders of people. They would not
have been useful to him or to the country in peace. This
Truman could not know. They were there. They had been
trusted; and an unbriefed successor, not understanding the
Rooseveltian method, had better accept them. This was the

natural conclusion of a small man following a big one. It was what Truman did conclude.

Roosevelt's concentration in his last months had been on the coming peace; the strategy of victory was already in the past. He had been failing fast and for some time it had been obvious that he could not go on much longer. Even his inauguration in January had been held not as customary at the Capitol but at the White House. The pictures of the big three at Yalta had shown plainly his exhaustion and the debilitation of his once strong body; but he was determined not to recognize that his weakness was permanent.

A President who is incapacitated in such a way as not to be prostrated can go on and on unless he himself chooses to resign. The Constitution had made no provision for such a contingency. Roosevelt had felt that his relations with Churchill and Stalin were such that no substitution was possible; and his scheme for the first years of the peace depended on their close collaboration. Besides, although he was thin and tired, his mind was not impaired; and his dedication to the purposes of his life was as strong as ever.

There was the consideration also that if Russia and the United States, each dominating a continent, could cooperate, the many dissensions among countries trying for advantage in troubled circumstances could be managed. He quite realistically felt that only he could bring that cooperation into a settled stage. Britain unfortunately did not count much in this. The Empire was falling apart; the war had been fatally impoverishing; and Churchill was vainly trying to arrest the decline. Stalin obviously respected the American President and saw the British situation all too clearly. With Roosevelt gone, the chance that collaboration would be of any use to Russia would be slight.

There had been work going on in Washington to shape an organization for world order. This was Roosevelt's return to the lessons he had learned from Wilson. The first of these had been in 1918 on the *George Washington* as Wilson returned from the first sessions of the peace conference in Paris. By accident Roosevelt had been on the same ship. Wilson had never appraised his Assistant Secretary of the Navy very highly; but on shipboard he came as close to opening his mind to the younger man as it was in his nature to do; and Roosevelt had been convinced. Thereafter his dedication to world order had many characteristics of conversion. It was among the large intentions he would do his best to see materialized.

From that time he never gave up the hope that an organization would be created that would guarantee the avoidance of further war and would implement cooperation. He had seen Wilson's political errors, and, in the years since, had thought much of ways to avoid making similar ones. Their central cause had been the attempt to enforce the principle of self-determination. There was much remaining sentiment for such an arrangement; it sounded so liberal to speak of independence, of peoples' rights to shape their own government, and to be free of colonial hegemony! Roosevelt understood, however, that only great-power collaboration could prevent the chaos sure to result from the struggle of every ethnic group not only to establish itself as a nation but to take in as many minorities and as much territory as it could grasp. Independence was something to be worked for; but, when minorities demanded what the majority had, it was different. They became rebels; and they must be suppressed to preserve union. He could see chaos in entrusting world order to an assembly of small nations all scrambling for advantage and all having dissident minorities.

The United Nations he visualized, and got agreement from Stalin and Churchill for, was expected to have as its central body a council of the great powers: Russia, the United States, Britain, France, and China—a horrid arrangement to the liberal view; and those who were working on the proposal—Pasvolsky and others—were unreconstructed Wilsonian liberals. They meant to reconstitute the League of Nations, now dead, in essentially its old form. The United States had never been a member of the League; and Roosevelt had long ago repudiated any intention of re-establishing it. His conception was, in effect, a return to the spheres of influence associated in liberal minds with minorities included in empires who claimed to have been exploited—"oppressed" was the favorite description.

That it was practically impossible to form a nation large enough to survive with no rebellious minorities was not a consideration that ever seemed to have weight with the collaborators at Dumbarton Oaks, where the United Nations Charter was being drafted. Roosevelt had agreed to an Assembly of delegates; but he meant the real power to rest with the permanent members of the Council. The Assembly might talk but would not be allowed to legislate. This was the essential, the irreducible principle, arrived at, as he thought, by enough, and sufficiently costly, error.

Truman had no sense of these differences and only superficial knowledge of the background Roosevelt was judging from. He was hopelessly unready; but he was suddenly President, and the decisions would be his to make, and the assistants would be his to choose.

For the implementation of Roosevelt's grand postwar design, it was necessary for the five powers to cooperate. In this the lead must be taken by the United States. No other nation had emerged from the war stronger than when it had begun. Productivity was immensely increased; military forces, relatively weak before 1940, and severely set back by Pearl Harbor, had grown to unprecedented size and had reached across both oceans; sharing with the Allies was well organized and was meeting the deficiencies caused by their losses and disorganization since 1939. Russia, in contrast, had been invaded, had been forced to fight mighty last-ditch battles as deep in the heartland as Stalingrad on the Volga. When winter and heroic defense had turned back the invaders, there had been left a lasting expectation of aggres-

sion from the west and a deep longing for secure borders.
These fears and hopes were not only in Stalin's mind but in
that of all those who had suffered through the experience.
The Germans, beaten, had to be Germans without power to
repeat the outrage.

Less than a month after Roosevelt's death, they surrendered. V-E Day was on May seventh; but less than two
weeks after his death American and Russian negotiators
(Harriman and Molotov) had fallen out over the regime to
be installed in Poland, the staging base for German armies.
The question was whether it should be the government in
exile, for years headquartered in London, or one chosen by
the Russians. The most sensitive element in the situation was
that Poland had been conquered with little opposition by
Hitler's blitzkrieg (as had France) and had thereafter been
helplessly subject to Nazi abuses. Memories of starvation in
Leningrad and the costly losses at Stalingrad were mingled
with those of massacres as the Germans had crossed the
Ukraine. The Russians were determined to prevent another
such invasion, and this, for them, meant domination of Eastern Europe all the way to Berlin. They were determined to
have buffers.

Roosevelt had understood the Russian trauma. He shared
the fear of German recovery and, in another twenty years,
the rise of another Hitler. He had allowed the Russians to
fight the last battle for Berlin when Eisenhower might have
been ordered to take it. He had suggested the four-power
occupation, calculated to keep the proven aggressors in disciplined subjection for as long as it might be necessary. Questions having to do with Southeastern Europe, with the Balkan
states, Greece, Turkey, Iran, Egypt, and the rest of the
Moslem lands remained to be settled; this was the old
British and French area of hegemony, monopolizing the
warm seas to the south of Russia.

What Roosevelt saw ahead was certainly a difficult time
with the suspicious and battered Russians. Their demands

for security would clash with the American belief in indiscriminate self-determination. Then too the British had not yet given up in India to the independence movement; and this required control of the passages to the East. He had told Churchill frankly that the empire east of Suez might better be liquidated peaceably and Churchill had been deeply offended, seeing the Russians as threatening what he spoke of as the British lifeline. He meant to follow the traditional policy of blocking that nation at the Dardanelles; and his view of India was well expressed in the books of Henty and Kipling, who had made the Queen's Own Rifles, the Himalayan passes, and resplendent Viceroys items in a romantic drama inviolable to American disapproval.

This was not the only issue disagreed on by the two statesmen; but it was the most important. Roosevelt wanted a situation relatively immune to disruption by the pursuit of national interests. For this purpose the British were the worst problem, since the French, whose empire in the East had been almost as extensive, were prostrate and obviously could not recover Indochina. The collapse of 1940 had canceled claims to postwar advantages such as Clemenceau had insisted on in 1919. Italy, as well, was out of consideration. Mussolini's inflated notions about a North African empire had been extinguished. Italy would be lucky to escape heavy reparations.

The two nations with consolidated power were the United States and Russia, the one stronger for the war, the other with territory unimpaired and with a recuperative potential based on solid unity. British control of the seas had kept together many separated territories—so far spread that the sun was never known to set on all of them at once. Without the empire Britain was "a few islands in the northern seas." Churchill would not acknowledge that an end had come to the empire and was furious that Roosevelt should suggest it. With Roosevelt gone, Truman remained to be worked on. How successful Churchill was would be revealed in a famous

speech at Westminster College in Missouri. With Truman
approving, he invented the metaphor of the iron curtain, and
together they welded its parts and extended them around
Greece and Turkey, again shutting the Dardanelles to the
Russians.

Truman, new in the White House, had many things to
consider; and the rescue of the British Empire was not high
on the list, if, indeed, he did not share Roosevelt's conviction
that it was inconsistent with what must now be done. He
might approve the effort to keep Russia out of Europe, but
this did not imply a defense of Britain's Far Eastern holdings.
Anyway, before the summer was over, Churchill's Conservatives had been defeated, and a Labor government had taken
over. It was the new Prime Minister, Atlee, who was to preside over the dissolution of the empire. The changeover took
place while the Potsdam conference was in progress (July
17–August 2). During that conference, with the least possible emphasis, Stalin was notified that the United States
possessed a new weapon of unexampled power and would
use it on Japanese targets.

That decision had been made during the preceding weeks
after Alamogordo had demonstrated that the bomb was
operational. Its existence had been news to Truman, conveyed during his first days in office by Secretary of War Stimson. Its power and consequences were only half understood;
but the recommendation for its use was made by a committee
of scientists who agreed with General Groves that it should
be used on live targets, not, as was suggested by a minority,
on a dead one—an uninhabited island—as a demonstration to
the Japanese. The development of the nuclear device had
been a tour de force initiated by Einstein in a letter to Roosevelt, describing it as the end product of scientific efforts extending far into the past. Roosevelt's naval adviser, Admiral
Leahy, had counseled against spending money on such a
scheme—it was, he said, only some damned professor's theory;
he was an expert in explosives and he ought to know. Never-

theless Roosevelt had approved the project and its development and had engaged the best talent of Britain and the United States and several expatriates from Hitler's Germany and Mussolini's Italy. Their racist policies were paid for expensively.

It was called the Manhattan Project and had had its first test in a temporary laboratory rigged up under the Stagg Field stands at the University of Chicago. Atom fission was first accomplished there on an occasion all who knew about it saw at once could end conflict as it had been known until then and would begin an era of maneuvering among nations with a fearsome genocidal weapon. At the moment, of course, it was enough that it would finish the Japanese resistance.

Some time after the Chicago success an actual weapon was put together at Los Alamos under the direction of Oppenheimer and others. It was then that the question of its actual use arose. The conflict with Germany had been concluded, and the Japanese had been trying for months to surrender on condition that the Emperor not be deposed (the condition included actually in the terms presented to them later). Nevertheless, for reasons never explained, Stimson convinced Truman that use of the bomb to destroy a city or two in Japan would end the war abruptly and would save the lives of a million Americans who would die in the invasion being prepared.

This argument, together with the recommendation of the scientists' majority, was sufficient. Its use was ordered; Hiroshima and Nagasaki were pulverized; and the United States was left with the guilt of an unnecessary genocidal attack that had overtones of vast consequences. Was it approved more easily because the Japanese were not white? Was it done to forestall the participation of the Russians in the Japanese defeat? They were getting ready to carry out the pledge exacted of them at Yalta on the insistence of General Marshall. After Hiroshima they were not needed; and the occupation became an exclusive American affair.

After twenty-five years the answers to these questions could only be guessed at; but the suspicions were stronger that issues other than Japanese defeat had entered into the calculations concerning the bomb's use. Whatever they were, they cannot have rested on saving American lives as Truman would persist in saying to the end of his life.

4. *Second Mistake: Disarmament Fumble*

Immediately after the war something had to be determined about nuclear weapons. Now that they existed, it seemed obvious that the overwhelming magnitude of their power had made lesser devices obsolete; but on second thought this appeared to be true only in such vast conflicts as had just been finished. In what the military referred to as "brushfire wars" they would be unsuitable. Only a third thought, a somewhat belated one, indicated that they could not be used at all. They were of no use even when they were an American monopoly; the revulsion after Hiroshima ensured that; and when the Russians also had developed similar weapons their use was doubly impossible since it would induce automatic retaliation. Pre-emptive strikes, talked about for some years by xenophobic haters of communism, very quickly faded out of public dialogue.

The simplest policy would be to develop the nuclear potential as an American monopoly and use it for keeping the peace. It was easily assumed that others would trust Americans as its guardian.

When the monopoly was seen to be a fiction, however, a reappraisal of policy was necessary. Others had to be considered as co-possessors of genocidal capability. Somehow the monstrous danger would have to be got under control; and it could only be by mutual agreements. It must be confined, otherwise its destructive power might very possibly destroy the world. This was a new and baffling problem for politicians to confront. They had become addicted to exchanges of bombast whose irresponsibility was relatively safe since threats could not actually be carried out. It had been a heady reliance for those who feared communism that it could be destroyed in one blow. There were unaccustomed silences while reappraisal went on; but there were some outbursts too, and they tended to be taken too seriously abroad.

For finding answers to many novel questions the United States was singularly ill-equipped just then with statesmen; such large issues had been Roosevelt's province for more than a decade. Among these was the need to find ways through the complexities of postwar divisions and irritations to some sort of policy for the further development of the awesome power now existent. It would not go away, and it seemed to enlarge from an inner momentum. There was soon talk of vaster destructiveness; a fusion rather than a fission weapon was hinted at.

The monopoly assumption had contributed to division and hostility in the world, making everything more complicated. Nevertheless an agency for its custody had to be devised. A bill sponsored by Senator McMahon finally became law on August 1, 1946. An individual who had survived as long as 1970 could hardly believe his own recollections of the dialogue concerning the bill or of that following its passage. The act was accepted with such reservations on the part of belligerent but confused legislators that it stood in danger of repeal during the year that followed. The commission of five it provided for was appointed by the President only after long delays for consultation, and its members were confirmed after even more protracted hearings. These were accom-

panied by ignoble political maneuverings and with a legislative history emphasizing bellicose emotions. Ideology over-
came practical sense. Communism was still conceived as a
monolithic organization directed from Moscow with a totally
unrestrained ambition to rule the world. It meant to use the
same infiltration by mendacity and subversion abroad that
had been used at home. Executions of dissenters by the thousands was reported bv correspondents in Moscow.

It was not even considered that Russians might be trusted
in international dealings. As allies in the war they had been
only as cooperative as they had to be; and there were many
who regarded any deal with them as something that must
be safeguarded with potential force and policed by American
watchers. It was of no importance that Russian interests co-
incided precisely with those of the United States; at least
no use was made of such a perception.

Truman's advisers were among those who were thus affected, and he, himself, if he had more sense of the dangerous
forces involved, still had the same convictions about communists.

There had been, for the past year, a United Nations commission at work on disarmament with special reference to
"the discovery of atomic energy and related matters." To
this commission Truman appointed Bernard Baruch as the
representative of the United States. The reason for such a
selection has never been quite clear; but it may have been
the fancied necessity for entrusting such a task to a thoroughly credible representative of the dominant group in
American counsels. Baruch was a very wealthy man who had
made his fortune in Wall Street, and so was recognized as a
member of the group so powerful in policy-making at that
time.

In November, 1945, Molotov, the Soviet Foreign Minister,
made a pronouncement to a Party Congress denouncing the
American "atomic diplomacy" being used to capture world

domination. He enlarged bitterly on refusal to recognize Russia's special relationships with the small nations of Eastern Europe. He ridiculed the demand that they be given immediate autonomy, including the right to hold instant elections; that, he said, would mean a return to power of the old capitalist-landlord classes—and orientation toward the West. The Russians had no intention of opening the Balkans to Western intrigue. He made it quite plain that, if Americans approached arrangements with the Soviets guardedly, the Soviets doubly reciprocated. It was basic to their view of the world, one they had impressed on faithful communists for two decades, that the capitalist-imperialists meant to overthrow the Russian government and impose a decadent democratic regime. American policy was now a confirmation. Baruch was a perfect symbol.

The retort to Molotov was made by Secretary of State James F. Byrnes. It was as vitriolic in denouncing the communist conspiracy as Molotov's was in ridiculing the capitalists' pretensions to the protection of liberty. Exchanges on this model were to proliferate and harden in future years; but the pattern of opposition was set at once. Presently, after an interlude when General Marshall was Secretary, Byrnes was succeeded by Dean Acheson, and that able lawyer would meet the Russians head-on with vituperation worthy of his clientele. That clientele was the business complex grown so powerful during the war and anxious to consolidate that power in the peace. Truman had their representatives in his cabinet; and their sycophants were a majority in the Congress. Democrats and Republicans alike had accepted the stereotype communist, and this concept was reinforced by domestic events.

In the postwar confusion, businessmen saw the best chance in years to escape from the entire network of regulations, and, at the same time, to re-establish the free-for-all of *laissez faire*. This was viewed agreeably also, strange as it may seem, by those who suffered from inflation and its ac-

companying hardships. Ordinary folk were tired too of unaccustomed restrictions—of rationing and shortages. They,
like the businessmen, had had a taste of government controls and shuddered at the thought of the more stringent
ones they heard about in Russia. It might be unrealistic to
think that the Russians might invade and conquer the United
States, but their reputed intention to do so caused violent
public reaction. Baruch as the American negotiator at the
U.N. was a high-style American adventurer. He was entirely
representative. There was little objection.

An international agreement to limit nuclear weapons was
most agreeable to Truman's circle, especially since an effort
to pass what had been called the May-Johnson bill had
failed. This would have consigned the control and development of nuclear energy to the military. But Senator Mc-
Mahon, backed by what could only be described as an uprising by the scientists who had made the bomb, and by a
certain number of liberals, had succeeded in establishing the
civilian commission. This presumably would be interested
in peaceful uses of nuclear energy as well as in its use for
warfare. If they could not have it as an exclusive weapon,
the military were agreeable to limiting its use by treaty. But,
naturally, that agreement would recognize the American
monopoly and would ensure its perpetuation. This the conservative politicians heartily applauded.

In this year the Acheson-Lilienthal report was produced
at Truman's direction; it was presumably to guide Baruch as
he dealt with the United Nations Commission. Acheson was
not yet Secretary of State but was in Truman's confidence,
and Lilienthal, who had been Chairman of the Board of the
Tennessee Valley Authority was Chairman of the Atomic
Energy Commission set up under the McMahon Act.

The report setting out American proposals recognized that
a small object with paralyzing effectiveness could only be
controlled under certain conditions. There must be revolutionary modification of national attitudes; and it must go to

the extent of mutual cooperation, if not trust. How could this come about with the Americans still having a monopoly of the weapon? In spite of this absurdity—as the Russians saw it—there was proposed a Development Authority to be entrusted with "all phases of the development and use of atomic energy, starting with the raw materials and including:

1. Managerial control or ownership of all atomic energy activities potentially dangerous to world security;
2. Power to control, inspect and license all other atomic activities;
3. The duty of fostering the beneficial uses of atomic energy;
4. Research and development responsibilities of an affirmative character intended to put the Authority in the forefront of atomic knowledge and thus enable it to comprehend and therefore to detect misuse of atomic energy. . . ."

This seemed at first reading to be generous; but accompanying the list of objectives there was disclosed the price for surrendering the existing monopoly: the Security Council must give up the veto power accorded its members in the U.N. charter; also there must be assurances of safety—"a guarantee . . . not only against offenders in the atomic area, but against illegal uses of other weapons—bacterial, biological, gas—perhaps, and why not—against war itself."

To the embattled, but still hopeful, nuclear scientists these initiatives seemed the realization of their desire to escape the heavy guilt they bore for their part in the creation of the genocidal weapon—one already used to exterminate two whole cities. Naturally the Russian response was awaited with anxiety. Perhaps the proposal was only intended to establish a bargaining position; but it could have been accepted only if the Russians agreed to American custody of nuclear weaponry. That custody was a fact, whether or not it was agreed to, and giving it up without guarantees would have been an unnecessary and unreasonable sacrifice—so it was argued. The reply, however, was a counterproposal. It came on June 19, 1946. Gromyko, for the Russians, offered:

> . . . a study of the conclusion of international agreements forbidding the production and use of weapons based upon the use of atomic energy for the purposes of mass destruction. The purpose of such an agreement should be to forbid the production and use of atomic weapons, the destruction of existing stocks of atomic weapons, and the punishment of all activities undertaken with a view to violation of such agreements.

The Russians saw in the Baruch proposal an attempt to establish American domination and to smother their communist ideology. While the international organization was being set up the Americans would keep control until satisfied that the Soviets had stopped all attempts to spread their philosophy—and this undoubtedly meant independence for their buffer states in Eastern Europe. They saw themselves caught in an intimate embrace with an enemy whose intention was to strangle them or, at least, to confine them, powerless, within their old, insecure borders. What they demanded was that the United States voluntarily divest itself of this power by getting rid, entirely, of all nuclear weapons—at once. That this would leave Russia with the advantage of vast manpower reserves and the huge armies they were maintaining on the borders of Europe was quite obvious; but also they demanded that the agreement be enforced by each nation *on itself*.

This last was recognizably the result of Russian suspicions. An inspection system had been part of the American plan to prevent violations. As they saw it this would amount to foreign outposts inside Russia; and, having given up their veto power in the Security Council, they could not prevent extensions of this espionage. The secretive Russians, who knew what Westerners thought of their government, their ideology, and their methods of maintaining discipline, were outraged by such a suggestion. Control from outside while disarmament was going on meant that the communists would be helpless.

The Americans were surprised, or at least disappointed, that the power of nuclear weaponry should not be acknowledged by a willingness to accept conditions for its gradual diminution until it no longer existed. Each nation was bargaining for an advantage the other would not grant; and unless some mutual giving way could be arranged there could be no agreement. In this the Americans could have afforded to be the more generous; but acrimonies reached irreversible offensiveness and no concessions were made.

The opportunity was wasted. Guarantees were demanded that the Russians would rather perish than give; the proposal was put to them by a representative of the hard-core capitalists they believed meant to destroy their system; and, even in the interest of future security, consent was not given to the abolition of nuclear weaponry. There were no mortal risks in this; the Russians were as yet years from capability; and they might never have developed it if the Americans had given up theirs.*

So the moment passed when the nuclear threat might have been contained. It was judged by Truman that the positions were too far apart for further useful bargaining, and, so, it was not seriously pursued. Presently Baruch resigned, and the United Nations Commission faded into obscurity. That the Russians would presently have produced a nuclear weapon themselves, and in a quarter-century would have at least an equality with the United States was not a consideration among the policy-makers of 1946. They simply could not believe it. They went on holding to the fantasy that the secrets of the bomb's production could be monopolized. If they could, it was confidently concluded, the United States would be secure and dominant in the world.

---

* A more adequate description of Truman's situation among his hawkish advisers and his White House circle was offered in the author's *Chronicle of Jeopardy*, mentioned in the introduction to this essay

In 1946, policies being shaped by misconceptions and emotional politics would persist through succeeding administrations. Then Nixon, who had based his career on the hardening of suspicions and the acerbation of relations, would find himself obliged to retreat. Only then would accommodation seriously be sought.

The interlude seemed the more foolish, looking back, because by then it was clear that the Russians had assessed quite accurately the effect of Hiroshima on the American conscience. Since they believed it would never be used again, the bomb was not really a threat; and they could go on developing their own with no concern whatever for belligerent speeches. Failure to understand this, and still to go on making threats, was, however inexcusable, the basis for a quarter-century of diplomacy.

Opportunity for a mistake of this colossal size is not given to many men. It was given to Truman, and it must be said that he made the most of it.

5. *Third Mistake: Containment*

> . . . *a school of academic criticism has concluded that we overreacted to Stalin, which in turn caused him to overreact to policies of the United States. This may be true.*
>
> DEAN ACHESON,
> *Present at the Creation* (1969), 753 (footnote)

The suspicion has grown with the years that excluding the Russians from any part in victory or occupation was indeed the reason for using the bomb on Japan. The long confrontation, presently to be called the "cold war," had begun. The United States' decision-makers certainly wanted sole control of Japan in the interest of hegemony over the whole of the Pacific. This was accomplished; the years of occupation were passed with MacArthur directing a military government; and the Russians were wholly excluded.

There was other evidence. During the war, assistance to the Russians by lend-lease had been accomplished by heroic means. The Murmansk run, through the Arctic seas past the German installations in Norway, had sometimes cost the loss of half the ships in the convoys. It was as dangerous as any duty ever exacted of seamen. Their ships were at such risk that it was later beyond belief that men could have accepted it. They were blown up in dozens, and life in the icy water was limited to minutes; there were very few rescues from the lost freighters. The other route, established by incredible engineering feats, ran from the Persian Gulf overland to southern Russia.

Both routes came into full use late in the conflict, and the Russians had throughout their development been ungrateful and demanding. They had suffered mightily and had withstood the battering of the *Wehrmacht* with stolid bravery; but it had been an ordeal of such magnitude that it seemed to them comparatively more than their share of a common conflict. They wanted more help. Stalin practically ended communication with the Allies when the channel crossing was not put into operation in 1943; and he considered the invasion of North Africa a mere diversion. He was only grudgingly pacified by the successful operation when it was undertaken in June, 1944. By that time the Russian armies had driven out the invaders.

There had been heated arguments in the Congress during the 'thirties about Pearl Harbor: should it be improved as a base? Had the United States any business in the Pacific? The argument extended to the Philippines. They had been given independence. Did the obligation inherited from the Spanish-

American war include defense of the islands? If so, the nation's reach would extend all the thousands of miles across the sea to Asiatic shores. There the two powers would have meeting lines if the Pacific and its islands were an American responsibility.

It had been Roosevelt's policy to give the Filipinos their independence; and when the Japanese had occupied the islands early in the war, he saw it as a responsibility to drive out the occupiers and restore the former status. This, however, was no more than an incident in the war with Japan. It was a job for the navy. The army became involved in this as in other battles for expulsion of the Japanese; but this did not imply that the Roosevelt plans included occupation of the Asiatic mainland. While he was President the Chinese were allies to be assisted, and the American intention was to free them as the Filipinos had been freed. He could not have imagined China as an enemy.

A whole series of failures began, it must be admitted, when Hurley, Roosevelt's envoy, failed to negotiate a coalition between Chiang Kai-shek and Mao Tse-tung. Afterward, Marshall, acting for Truman, failed as well. It would not have happened if a more careful assessment of the situation had been made and more attention had been given to China's internal struggle. By the end of Truman's regime, the communists had won that struggle and were denouncing Americans as enemies. Chiang Kai-shek's faction was reduced to a government in exile on Formosa (Taiwan), to be a liability far into the future.

It has not been argued here that Roosevelt always made the right decisions or that he never made mistakes. He certainly should have understood that Mao was something more than an agrarian reformer; and, of all those who might have been available, General Patrick Hurley was the worst choice for bringing factions together and assisting in the formation of a Chinese government more friendly to the United States. What is argued is that Roosevelt recognized his mistakes and set about to correct them. He was an experimenter, not much worried if things went wrong temporarily; something else could be tried until a tolerable situation had been achieved. The difficulty was that he left to Truman many situations in flux with no more than tentative solutions and that nothing was tentative to Truman. Once fixed he turned away and refused to reconsider.

Truman not only considered any decision final, but belligerently regarded this as a virtue. It was his executive method. The way he put it was that he slept well after it was done and woke up to something else. For Roosevelt, nothing was ever quite done. Public matters were too complicated. There were too many fermentations. Adjustments always had to be made. It was only the end in view that was important.

One of his important ends was friendship with China. He was indignant about the Japanese attempt at conquest and wanted to see a new and more stable regime there. It was one thing the war had been about; and he would not have rested until such a solution seemed to be in prospect. When the Hurley mission failed he looked around for something else; he might even have recognized Mao and supported him in forming a new government. This is speculation; but it would not have been surprising.

On both fronts, across the Atlantic as well as the Pacific, initiatives were eventually crushed by irresistible forces. American ideology gave rise to impracticality. The venture in Vietnam would be no more successful than that in Korea. American soldiers would in time come home, having built vast installations costing billions. These would be left either to a military dictatorship or to the communists, if they should dominate an evacuated South Vietnam. By 1970 self-determination was a bankrupt policy, after having been endlessly preached by a stony-faced Rusk until his credibility was weaker than that of the Presidents he had served. The policy was containment, or it was nothing; but the lines had been

drawn in defiance of geography. Control of the seas could be
made good; invasion of the land beyond was a military impossibility.

In Germany there were still occupation forces whose presence there was becoming harder and harder to explain.
NATO headquarters had been expelled from France and
was now in Belgium. American troops were deployed to
defend West Germany; their number was no more than a
quarter of those the communists maintained within a few
days' march; only by the use of nuclear weapons could they
make a convincing show of ability to resist a determined
onrush toward the West; but American statesmen had said
repeatedly that they would not be the first to use nuclear
weapons. By 1970 it was not at all clear whether this pledge
included the tactical ones by now perfected. If it only referred
to intercontinental missiles it was of no use on a possible
battlefield in Europe; and the distinction between "tactical"
and "strategic" was difficult to make.

If Stalin had been given in to about Poland in 1945 he
might not have felt it necessary to advance as far as East
Germany. At any rate the Poles, as well as the rest of Eastern
Europe, had not been protected by the Truman policies.
Poland was a dictatorship under Russian control; the other
countries (with Yugoslavia somewhat of an exception) were
harshly dominated in the communist manner; and it was at
least arguable that this might not have happened if the
Russians had not felt themselves threatened by encirclement,
and especially the fear of a revivified Germany.

As for West Germany, a remarkable economic recovery,
with American help, had given it a position of comparative
superiority among Europeans, but this was behind the allied
armies still being maintained theoretically to prevent renewed aggression, but actually for protection against Russian invasion. As 1970 opened, Brandt, the Prime Minister,
was beginning discussions with Russia to modify the hostility between East and West. This, if at all successful, would

leave the Allies with nothing whatever to show for twenty-five years of costly occupation.

It might be argued, in fact, that NATO's containment had been for the Russians a favorable policy. It had given them reason for building a vast new army and navy, for holding Eastern Europe in fief, for establishing a communist regime in East Germany, for penetrating the Mediterranean and making subjects of the Arabs, for putting North Korea and North Vietnam in their debt, and for holding on to, and possibly expanding, their Asiatic empire with inscrutable determination.

All this the United States had opposed, but never with the force to sustain the policy. Deployment thousands of miles from both coasts was simply an impossible logistical task; and what had been done had been at the cost of ruinous neglect at home and the accumulation of problems it had begun to seem almost too late to overcome, even with quick and complete reversal. The results seemed to many young people who must furnish the manpower and pay to support it, a failure not worth going on with. It could be seen how Russia and the United States together could have unified the world, at least to the extent of stabilizing the situations that broke out into small wars in many places; but neither could do it alone. Especially, if they used their resources to oppose each other, this was all they could do. A common policy toward China might even have prevented its retreat from the affairs of the world outside.

The first President after Truman's policies were clearly exposed as bankrupt would have to abandon the whole undertaking and do the best he could to create a new strategy. It had taken only two years after Roosevelt's death, and with Truman's management, to turn two great victorious allied powers into aggressive enemies. Russia and China would, in future, far overbalance the United States in population—in 1970 about a billion to two hundred million. Neither would be so productive per person, but neither would be in danger of starvation. Each would have drawn the United States into futile containment activities with troops deployed abroad on both fronts and actually fighting in Asia. Neither Russia nor China had soldiers in combat.

Could the situation have been avoided? To conclude that it could have been, it has only to be assumed that the Soviet Union and China might have been induced to remain American allies for the purposes of peace as they had been for the purposes of war. This would have required consent to the extension of Russia's sphere of influence into Eastern Europe short of Germany but with the Germans under compulsion not to rearm. For China it would have required recognition that the time had come to rid the nation of the reactionary— and corrupt—regime of Chiang Kai-shek, and bring that vast country into the twentieth century. Neither of these policies was tolerable to those in charge of American foreign relations; and in disregard of all reason they undertook the impossible.

The two most praised initiatives in the years immediately following Roosevelt's death were the Truman Doctrine and the Marshall Plan. Both were part of the general containment policy—the one to shut Russia off from the Mediterranean and the other to set up opposition to supposed communist designs on Western Europe.

The exclusion from the seas to the south had two obvious motives. One was to protect the British lifeline to the east; the other was to ensure that oil from Arabia would continue to be an exclusive Western resource. In spite of the enormous expenditures for these purposes the whole area had by 1970 fallen into Russian hegemony. The British had been forced to liquidate their imperial interests beyond the Red Sea, and so had no further use for a lifeline, and the oil for Europe was at such risk that new sources were being sought with frantic intensity. Both were therefore mistaken efforts. If they had never been undertaken the result would not have been much different; it might even have been more favorable. The

Russians had no need for Arabian oil, having plenty of their own, and they might well have agreed to a sharing arrangement; the Suez Canal might have been open, and shipping not diverted to the tedious route around South Africa.

After years of effort neither Russia nor China would be contained. It would not be fair to blame Truman alone for these vast misfortunes. Only their beginnings and their early phases, when allies were turned into enemies and enemies into allies, are chargeable to him. That, however, may be the most serious criticism that can be made of any American President except Buchanan, who allowed the Civil War to develop. Even then it has to be recalled how many collaborators and what almost universal support Truman had. Still, he was the President who kept on his desk that inscribed motto saying "the buck stops here." He cannot be exonerated; nor, to do him justice, would he want to be.

The policy once begun, wars with communists on the Asian mainland were inevitable. Confrontation with Russia having been undertaken, it proved difficult for Truman's successors to abandon it. Instead, the confrontation was enlarged, and this would go on until Johnson faced failure in 1968 and Nixon, because of Johnson's forced abdication, was obliged to find means for liquidation. Seldom had people paid a higher price in dissension at home and lost opportunity abroad for decisions made in pursuit of futile aims.

It is impossible to exonerate Dean Acheson from a large part of the responsibility for these results. He was Assistant Secretary of State from 1941 to 1945, when Roosevelt was busy with the war, and he had much to do with drafting a United Nations charter that Roosevelt did not approve but thought could be modified. He was then Undersecretary from 1945 to 1947 and was Secretary from 1949 to 1953. He was the proximate author of the Truman Doctrine and of the Marshall Plan. His assistants in the Department included Rusk and Rostow, who went on after he left until Johnson was through. His influence was pervasive all this time. He persisted into the Nixon age in defending his part in making policy during the Truman years. Throughout his service, and even later, he continued to identify Russian communism with imperialism and to claim that the measures of those years were no more than an essential defense of the "free" world.

A necessary part of that defense gradually became the insistence that all disturbances, especially revolutionary ones, were instances of communist aggression and that they must be met everywhere with military opposition. This was true in Germany, in Persia, in Greece, in Asia, and in the Near East. This came to be called the domino theory and was used effectively to justify intervention in Southeast Asia.

George Kennan, who was ambassador to Russia in 1946, was the author of the "X" article in *Foreign Affairs* that first outlined the containment doctrine. In dispatches to the Department he spoke of the "Kremlin's neurotic view of world affairs." The Russians meant, he said, to "infiltrate, divide and weaken the West." Kennan, however, offered various proposals for accord with the Russians. These, Acheson rejected as useless. Kennan afterward said in his *Memoirs* (Boston: Atlantic, Little, Brown, 1967) that they failed because no other way to deal with the Russians was found than military opposition. There should have been a political solution. He said, also, looking back, that there had been a faulty interpretation of the North Korean attack on the South as inspired by Russia; actually the Russians had tried to stop it. This was an example of failure

> . . . to take advantage of the opportunities for useful political discussion, when, in later years, such opportunities began to open up, and exerted itself, in its military preoccupations, to seal and perpetuate the very divisions of Europe which it should have been concerned to remove. . . .

The author of containment lived to regret the rationale he provided for the politicians who had their own reasons for exaggerating his warnings about Russian intentions.

6. *Fourth Mistake: Korea*

Very soon after his accession in 1945 Truman was obviously in trouble with the American people. Before two years had passed he had lost the support of the Roosevelt coalition; and it would not show its former strength until, in 1961, Kennedy followed Eisenhower.

The Congressional election of 1946 returned a Republican majority to the House of Representatives for the first time since 1928, and, after that, Presidential suggestions were regarded even more lightly than was customary. Truman may have appealed to the city bosses, but they no longer had large loyal followings; and workers were showing the independence given them by collective bargaining and their more secure situations. Besides, there had begun to boil up the really serious protests of the black community, now crowding into city slums, having become unwelcome as sharecroppers in the cotton country. Truman was inclined to make little of this; he spoke of the freedom riders, forerunners of black liberation, as "trouble-makers" and, to sensitive ears, this was unmistakably a signal of racism.

The loss of the House, curiously enough, was, in a narrow political way, fortunate for Truman; he could blame Congressional opposition for every ill besetting a now thoroughly irritated nation. It could later be seen that the blame was more his own than he admitted; or perhaps it was the fault of a political system that made so sleazy a preparation for succession to the Presidency. This constitutional fault was never more evident than in the original choice of Truman for Vice-President. Measuring up to a position "only a breath away from the Presidency" was not a consideration. An adequate choice was, in such a procedure, so unlikely as to be accidental.

One thing that was wrong by 1948 can be illustrated by the cost-of-living statistics. At the end of 1946 the index had risen ten per cent over 1945; and by 1948 it had risen to more than twenty-five per cent above 1945. No such pressure on a people had been known since the Civil War. The most visible cause of this abrupt rise was the abandonment of wartime controls and the return of economic management to the mercies of a "free" market that no longer existed. Immediate advantage was taken of their freedom by big business and big labor alike. Consumers suffered; and naturally they held it against Truman. It had always been so even during times when there had been no governmental responsibility for the management of economic affairs. Now resentment was intensified because, since the New Deal, there *had* been such a responsibility. Lightening wartime controls might at least have been more gradual, and time might have been given for adjustments. There naturally followed a period of industrial unrest as workers sought to keep wages within sight of rising prices. Those with fixed incomes were quite helpless. They had to reduce their living levels by the twenty-five per cent shown in the cost-of-living rise, and they did not take kindly to the necessity.

Truman, presiding over domestic turmoil as he was also presiding over a debacle abroad, was on the defensive. He was opposed for election in 1948 by Thomas E. Dewey, who had also opposed Roosevelt in 1944 and was a formidable and confident candidate. His worst handicap was explaining the behavior of the Republican majority in the House during the past two years; and this Truman took full adavntage of. It had been more responsible than he for demanding the liquidation of economic controls, for the disordered rush to bring home American troops, and for rejecting all proposals for measures calculated to meet the problems of postwar adjustment. There had been an epidemic of strikes, with John L. Lewis staging a verbal brawl with the President; there was rent-gouging and a holdover of black markets until the Office

of Price Administration was liquidated hastily and all restraint abandoned. Generally the country was in an uproar.

Truman was the victim in much of this largely because he
was lost in national politics. He had been much longer in
learning what every President must know than he need have
been. Long after he ought to have gauged the implacable
opposition of legislators to chief executives he was still trying
to persuade them to "cooperate" and continually being frustrated.

Truman's performance confirmed the conclusion of many
observers that service in the Senate is a peculiarly unfortunate
preparation for the Presidency. Senators have a singular im-
munity to the consequences of what they say and do; they
have little difficulty in escaping blame and claiming credit.
Besides, they are elected not on national, but on local, issues
and so are not schooled in responsibility for the general welfare. They learn to be talkers, showmen, not leaders or doers.
To subject one of them to the pressures of the White House
is to risk a breakdown in policy-making and calculated strategic planning.

It is hard to find an exception to the rule that long legislative experience unfits a person for the Presidency; it can
almost be said to warrant ineligibility. Truman was a case in
point. He unnecessarily added to his own difficulties by be-
having in the White House much as he had in his Missouri
job before going to the Senate. He illustrated perfectly the
risks involved in an unconstitutionalized political system. The
truth is that a convention for choosing candidates is a gathering of local political leaders without general experience,
completely concentrated on local affairs and with minimum
concern for—or knowledge of—national ones.

It has become usual (since the advent of television) for
the delegates to pick a senator for the obvious reason that he
has been able to command air time enough to make himself
known to a wide public; and if he has been careful in choosing issues there will be much for and not much against him.

In 1944 Truman had been a very popular choice for Vice-President with the delegates to the convention. He was one of their own. If he should succeed Roosevelt he could be trusted to cooperate with the party leaders. There would be jobs in large numbers distributed to the faithful. With him in the White House, the old days would be revived.

When he became President he exhibited a quite unjustified cockiness. The incident related by Acheson about Oppenheimer's concern over the bombing of Japan was typical. It said much about Truman—and perhaps more about Acheson, who was by then his Secretary of State.

The volume of memoirs, written by Acheson, called *Present at the Creation,* published in 1969, was accurately named. Since he had been Undersecretary of State until June, 1947, then after an interval had become Secretary (in January, 1949), he had been Truman's most trusted policy adviser. He had not only accepted containment but had energetically reinforced and defended it. His exhibitions of extravagant invective in the United Nations appearances and elsewhere seemed incongruous in so restrained and gentlemanly an individual; but he had an unexpected talent for it. If the "establishment" could be personified in one individual, Acheson would come as close to the model as anyone who could be named; but when it came to trading epithets he easily bested the crudest individuals produced by the Russian proletariat.

The "settlements" of the postwar years were these: the communists had expelled Chiang Kai-shek, Kennan had written his famous dispatch from Moscow, and Harriman had reported from Paris that there was in progress "a new barbarian invasion of Europe." In August, 1947, a naval task force had been sent to the Mediterranean, and it would still be there, as the seventh fleet, in 1970. Britain had given up in Greece and Turkey, and the United States had taken over. Marshall had made his speech at Harvard and the famous plan had been accepted by sixteen nations—but not by the wary Russians. Bevin, the Labor government's Foreign Minister, had proposed defense treaties, and the Brussels Pact had been signed, to be followed by the North Atlantic Treaty with its military establishment in Europe.

In the midst of all these events reordering American policy toward Russia and implementing containment with rebuilt military forces, and with the country divided and unhappy, Truman was re-elected by a narrow majority. There still remained a recalcitrant Congress, but it was quite as anticommunist as Truman, and his inaugural, emphasizing the U.N., the Marshall Plan, and NATO, as well as his "Point Four" plan for foreign aid, was well received. This Point Four was intended to assist in the recovery of friendly nations, and appropriations for it were made without difficulty. It would still be an item in the budget for 1970 although much reduced, and with Europe eliminated. It would be passed with many reservations and diminished annually as retreat from the Truman commitments proceeded.

It has to be said that Truman, being from old Populist country, and a Democrat, after all, made many proposals to the Congress for an increase in funds for welfare, education, and other domestic necessities; but these were ignored, and his administration ended with little done to meet the problems even then visible as ones the nation must eventually solve. As commander in chief, however, he could finish what Roosevelt had begun during the war. He could end racial discrimination in the armed forces, and he could enlarge the Good Neighbor policy with Point Four money. His frustrations were finally hidden by the Korean conflict when he could make use of emergency Presidential powers.

In June of 1950 the North Koreans invaded South Korea in an attempt to overrun the country before a defense could be organized. Truman reacted at once and, with United Nations backing (the Russians having some time before boycotted the Security Council), entrusted the joint command to MacArthur. A combat team opposed itself to the full force of the invaders and delayed them until two divisions stationed in Japan could arrive and begin effective defense.

There was something curious about the immediate undertaking to defend South Korea. It followed almost at once on the expulsion from China of Chiang Kai-shek and was, therefore, on the border of a hostile nation. It was assumed that the attack was inspired by Russia, although this assumption later appeared to have been false. Truman treated it as a provocation and met it as such even though there had been no promise of defense and American forces had been diminished. It had been omitted by Acheson himself when he had defined the defense perimeter of the United States in a policy statement; in April, 1948, he had said unequivocally that the nation should not become so involved in the Korean situation that an action taken by any faction in Korea or by any other power could be considered a *casus belli.*

The Joint Chiefs had felt, as General J. Lawton Collins reported later on, in *War in Peacetime: The History and Lessons of Korea* (Houghton Mifflin, 1968), that, in the context of a general war, Korea was indefensible and "of little strategic value to the United States." Acheson had confirmed this conclusion in his speech (in 1950) drawing the defense perimeter. The line, he had said, "runs along the Aleutians to Japan and then goes on to the Ryukus . . . and from the Ryukus to the Philippines." Both Korea and Formosa were outside this perimeter. The defense of Korea was, then, a reversal, undertaken as a riposte to what was supposed to be a Russian thrust outward. It was unjustified either by the supposition supporting it or by the defense of any American interest.

The military tragedy in Korea was attributable to MacArthur. When reinforcements had driven the North Koreans back across the eighteenth parallel, MacArthur was not willing to stop there. As a military man he saw that if the territory across the Yalu remained an enemy sanctuary, there would never be an end to the threat of invasion. Besides, it seemed to him an opportunity to eliminate the Chinese communists from the world scene. He would not accept the confinement of a limited war. He grossly miscalculated the Chinese reaction and found himself facing hordes of foot soldiers, whose numbers and carelessness of losses he could not defeat. In March of 1951 Truman relieved him of command, and he returned to an outpouring of support and sympathy, in defiance of Truman, that had no match in American history.

The Korean conflict was still going on, but was somewhat stabilized, when Truman announced his intention not to run again. The Democrats nominated Adlai Stevenson—although Truman preferred his cold war assistant, Averell Harriman. Stevenson made a brave try but was defeated in a hopeless contest with General Eisenhower, who, in the multifarious troubles besetting the nation, appeared as a father figure who would become the stabilizer everyone was longing for. He had made that unfortunate statement about soldiers sticking to soldiering; but he allowed himself to be persuaded that a crusade to save America must be undertaken—and that only he could undertake it. His winning promise was that he would end the now unpopular war in Korea—and, because he was a victorious general, he was believed.

Truman retired to Independence, Missouri, having been President for nearly eight years. During that time the world had been divided with such zeal on both sides that Churchill's iron curtain speech was accepted as an inspiration. The acceptance of this view continued to be practically unanimous; and Truman, in retirement, was a statesman who had held off evil forces and deserved well of his countrymen.

What must be said about these strategic decisions at the opening of the nuclear age is this: there is a choice between two views; either there were colossal misjudgments or what happened was inevitable because of Russian intractability. What there is no doubt about is that the communists came out ahead. By 1970 that was what the inheritor of Truman's policies had to face. Nixon had to escape a dilemma that ought somehow never to have happened. This was ironic, since he had been, as a member of the Congress, and as Vice-President, one of the most active xenophobes. Because of his record it was fair that he should have to deal with the consequences. Only occasionally does a politician find himself thus confronted with his past; he can usually blur the record in some way; but Nixon had built his career on the exposure of a communist conspiracy. He had won his congressional campaigns on this issue; and he had been the most prominent figure in the immolation of Alger Hiss as a conspirator. But for these activities he would never have come prominently into notice and been found acceptable as a running mate for Eisenhower.

There are these questions: would the Russians have been able to establish satellites in Eastern Europe and dominate the Mediterranean and the passages to the East, if they had been more sensitively dealt with? If the United States had not used its monopoly to demand that, in return for eventual disarmament, the communists must accept surveillance as force was reduced, would they have consented to an arrangement for coexistence? Could mutual interests have been made to prevail then and there?

It is arguable that Roosevelt might have been able to do it. Truman did not—and all his life was proud that he had not conceded anything. So, in fact, was Acheson. His *Present at the Creation* was one long rooster-crow over the results of his hard-line policy. It had cost by 1970 a hundred thousand American lives and well over a hundred billion dollars. It is hard to assess the result achieved as worth all that, especially if it is suspected that Roosevelt—or other American statesmen —might have made it unnecessary.

There is a caveat to be entered here. The faults were not all American. The Russians were intractable, unreliable, ill-mannered, and inscrutable. It required patience and almost saintly forbearance to deal with them in decent exchanges.

Such virtues, however, ought to have been easier to cultivate for the representatives of the one nation in the world possessed of absolute power. The United States in those years could have forced Russia into submission. It would have required a holocaust to do it; but a holocaust was available. The difficulty was that the Russians correctly calculated the Americans' adherence to an ethic that would not allow the genocidal weapon to be utilized. They therefore felt free to act as though it did not exist.

All through the fruitless exchanges between Molotov, Vishinsky, Gromyko, and other Russians and the various American negotiators, the Americans were unable to understand why their monopoly of force was not recognized. They were obviously dealing with an inferior power; but its representatives refused to behave as they should; and the Americans never reached such an understanding as would have permitted the concessions to the Russians' surly suspicions needed for an approach to mutual conciliation. Negotiators from the American elite, with a background of democratic experience, cannot really be forgiven for allowing the time to pass when invective should have given way to forbearance. If the Russians had been allowed their overbearing pride and their brutal denunciations and if their affronts had been met with patient silence, the outcome might have been different. There was nothing to lose by such a policy except face. Words could not change the fact of power. But it was not done. American manners tended to match those of the Russians, and there were no agreements.

There is something else; if the invasion of South Korea was not what it was assumed to be in Washington, then it ought not to have roused American emotions as it did. There seems to have been faulty intelligence in this as in so much else having to do with that crisis. MacArthur, it will be recalled, was quite certain that China would not meet him at the Yalu with overwhelming force appearing out of nowhere.

Korea, therefore, was a strategic mistake, ending in an

occupation to be maintained for years. If it was not one of those Russian attempts to challenge the United States on the periphery of the American sphere of influence that became a fixed point of departure for American policy, then it was undertaken under a misapprehension still being paid for in 1970.

7. Fifth Mistake: Assisting the French in Indo-China

As the Japanese retreated from their conquered territories, Roosevelt had tried to persuade the colonial powers that they must divest themselves of their Southeast Asia holdings or be expelled. The British recognized the inevitable; the French and the Dutch had to be forced out. The general result, after years of turmoil, was that several small nations emerged whose borders defied all geographic sense. This would seem to have been in accord with the ideal of self-determination, so much prized by American progressives; but it must be recalled that, at the same time, Roosevelt was trying to negotiate the acceptance of world order to be maintained by those who had the capability of repressing aggression. Since he relied on accord among the great powers to keep the smaller nations from squabbling among themselves and drawing the big ones into taking sides with the hope of gaining some advantage—access to resources, perhaps, or the extension of an ideology—the postwar arrangements among the victorious allies should have been made with this in mind. The moment for persuasion was then, before opportunities for making trouble had arisen.

Self-determination was not, in his view, a wholly unworkable principle; but once a people had agreed to live together as a nation, minorities with grievances, whether ethnic or economic, ought not to further break down the arrangement into progressively smaller national units. If every minority could make itself into a nation the world would become impossibly fractionalized. Such disaffected minorities would not be able to establish viable states, and their attempt to maintain the posture of nationhood would inevitably fail, with just such spreading disturbance as had happened repeatedly in Eastern Europe. Consolidations by the colonial powers were in this sense a more efficient arrangement; but some of the associated peoples simply would not live together if separatism was a possibility. Subsequent troubles in India showed how difficult it was; those in Indo-China were even more illuminating; and Africa illustrated the consequences of tribalism transformed into nationalism.

The demand for independence would obviously have to be satisfied whenever it was possible; but it would need a strong organization of the great powers to prevent further rebellions so serious as to engage the powers themselves in defense of dissidents and perhaps in competition with each other.

It was Roosevelt's intention that small nations should be allowed autonomy unless they threatened the disruption of world order; but if they caused serious trouble the great powers must enforce settlements. This should not be done, however, by each separately, but by all in concert. This was not a proposal to divide the world into areas where one or another of the great powers would be recognized or dominant by the others and expected to exploit it as seemed best. On the contrary, no power would have authority beyond its own borders or would try to extend them. The third world would be collectively overseen by the Security Council, where the great powers met.

This was the essential scheme of Roosevelt's United Nations.

The Assembly of that body would be able to debate and recommend; but only the Security Council would be able to act, and every action must be unanimous. That is to say, no members would be able to discipline small nations or dissident minorities by itself, only when the others agreed that it was necessary; then all would act together, presumably having as their agents a United Nations conciliation service and such a neutral police force as might be necessary.

It was clearly assumed in this that any Assembly of small nations with legislative powers would engage themselves in intrigues for advantage, in the forming of ethnic or geographic coalitions, and in the formulations of demands on each other. Solicitation of assistance from one or the other of the great powers would be likely to be successful if those powers had not formed a firm coalition with commitments not to encroach on each others' spheres of influence. There would certainly be proposals to tempt them separately with offers of trade preferences or exclusive access to resources, perhaps even alliance. This would lead to desire for the extension of borders; and dependency would follow. Presently they would find themselves in the business of selling or otherwise furnishing arms, and these would be used to start small wars. If adopted satellites were supported those small wars could quickly enlarge. How the Russians extended their support for East Germany was a frightening confirmation of this possibility.

Truman did not explicity abandon the Roosevelt conception; he simply never attempted to effectuate it. Perhaps he did not understand it; or, if he did, he considered that close association with the Russians would be an ideological impossibility. At any rate, almost at once he exhibited an implacable hostility; and this became the central principle of American policy in direct contravention of the Roosevelt strategy he professed to be following.

A national policy may be allowed to die, or it may be reversed. The first is a mild kind of change, the other an aggressive one. Truman did not merely stop cooperating with the Russians; he became their enemy. He would say—did say —that it was all the Russians' fault. No one could claim that they were not exasperating; the manners of their representatives were boorish; and they never spoke of the United States without using the clichés of communist intercourse with others—sometimes very hard to bear. It would have required a stopping of speechmaking for political effect to have made possible calmer consideration of mutual interests. This was not done; conciliation was not attempted; and presently the situation had got beyond the possibility of reversal.

There is no evidence that any effort was made on the American side. The guiding notion was that there could be no dealing with communists. They were liars and cheats. No doubt they were; but they were still immensely powerful, and American interests required that ways should be found to reach reasonable exchanges. Interests, however, were less important than emotions.

The long-continued pursuit of containment emerged eventually into perilous situations all around the world—in Germany, the Mideast, Southeast Asia, and in Africa—of the kind Roosevelt had clearly hoped to prevent. In Asia it began by, of all things, assisting the French, who were trying to re-establish their colonial power in Indo-China as the Japanese withdrew. This was about as complete a reversal as could possibly be imagined. Truman was quoted in a *Department of State Bulletin* on July 3, 1950, as saying:

> The attack upon Korea makes it plain beyond all doubt that communism has passed beyond the use of subversion to conquer independent nations and will now use armed invasion and war. . . . Accordingly . . . I have directed acceleration in the furnishing of military assistance to the forces of France and the Associated States in Indochina and the dispatch of a military mission to provide close working relations with those forces . . .

There thus began an involvement that would reach a nearly complete American takeover of the anticommunist war on the Asian mainland in 1965 and would have gone on from there to vaster efforts if the American public had not by then begun to question the necessity for protecting a population with no very strong wish to be protected. That this last was true was recognized by Acheson himself in 1952. He advised the incoming Eisenhower administration:

> The central problem in Indochina was fence-sitting by the population. They would never come down on one side or another until they had reasonable assurance of who would be the victor.

He went on to inform his successor:

> We are helping France to the extent of carrying between one-third and one-half of the financial burden.

It was not until years later that it became apparent on what flimsy foundations the assumption was made that the Russians instigated the North Korean or the North Vietnamese invasion of the southern halves of those countries.

Lackadaisical self-defense on the part of the South Vietnamese, and, earlier, the South Koreans, was the reason why, once begun, their defense became so largely an American enterprise; but this did not explain the strategy. This, of course, rested on the conviction that the communists meant to dominate Southeast Asia and that, if they did, American interests would be so seriously injured that it must be stopped at all costs. These costs were not known at first, but not counting them was deliberate. Whatever it required was to be invested. When, however, it ran to half a million men and perhaps one-third of the national budget, there was general insistence that the costs *should* be counted and that they should be weighed against the possible gains. The discrepancy was appalling.

These were all too plainly the kind of dangers Roosevelt had anticipated. The Russians, as well as the Chinese, were drawn into support of satellite communists against other great powers—except that the Russians always managed to let someone else do the fighting, a lesson learned also by the Chinese after Korea. They only furnished the munitions and the rhetoric.

It has to be said for Truman that the earliest involvement in Southeast Asia was urged on him by all those around him. There must have been practical unanimity among the White House coterie that the Russians were attempting the sort of thrust assumed in the accepted theory of aggressive expansionism. That the Chinese did help the North Koreans, and that the Russians stood aloof, was considered to be no more than a typical wily maneuver of Stalin. The Chinese and Russians were not differentiated then as they came to be later; they were both communists, and communists were assumed to be a unified horde committed to world conquest; and they had to be stopped at its beginning. Containment was the rubric.

That Truman accepted this general conviction and its policy implications is not strange considering his origins and experiences—but he was President and, so, responsible, as others were not. There must have been intelligence available to him showing at least the beginning of what became so significant within a short time—that the Russians and Chinese were divided in what seemed on the surface merely ideological differences, but were better explained as geopolitical. They had the longest mutual border in the world, and Chinese maps showed extensive territories now occupied by the Russians.

The Truman decisions, from using the bomb on live targets in Japan, to supporting the French in Indo-China, were thus preceded by what later would seem either shallow explorations or faulty intelligence, as well as failure to evaluate future consequences in any significant depth. His advice came from those who were biased in these ways; but frequently, he needed none. Someone must have told him, or he must have read—he was an assiduous student of American history and often expressed admiration for James K. Polk—that strong Presidents acted decisively. They were responsible; they made up their minds; they must not appear to have doubts. It was better to make mistakes than to hesitate and give the impression of uncertainty.

Or, perhaps, it was just Truman's nature. After ten years in the Senate, after being a county official, he had power to dispose of. It was a heady possession. He used it freely.

Oppenheimer might agonize over the dead Japanese at Hiroshima and Nagasaki, but Truman never agonized over anything. He had no afterthoughts and no regrets. If that is not the careful weighing process expected of one entrusted with decision-making for a great power, it was the method of the American President who presided over the war's end and the arrangements for what was to follow.

He is said to have been annoyed that so little happened after his decisions—that the bureaucracy found so many ways to diffuse his authority. He once said that Eisenhower, following him, would be surprised by this frustration; but this was at the end of his Presidency. The fateful decisions were made when he was new in office and inflated with the opportunity to show his executive style. Since they were what his subordinates happened to approve, there was no holding back. Action followed all too quickly whatever foreign policy conclusion he arrived at.

Later on, he discovered that his Populist proposals did not result in quick approval by the Congress—or even the Democrats in the Congress—but these were other matters, not those wanted by the conservatives; and if he might have made a respectable record on domestic issues, there was no way of knowing. Very little got done.

8. *Eisenhower: Drifting*

Politics is a profession, a serious, complicated, and in a true sense, a noble one. In the American scene I see no dearth of men fitted by training, talent and integrity for national leadership. On the other hand, nothing in the international or domestic situation especially qualifies for the most important office in the world a man whose adult years have been spent in the military forces. At least, this is true in my case.

EISENHOWER, to a New Hampshire editor,
as he assumed the presidency of
Columbia University and was being talked of
for the U.S. Presidency

I have a problem in assuming the presidency at Colum-bia; but what could I do? I did not want to be head of the Boy Scouts; and I did not want to capitalize on my army connections in business.

EISENHOWER, to R. M. Hutchins, with the
University presidency in prospect

The Eisenhower Presidency was a relatively uneventful one. It seems curious to say so, but it is true that this conservative military man had much the same place in people's esteem as Roosevelt the innovator. He was what they wanted their President to be: informal, kindly, decent, somewhat confused by the more difficult problems of finance and even the daily doings of government, but trustworthy in making the big decisions they wanted made. Truman, following Roosevelt, had never become the respected figure a reliable President must be.

With Eisenhower in the White House a sort of calm spread

across the land, differences were less sharp, compromise
seemed easier, and the settlement of problems was postponed. The problems were still there—racial, economic, and
all the rest—but there was little hysteria about immediate settlements, and few harsh demands on some by others. Americans cannot afford this kind of President. The accumulation
of issues that sometime will have to be settled goes on in-
exorably; but it is the kind of President they like. They like,
also, never to hear about foreigners—they are always the
source of trouble. And Eisenhower, paradoxically, was a
man of peace—far more so than Truman or his own Secretary
of State, John Foster Dulles.

This cessation of activity was understandably annoying to
liberals who had hoped to resume New Deal progress with
Stevenson; but there were many others to whom Eisenhower
did seem to recall old faiths, old loyalties, and Americanism.
They accepted the virtual standstill with relief.

When Eisenhower was first being urged by the Republicans to be a candidate he said to some of them that he
would accept only if both parties wanted him. If this showed
an appalling ignorance of American political processes, there
was the excuse that some prominent Democrats also had
thought he might be their nominee. Until he finally made a
choice no one knew what party he favored. Apparently he
had never cared to vote; moreover there was that apparently
decisive statement that it was quite out of character for a
professional soldier to hold high civilian office. What he had
said ignored several precedents, Grant being the most
prominent, but there was the truth in it that generals are not
politicians—or ought not to be—and, when chosen, have
usually been used for party purposes without regard to national interests; and have been among the worst of Presidents—Washington being the exception. Still, Eisenhower
did manage, once in office, to be the least partisan President
since the father of his country, much to the disgust of Republican leaders.

The popular acceptance of Eisenhower, and the approval of his Presidency in spite of the standstill in domestic progress, showed how much Americans needed a chief of state who stood above battles among themselves, representing their more decent impulses and always being there to remind them of their duties to one another.

The framers had had something like this in mind when they had created the Presidency under the chairmanship of Washington. They had ignored the existence of political parties—even though they did exist even then, as soon became all too evident. They intended the President to preside. He was to be chosen by a college of the best people, not by a nationwide adversary proceeding, sure to arouse the mobs they hoped to subdue.

Even Washington, before the end of his second term, was being savagely attacked, and Jefferson was deep in machinations to discredit him. John Adams had no peace; he caused furious controversy, and, when defeated, he left office so embittered that he ignored the amenities and refused even to greet his successor. The above-the-battle President has seldom been a reality.

Hamilton had foreseen this and had done his best to convince the convention that a monarchy was needed. He had been ignored. Everyone just then had had enough of kings.

The President was described in the Constitution as a "Chief Executive." That he was to be chief of state was only inferred from his duty to appoint not only domestic officers but ambassadors, and to negotiate treaties; also he was to be commander in chief. This consolidated in his person two hard duties—to manage the government, even the military forces, and to be the only symbol of union. The Congress was to possess the purse, but he was to *do* everything. No other figure could become the center of attention, the principal American.

The resulting ambivalence was for Eisenhower as for his predecessors an immense difficulty; but if he expected to be

a nonpartisan President he was given the opportunity; the
same people who elected him returned a Democratic majority in the Congress after two years; and after 1954 he had
them to deal with in legislative matters. There had, however, grown up a tradition of solidarity in foreign relations,
and there was, in fact, general agreement on containment;
consequently he had no more trouble with the Senate majority controlled by Lyndon B. Johnson than Truman had
had when Arthur Vandenburg had been majority leader.

If he had been belligerent instead of peaceable he could
have had ample support for the preventive war Dulles
seemed always to be suggesting, but, having ended hostilities in Korea by letting the other side know that if they did
not stop their aggression he would resort to the nuclear
weapon, and having to deal with Russians not yet ready with
such weaponry of their own, he had only to check his Secretary of State at intervals. The army was allowed to run down
because no more land wars would be fought and because he
had considerable confidence in the Russian generals he had
dealt with in Europe. Some of them he regarded as friends.

In spite of the nuclear threat latent in many minds, there
was a feeling that so long as the American finger on the
button would have to be Eisenhower's, it would never be
pressed; and somehow he would keep the Russians from
pressing theirs.

There was more trouble about the economy. Inflation continued and organized labor, trying to cope with inflation,
made appropriate demands resulting in occasional disruptive
strikes. Inflation also resulted in lower and lower living
levels for the unorganized. During Eisenhower's eight years
there were three distinct recessions, resulting from the obsolete policies of the men he had chosen to manage the
Treasury. They had succeeded in business and it seemed
reasonable to Eisenhower that they must know about finance.
What they knew was what they wanted for themselves, not
what was good for the country. He had better advice from

the Council of Economic Advisors; but he was slow to accept it.

There was a certain letdown along with the placidity, in the later years of his incumbency, and with it there was increasing unhappiness with the national condition; but the President was not blamed. If he could have run again—the twenty-second amendment, intended to prevent Democrats from keeping another Roosevelt in office practically for life, now had the ironic result of preventing the Republicans from keeping Eisenhower there—he would have been re-elected without difficulty. In spite of their disappointment with his political lassitude, possession of the White House was all important.

The same protective sentiment that had kept Roosevelt safe in many people's regard worked for Eisenhower. When Roosevelt grew impatient with labor leaders who were unreasonable and importunate, they said to each other that it was a failure on their part—they just hadn't made him understand; and the same attitude was prevalent among the others in his coalition of the disadvantaged. Such loyalty is the most valuable resource a leader can have; and Eisenhower had it too. These sentiments are never unanimous; there are always carpers and critics. They said Eisenhower did not attend to business—how could he with all that golf to play? They said all those presents from his wealthy friends were not given without expectation of return in good will. They said he was ignorant of economics to an incredible degree. They said many other things, all of them more or less true; but not many people were listening. The intellectuals were amused by incredibly garbled grammar when he spoke without his speechwriters' drafts before him. When they were there to be read, he sometimes could not pronounce the words or make it seem that he had the least understanding of what he was reading.

All these devastating evidences of incapacity somehow did not result in much if any loss of popular affection. He was easy and plain. He made nothing of his vast powers. He accepted the luxuries and attentions of the enlarged Presidency without any fuss; he had become used to this sort of thing as Supreme Commander and as President of Columbia. Truman had never behaved in the White House as though he belonged there. His style had been such a contrast with that of Roosevelt that it had become a problem in his role as chief of state. Eisenhower took it all easily; he presided over the occasions arranged for him with informal formality that never became condescension. When absolutely necessary he rose to occasions in ways natural to a disciplined but not a strained or constricted soldier.

Perhaps the most celebrated series of events during the Eisenhower regime were those associated with the name of Senator Joseph McCarthy of Wisconsin who set out on a crusade of his own to purge the government (and other institutions) of communist influence. The Senator was a reckless demagogue. His accusations were groundless, and his investigations ignored the rights of his victims. He let innuendoes substitute themselves for facts, and he played mercilessly on the current fear that Russian spies were everywhere. The few years of his activities are spoken of by historians as the McCarthy era. He was capitalizing, of course, on the preparatory work of the Un-American Activities Committee of the House of Representatives and of Richard M. Nixon, while a legislator. He had a following of some size among fascistic and xenophobic citizens, and for a time he terrorized the liberal community.

McCarthy was eventually rebuked by his senatorial colleagues; but Eisenhower had pretended throughout his period of notoriety not to know of his existence. He might at any time have stopped the dissension caused by the McCarthy behavior, but he serenely ignored the whole affair. Even when the army was accused of harboring traitors, and General Marshall's reputation was called in question he was not moved to protest. The excitement died, the Senator was discredited, and those who had been injured were left to recover their reputations as best they could.

Such incidents had happened before in American life, but none so traumatic and at the same time so unnecessary. Eisenhower was neither blamed nor commended. He blandly pursued his unexciting routine.

In one matter, however, Eisenhower left a lesson for his successors if they had known how to profit from it. He knew how to use a staff. Roosevelt had known that he needed one but could never keep to the rules necessary if assistants are to work effectively. The General behaved in the White House just as he had in his command vehicle in Europe, using his disciplined aides effectively, reaching down the lines to lower levels, and insisting on keeping everything simple— and short. He would not read a position paper more than a few paragraphs long. If he did, he could not read the others —and have any time left for recuperation.

He was incapacitated much of the time. He had a heart that was failing and an old ileitis that gave him trouble. He was no engine of great power. But he had the most careful attention, and he let all his ills be known. He had sympathy and no suggestion from anyone that he was not in complete control.

If all this sounds like the nearly ideal American President, it was. The only difficulty was that nothing much was being done to anticipate coming troubles. There was no satisfactory debate about the national future. The result was much the same as that of the Coolidge Presidency. The era of "Silent Cal" ended in the debacle of the Great Depression. When Eisenhower left, peace and satisfaction left with him. An appalling number of issues rose to the surface, and there to solve them was an inexperienced youngish man who had demonstrated political potency but whose preparation for managing the affairs of state was even more elementary than

Truman's had been. The likelihood that in the process of learning he would make dreadful mistakes was more than likely; it was practically certain.

9. *Eisenhower: Massive Retaliation*

You had a row of dominoes set up, and you knock over the first one, and what would happen to the last one was the certainty that it would go over very quickly. So you have a beginning of a disintegration that would have the most profound influences.

EISENHOWER, news conference,
New York Times, April 8, 1954

The important thing from now on is not to mourn the past but to seize the future opportunity to prevent the loss in northern Vietnam from leading to the extension of communism throughout Southeast Asia and the Southwest Pacific.

JOHN FOSTER DULLES,
Department of State Bulletin, August 2, 1954

It can be seen why there is less to say about Eisenhower than about Truman: during his time so little was really begun! There was, however, one important change. This was the conclusion that the long-reach nuclear weapons had revolutionized warfare, and, at the moment, were, as well, an American monopoly. Until the Russians also possessed the same capability this would serve for defense policy. It was, however, a tactical, not a strategic change. The acceptance of containment was complete; it was a crusade with Dulles, the Secretary of State; but, for the most part, it is fair enough to say of Eisenhower that he merely acquiesced. Such mistakes as he himself made in foreign policy were not really ones of commission. There were, however, limits to his approval of aggression, and beyond them he stubbornly refused to go. This may have been illogical, but in fact he simply would not undertake a preventive war that, strictly considered, the policy called for. From 1952 to 1960 he had such public prestige that his decisions were not challenged in any important way; and he had no cause to be worried by noisy dissenters. He drifted; but not over the edge. The word "brinkmanship" was appropriately applied to Dulles; but Eisenhower always pulled his associates back from the brink.

There was, however, deep in what often seemed an indecisive Presidential mind, a conviction that the apocalyptic proposals he was presented with were too extreme for acceptance and too fearsome to entertain; so, although he allowed Secretary Dulles to run loose around the world and seem to make commitments of the most horrific kind, and although he recalled—in a curiously intimate and naïve review, published in 1969—that he had often sat, at the end of a day in the White House, relaxed, talking at length with his friend Dulles, the fact is that he mostly listened; and ultimately he never let Dulles go too far. He was again and again urged by his Secretary of State and by Admiral Radford to open an attack; force must be used, they said, to save the world from the communist conspiracy. Now, they told him, as MacArthur had told Truman, was the time to destroy the growing menace.

General Gavin described one such round of urging and refusal—perhaps the most important one (in *Crisis Now*, 1968, pp. 48–49):

> Again, as at the time of Dien Bien Phu, the Joint Chiefs divided. Admiral Radford (the chairman) was emphatically in favor of landing a force in the Hanoi-Haiphong area, even if it meant risking war with Red China. In this he was fully supported by the Chief of Staff of the Air Force and the Chief of

Naval Operations. In my opinion such an operation meant a
great risk of war. Just southeast of Haiphong harbor is the
island of Hainan which is part of Red China. The Navy was
unwilling to risk their ships in the Haiphong area without first
invading and capturing the island. Admiral Radford and the
chiefs of the Navy and Air Force felt that, faced with our
overwhelming power, the Red Chinese would not react to his
violation of their sovereignty. General Ridgway and I had
grave doubts about the validity of this reasoning.

. . . Again, fortunately, the President decided not to commit
U.S. forces to Southeast Asia.

However, there was a compromise. We would not attack North
Vietnam, but we would support a South Vietnamese government that we hoped would provide a stable, independent
government.

Eisenhower was not alone in this final reluctance. There
were others who did not share the Dulles zeal. They might
—and did—fully accept the necessity for containment, believing that the communists intended world conquest, and,
when Chiang Kai-shek had been expelled, that all communists, including the Chinese, were unified and under one
discipline; but there remained some sense of practical possibilities, perhaps also unwillingness to risk so many lives
and so many billions. Besides, the deep isolationist sentiment,
so evident before 1941, was still alive. Foreign adventures
were to many Americans suspect. So, in April, 1954, when
Dulles asked leading members of the Congress to approve
a resolution permitting the President to use air and naval
forces in Indo-China, he was advised that he had better lo-
cate some allies before undertaking such a venture. Whether
Eisenhower really wanted that permission is not of record.

When Dien Bien Phu had settled matters for the French
colonialists, and there took place in Geneva the conference
of great powers, the outcome displeased Dulles. In that
meeting a settlement of the Korean dispute had proved quite
impossible, and it had been left as confused as it had been

since Eisenhower had undertaken to make a settlement and
had achieved no more than a cease-fire; but about Indo-
China there had resulted what were afterward called the
Geneva Accords. These had provided for a cease-fire, but
had ended (in August) in a declaration reiterating the temporary nature of the separation between North and South
at the 17th parallel and had said that democratic freedoms
should be achieved by election—a secret ballot.

Neither the United States nor Vietnam signed the declaration; but France, the Soviet Union, and the United Kingdom did. Afterward there was a grudging unilateral statement, however, saying that the United States would not
disturb the agreements by force and endorsing the suggested
free election.

The world was accommodating itself as best it could to
the A-bomb, without much assistance from the United States,
when the H-bomb figuratively burst on an already appre-
hensive public. This was more terrible than its predecessor
had been in comparison to the artillery of World War II.
Dulles regarded this new reinforcement as a final capability
to contain communism. That was not precisely what he said,
but that was what he meant. There would be, he said, no
more small wars of the Korean kind. If aggression originated
anywhere in the communist world it would be accepted as
an invitation to World War III; and there could be only
one outcome. The threat was plain.

Only gradually did Americans become aware that they
were committed to strike at the Russian heartland with
genocidal weapons if there should be a border dispute in
Turkey, for instance, or somewhere in Indo-China; but Governor Stevenson, spokesman for the opposition, saw the
implication:

We are told, and I am quoting Secretary Dulles, that we have
rejected the "tradition of meeting aggression by direct and
local opposition." We have taken the decision "to depend pri-

marily upon a great capacity to retaliate instantly, by means
and place of our choosing . . ."

. . . this means, if it means anything, that if the Communists
try another Korea we will retaliate by dropping bombs on
Moscow or Peking.

This provoked Eisenhower, who, although, as afterward
became known, would never have used the bomb, evidently
thought it good policy not to say so. He took a high position,
saying that Stevenson's was a "demagogic" attack. He then
called attention to his own expertness in military matters;
compared with Stevenson's it was obviously overwhelming.
Since this was obviously a political issue rather than a military one, and his annoyance had shown all too plainly in
the off-hand press conference reply to Stevenson, it was not
well received. Presently Vice-President Nixon sought to
modify its effect. On March 13, after acknowledged consultation with the President, he elaborated the argument. Russian strategy, he said, called for starting numerous small
wars all over the world. This would force the United States
to stay armed to the teeth, ready to fight whenever the enemy
chose. The Security Council, after long discussions, had
adopted the "new look" as a principle: "Rather than let the
communists nibble us to death, we will rely in future primarily on our massive mobile retaliatory power which we
can use at our discretion against the major source of aggression at times and places that we choose."

Dulles' doctrine horrified so many people—in other countries as well as in the United States—that he began a retreat
ending in a position hardly distinguishable from that of his
more moderate critics. He explained that "our" meant "only
after consultation." It was well known that he had made a
hasty journey to Britain before the Geneva meeting to see
whether an ally could not be found for intervention in Vietnam. He had been making violent speeches and the President had been persuaded to make the "domino" speech;
Nixon had hinted that military measures were not far off;

and it was rumored that Radford had a plan for a nuclear attack from the air. Everything seemed prepared for action as Dulles had planned.

Backing away from this position was not easy; but Eisenhower, suddenly awake to his subordinates' intentions, simply but absolutely refused. It was extremely awkward; but they had to accept; and an alternative was hastily invented. Unfortunately, in a partisan sense, what was put forward recalled Truman's Fourth Point—the rescuing of peoples from the conditions that made them vulnerable to communist appeals—but that was not much noticed. Truman had not been able to get from an isolationist and obstructionist Congress funds sufficient to make such a policy operative; and Eisenhower was no more successful. He now had a Democratic majority to deal with. It remained a paper proposal. This was inevitable since neither President had created such support for the scheme as would impress reluctant legislators. They had allowed the military—especially the navy—to usurp such funds as could be got by tolerable taxation, they had failed to make an accommodation with Russia, and they had encouraged the belief that nuclear superiority made the nation safe. The policy seemed accepted and permanent.

Eisenhower had this unhappy stalemate to live with from the earliest essays of his Secretary of State. He made a number of proposals for conciliation and even for coexistence; but he was hampered for a long time by the McCarthy harassment and by his own acceptance of the communist conspiracy theory. When his eight years ended he left to Kennedy, his successor, a situation not much different from the one he had himself inherited from Truman. The nation was no safer; it was in fact far less safe, since commitments had been made, through treaties, in Europe, Southeast Asia, and the Middle East to support militarily no less than forty-three nations if they should be attacked; or if communists should start a "liberation war." Already in Vietnam there was a fomenting revolution in the South, and what was invited was what would readily enough develop within a short time. The Vietminh had not yet been adopted by Ho Chi Minh, but they were giving the American protégé, President Diem, plenty of trouble.

Kennedy claimed to know, as he campaigned, that the development of missiles to carry nuclear warheads had been neglected and that the United States was open to Russian attack; in his speeches this "missile gap" was referred to again and again. As a legislator, Kennedy had not been a notable conciliator and had not made much effort to study or understand the events of the Eisenhower years. He had fully accepted the going view of the communist conspiracy, and, actually, there had not been much to choose between him and Eisenhower's Vice-President, Nixon, who was the Republican nominee. He won by an almost infinitesimal margin. No one had any reason to believe that he would break out of the freeze so long maintained by the nuclear powers. It could be said for Eisenhower that he had kept nuclear war in the threat stage; but he had allowed "brinkmanship" to become so much a habit with his associates that the outbreak of hostilities seemed always an imminent possibility. Only he, himself, much of the time immobilized by successive illnesses, was there to veto the last decision necessary to initiate nuclear war.

10. *Eisenhower: The New Federalism*

If Eisenhower without hesitation adopted containment as an adequate controlling thesis for foreign policy, with Russia as an implacable enemy, he also accepted quite naturally a permissive policy in domestic affairs. This was in character.

That part of his life not spent on military posts among professionals had brought him into contact with successful and opulent industrialists, financiers, and speculators. Even as President of Columbia University he had known more of the trustees than of the faculty; they were among New York City's most influential people; and in his view there must be a reason for their positions. Military officers are likely to feel that business success is a guarantee of wisdom and also of public interest.

His experience as a career officer in the army had given him genuine sophistication about bureaucracy but left him with a hardly believable innocence about politics and politicians as well as about business. His abstraction from money-making and his ignorance about money-makers had led him to accept the contradictory theories that free competition was the life of trade but that it was acceptable for big businessmen to extinguish it at will. During his lifetime the suppression of small competitors by bigger ones had been very successful. American industrial and commercial facilities had been gathered into fewer and fewer organizations. Hundreds of automobile manufacturers had been absorbed into four; scores of steel, oil, and chemical companies had come into the control of very large ones; a few firms whose branches spread across the country carried on three-quarters of the retail business; financial institutions had merged and merged again. The word "conglomerate" had not yet been heard but the condition it described was far advanced.

That free competition was any longer operative in the classical sense was a myth, but a convenient one for those who had a talent for exploiting the risks and uncertainties of the economic system. For this it was necessary that a hands-off policy should be maintained. Big businesses demanded a freedom denied to their real or potential rivals. They wanted, in fact, more than this. They were vigilant to prevent public ownership. No other source of capital was large enough to provide the competition they professed to support; but any advance into this area would be an intolerable threat. They therefore expected to use the government's resources on their own terms and to prevent its regulatory powers from interfering with their procedures.

There were some difficulties about this. Roosevelt, against intense opposition, had persuaded the Congress to authorize the experimental Tennessee Valley Authority for harnessing a system of rivers to produce electricity, thus providing competition for one of the largest private industrial complexes. It showed how cheaply power could be produced when relieved of the lavish irrelevant expenditures characteristic of the industry. Preventing any further demonstrations of this sort was a cause worth fighting for. Truman had given no trouble; he came from old progressive country, where free enterprise was still a religion and business was supreme. The enlargement of its units gave him some reason for thought; but regulation during his Presidency was ineffective. He made some liberal speeches, but their translation into action was always somehow impossible.

Stevenson, who was Eisenhower's rival for the Presidency, was undependable from the businessmen's point of view. He came from Illinois; but he had inherited money and position. He certainly had no interest in preserving the competitive system; and he might be hard to handle. Eisenhower, on the other hand, was exactly what was wanted. No more perfect candidate could be imagined. He shared every belief of most use to the financial and industrial giants. He spoke of TVA as "creeping socialism"; and he admired those who, like himself, had risen to power from unlikely beginnings. He knew how to preside over a three-million-man army with an enormous logistical spread; he knew what abilities were required for managing a knotty operation; he was not a politician and would occupy a position above partisan interests; and, best of all, he was the father figure needed by a people just finished with nearly eight years of Truman, who had been more like a country cousin than a hero.

In office Eisenhower performed perfectly in the conservative pattern. There were still those who recalled the depression resulting from the chaos of unplanned business; but there had always been general complicity in the avoidance of responsibility for that terrible ordeal. Blaming businessmen had run contrary to the myth that free competition resulted in the good of all, and what anger there had been had vented itself on a few malefactors—Insull, Sinclair, Whitney, Grace—and not on the system itself. So when Eisenhower appointed "Engine Charlie" Wilson, a General Motors executive, Secretary of Defense and when Wilson ventured the aphorism in his examination for confirmation that what was good for General Motors was good for the nation, it was accepted as a truism by all but a few liberals. George Humphrey, for Secretary of the Treasury, was a big businessman from Cleveland whose zeal for orthodox finance produced the well-marked depressions of the Administration, and the welfare system Roosevelt had begun was entrusted to a woman who was as little likely as any woman in America to favor generous administration, much less expansion.

With such associates, with the White House facilities available for frequent gatherings of the powerful, and with a Security Council made up of military men he trusted, together with State Department and Intelligence operatives who were faithful to the belief that Russians were conspirators, Eisenhower's "establishment," as it was now being called, felt itself safe; and, until the Russians, defying the theory that communism was incapable of any considerable feats of enterprise, produced the bomb, it was. Suddenly the fancy that nuclear knowledge was an exclusively American secret was no longer tenable.

A series of spy trials exposed one way of exporting such secrets as there were; but it was not the most important one; communication among scientists was carried on over a network no layman could understand and consequently could not prevent. When the basis existed for further advances, those advances were likely to be made in many different places. It was that way with nuclear knowledge.

Politicians could not understand this; and the conviction that communism must be a failure was unshaken. That this did not accord with the simultaneous conviction that it was dangerous, was one of those paradoxes democracies absorb with ease. Both managed to exist together. So there were more contracts to be let, more arms and munitions to be manufactured, and a very satisfactory customer created. Adaptation of armed force to the nuclear-missile age was a major project and an extremely profitable one.

As for domestic matters, Eisenhower had one scheme that was very dear to his heart. It seems to have arisen from the practically unanimous naïve belief that federal bureaucracies are worse than any other kind. This defied all the facts disclosed by two generations of muckrakers, amply exposed by the press, concerning corruption and inefficiency in state services; but this, again, was impervious to exposure. It was encouraged by all those who wanted federal size and strength reduced. Decentralization of government operations, with the states taking up the duties of the federal bureaucracy, was the answer to all the Presidential difficulties in controlling swollen departments and other agencies. Also it was in the American tradition of strict construction, strangely enough no longer a Democratic, but now a Republican, theory. It promised the advantage to business of passing on to state capitals the rising threat of regulation; and they knew, if no one else did, that the states were inherently incapable of serious interference. Many enterprises were bigger than any state, for one thing; but, for another, most of them could easily be kept under control; especially their legislatures were open to persuasion.

Eisenhower's single most publicized failure was his seizure of the states' rights issue and the attempt to shift out of Washington the bulk of federal operations. His first proposal was made with uncharacteristic fanfare; he was certain that he had a popular issue, and it was, for once, one that he heartily believed in. With all the talk about bureaucracy and the heavy hand of Washington, there must be a widespread demand for action.

It was comical to see how quickly the politicians who had talked loudest in this strain now found avoidance and silence convenient. They had not expected to have the cause actually taken up. It would not have been pursued by a professional, who would have understood that such issues are not meant to have anything done about them; but Eisenhower was not a professional. He believed it ought to be done, and he did his best to see that it was done. He even went personally to meetings of governors to offer his plan. He was amazed and disconcerted to find even these state executives were cold to his proposals. They saw in them only more duties they knew very well they could not carry out, more scandals they would have to explain. The venture gradually died. For Eisenhower it was a surprising defeat; he never understood how it could have happened. It would be revived by Nixon when he became President; but he, being a professional, would give it the verbal treatment due so old and well-accepted an assumption. He would not expect anything to come of it; and nothing would.

Those liberals who demanded more regulation of business were perennially in a dilemma about this. They knew well enough that it was an escapist ploy on the part of the conservatives; but they also saw that centralized government was becoming unwieldy if only because of its size, and they felt forced to preach about the evils of bigness. Another thing was happening, however, that changed attitudes considerably; it was being discovered that even federal regulatory commissions could be controlled by packing them with friendly members. For this it was only necessary to have Republican Presidents who would take advice about appointments. Even this was changing. Johnson would prove as amenable to advice as any hard-shell conservative. The

Democrats had no desire to be excluded from the generous campaign contributions offered by corporate donors; but until Eisenhower, the Democrats had seemed intractable.

Before long the regulators had become expediters. They not only allowed the practices considered desirable to go on, they included them in their rules. Big businessmen lost interest in states' rights; they were having easy federal relations under Eisenhower's benevolent eye. Liberals, betrayed by their favorite means for disciplining business, and having lost their states' rights cause to the conservatives, could only criticize Eisenhower and his administration, something that was not very profitable; he was too high in the regard of Americans.

Like his refusal at the last moment to accept Dulles' demands for preventive action in the cold war, however, Eisenhower refused to move backward in welfare matters. Social Security was not touched, for instance, and although he approved certain restrictions on organized labor so violently opposed by the union lobbies, collective bargaining was not abandoned.

What Roosevelt had created was not destroyed. There was no advance; but there was no backward movement, either; and it only remains to be noted that Eisenhower's farewell to the nation at the end of his term carried a startling warning against the military-industrial complex he had allowed to develop. How long he had been aware of the growing danger that the economy might be growing too dependent on military production is not known. Certainly he had done nothing about it during his Presidency; and his late warning was only that; he offered no means of escape from the coalition he deplored.

There was more to be worried about than the military-industrial complex. Under the calming ministrations of the General the economy had slowed down, and as Kennedy would remark in his first State of the Union message:

. . . the American economy is in trouble. The most resourceful industrialized country on earth ranks among the last in economic growth. . . .

The security and confidence Eisenhower had provided seemed to have become lethargy. Kennedy's promise "to get the nation moving again" was very much in order.

11. *The Kennedy Interlude*

Let every nation know, whether it wishes us well or ill that we shall pay any price, bear any burden, meet any hardship, support any friend, oppose any foe to assure the survival and success of liberty.
> JOHN F. KENNEDY,
> Inaugural, January, 1961

I think these are proud and memorable days in the cause of peace and freedom. . . . Our task now, and the task of all Americans is to live up to their commitments.
> KENNEDY, annual message,
> January, 1963

Kennedy's Presidency began with too little support and lasted too short a time for any substantial achievements to have been made. In foreign affairs he accepted the policy of containment and diminished confidence by consenting to a bizarre attempt, ending in miserable failure, to overthrow the Cuban Government. He gained only a little of it back by a successful interposition when the Russians attempted to place missile installations on the island.

He saw Vietnam as only one part of a general commitment

to protect democratic nations in the pattern of the Korean and the West German defenses. The United States might be called on at any time and in any place to oppose communist expansion. It could not be done by the massive retaliation called for in the Eisenhower-Dulles strategy, since the Russians were well able by now to retaliate. If the walls of liberty were not to be breached at some spot chosen by the enemy for a test, it would be necessary to re-create "conventional" forces while continuing to maintain a lead in nuclear armament. He, with Secretary McNamara, therefore set out to create a police force for the free world, reconstituting the army, neglected since 1945, adding to it units trained for guerrilla fighting, and making it mobile with newly designed planes able to land troops anywhere at short notice. This system of armaments, including, as well as the navy, fleets of constantly airborne bombers, was enormously expensive; but it did keep a temporary lead over the Russians. Inevitably, however, they felt forced to compete; and what resulted in a very short time was spheres of interest, reluctantly recognized, and with provocative borders where confrontations were all too likely to take place.

This was an ideal situation for smaller nations plotting to use the superpowers in their own interests—in Africa, in the Middle East, in Europe, and in Southeast Asia. In Vietnam and in Egypt immediate advantage was taken of this weakness to lure both superpowers into courses they would not otherwise have followed. North and South Vietnam were supported, and both Israel and Egypt were massively armed. Neither superpower seemed able to negotiate or to do other than increase its commitments.

In Vietnam Kennedy enlarged Eisenhower's "limited involvement." He notified President Diem in December, 1961, that he had given orders to increase American aid for defense. A year later he wrote to Diem that he was "deeply disturbed" by the assault of the Liberation Front. "Our indignation has mounted," he said, "as the deliberate savagery of the communist program of assassination, kidnapping and wanton violence has become clear." When he was shot to death in Dallas this increased aid was in progress.

He had agreed to send 10,000 soldiers to support Vietnam's forces in addition to the considerable number of "advisers" already there. They were not supposed to do more than assist in logistical and counterguerrilla operations, but actually they were often in combat, and lives were lost. One effect of this was abandonment of any pressure for implementing the Geneva agreements by elections. This was because it was quite clear that the Diem regime, growing more and more dictatorial, was losing ground. The countryside was rapidly becoming a general battlefield. Neighbor was betraying neighbor, and attacks in the night were regularly expected. It was one of those most terrible of conflicts—civil war, with constant resort to torture, killings, and forced service.

Hardly anyone asked any more why it was necessary to send armed forces to Vietnam. It was accepted that they were sent to assist in establishing a barrier state against communist expansion into the rest of Southeast Asia, and the expectation, by 1963, was that whatever force was necessary would be used, although, of course, that would not be much. Dulles was gone, but the domino theory remained. Kennedy, on the advice of General Maxwell Taylor, Secretary Rusk, Allen Dulles, and others of his Security Council, set in motion the operations necessary to the cause. The enlargement of conventional forces was immense and rapid.

The most notable of Kennedy's other foreign ventures was given a stirring name—the Alliance for Progress, a resumption and expansion of Roosevelt's Good Neighbor policy, using also the techniques of Truman's Point Four program. Its charter was signed in 1961 by twenty members of the Organization of American States. All the countries were to share the financing, but the United States was to invest the largest amount; and an Agency for International Development was set up to be responsible for its administration. Industry was to be financed, agriculture was to be improved, education was to be enlarged, and welfare measures were to be subsidized.

An energetic beginning ran into resistance from the Latin American upper classes who objected to land reform, and to almost any other change likely to threaten their position; and the opposition was so effective that such progress as was made was of little use to the most needy. Besides, the Latin republics lacked the technologists necessary to such a program. Expert assistance in agriculture and some industries had been in operation for some time—it was the central idea in earlier programs—but it was slow, since it depended on new generations of better-educated people. The attempt to stimulate and hasten the process resulted in more resentment than progress.

What Kennedy bequeathed to Johnson was an agency already discredited in the Congress and having difficulty in getting annual appropriations. Latin America had problems requiring a far more massive infusion of funds and a far longer time than had been contemplated by the organizers of the alliance. One by one, most of the republics became military dictatorships and, as their populations grew, sank further and further into such chaotic poverty that rescue began to seem beyond possibility.

In domestic affairs nothing of note was accomplished. The single considerable victory in a contest with the Congress was the passage of a bill reducing taxes, and that came after his death. He was a convert to the newer views of the economists he consulted. They believed prosperity and depression were controllable by government policies, fiscal and monetary. They were largely right, of course, except that manipulation of such forces required the collaboration of some five hundred legislators who had other views and other aims and would never do the economists' bidding in time to effect the result wanted. Kennedy was not so naïve as to think that all problems would be solved by higher and more sustained productivity, but he was convinced that this was the source of capability to do what was necessary in society.

In his campaign, Kennedy had made a repeated promise to "get the country moving again" after years of Eisenhower stagnation; and it could only be done by temporarily ignoring conservative prejudice. If the economy was to be stimulated, purchasing power must be increased, and reducing taxes would leave more income for purchasers. The theory would also call for contracting purchasing power when the economy speeded up, in order to avoid inflation; and this was even more difficult. The partisanship in the Congress ought to have been a warning that any accommodation requiring legislation would be slow, and, if the President could not bring pressure to bear, impossible. One of the two Kennedy years was devoted to this struggle, and no considerable progress in more permanent reforms was made while it was going on.

Especially he failed to assess the pressures building up in the cities as a consequence of the massive but unspectacular movement of displaced farm workers—and even farmers themselves—into cities everywhere, but mostly into those of the North. Nothing was done to prepare for this or to prevent it. As a result already overcrowded slums presently held several times as many people as they had held before.

The obvious problems of housing, schooling, and of somehow providing for all this migrating population was immensely complicated by racial strains. Many of the rural workers had been black, and when they moved into the cities they were forced to crowd into black neighborhoods. The inconvenienced whites were resentful, and a troubled period began that would not end until genuine national efforts to replan and rebuild were made and until funds were appropriated. The situation had been worsening for years without recognition in Washington. Truman, Eisenhower, and Kennedy were, if not indifferent, neglectful.

Kennedy's was a curiously small achievement considering its spirited beginning and the hopes of those who had been his most prominent associates. In the White House itself were such liberals as Theodore Sorenson, Arthur M. Schlesinger Jr., Walt Rostow, and Pierre Salinger; the Secretary of State was Dean Rusk, former foundation president; the Secretary of Defense was the brilliant Ford executive Robert McNamara; the Secretary of the Interior was Stewart Udall —so it went. There was the same sort of gathering in Washington of intellectuals anxious to do something in public service as there had been in Roosevelt's time, and actually they did regard themselves as the inheritors of that spirit. For a time it seemed that, after the Eisenhower dullness, the Roosevelt *élan* was again infusing the centers of power. The obstructionism would be overcome; leadership would ignite new fires; and the country would indeed "get moving again."

Almost from the first, however, the brave words of the inaugural "ask not what your country can do for you; ask what you can do for your country"—so inspiring to those who hoped for a renewal of national concern for liberal causes—were emptied of hope by what the country seemed to demand: mostly military service in a doubtful cause.

Attention was fixed on what was happening abroad, and the deployment of forces to meet new crises required energies and funds far beyond any former allocations. What was happening in the cities at home could be taken care of later. Discovery of black wrongs and resentments was perhaps less likely for one who had sprung from Irish ancestry in Boston. As a legislator he had thought first of his own people; it was to them that he owed his early successes. At any rate explosive racial issues were bequeathed to his successors with nothing even begun that would meet the coming crisis.

In the speech to have been made on the day of his assassination, Kennedy was still to have spoken of "manning the walls of liberty." It was a phrase that might have been found in one of the James Bond books he read so avidly; but his preoccupation with communist designs was certainly not so exclusive as Truman's or Dulles'. What was happening closer at home he heard about from his associates; and he may have been concerned; there were evidences of change. He made an eloquent speech at Amherst College about education, for instance, and was negotiating the sale of wheat to Russia when he was assassinated.

In spite of the gracious glow that infused White House entertainment, there was little light in the rest of Washington during the Kennedy years. Especially on Capitol Hill, there was more fog than sun. The informal alliance between Northern and Southern conservatives, ignoring party affiliations, had not been in the least modified by Kennedy's election; anyway, he had beaten Nixon by an infinitesimal margin, and so could not expect any impressive public support for liberal measures. Lacking it, his own Congressional party, dominated by the reactionary Southern committee chairmen, stood in the way; and he had no power to move them.

In retrospect, and considering liberal expectations, there is a melancholy dimness about the Kennedy Administration. The release from Eisenhower and the escape from the Nixon threat had seemed so promising to liberals, and yet so little had been done—except to confront the other superpower in a pointless competition to see which could accumulate the larger store of genocidal weapons that neither could use; and, of course, to offer assistance wherever the conspiracy showed itself. There was a gathering storm at home whose violence was not anticipated.

Roosevelt had started off with a magnificent array of legislative achievements in his legendary first "hundred days." Kennedy was to finish his "thousand days" with almost no similar accomplishments. The Congress had not listened when he spoke; it had dallied; and he had had no leverage to start it going. When he made the fatal trip to Dallas, there was disillusion among his most faithful supporters and even the possibility of rejection by the party he had blitzed in 1960 and whose older leaders had never forgiven him for it. He was trying desperately to hold the support in the South he had once bought by giving the Vice-Presidency to Johnson. Of course, if he had known that the Republicans would nominate Goldwater and, with him, invite the electorate to approve retreat from governmental responsibilities, he would have had no need to worry; but how could anyone have anticipated such a folly?

If Kennedy had had a longer time in the White House, and if he had had the liberal Congress of 1964–66, he might have done all that Johnson did and have done it in more orderly fashion. He was intelligent, industrious, and dedicated. He might have reached an understanding with the Russians in spite of the past; there were some signs of softening; Khrushchev, with whom he had to deal, was not wholly intractable.

As to the involvement in Southeast Asia, so fatal to Johnson, there is evidence that in 1963 Kennedy considered a complete withdrawal but that it seemed politically impossible without more support than he had. MacArthur told him, in a conversation he took seriously, what he was in for, reiterating the conviction that involvement on the Asian mainland had no advantages worth the costs. If he had lived, been re-elected, and had had a Congress he could depend on, the nation might have been saved the immeasurable agonies of the next decade.

After his assassination, there was more appreciation for Kennedy's quality than there had been while he had been President. It was seen then how distinctive his style had been. His sharp communications had been a striking change from Eisenhower's fusty blandness; it had taken some getting used to; but pride in his grace and style had grown. The Roosevelt agenda that Truman had neither comprehended nor had the power to go on with if he had, and that Eisenhower had regarded as un-American, might have been resumed. What the country needed, after these postwar fumblings, was just the sort of hard, realistic adaptations to the technologized world Kennedy understood and perhaps meant to carry out.

He had not had time to become the great President he had hoped to be; and his successor, chosen as most Vice-Presidents are chosen, because he would attract votes to the ticket, was as different from himself as could be imagined. He had had long experience and was known to be an admirer of Roosevelt, however, so there seemed a chance that the decline since 1945 might be reversed and Presidential leadership resumed. Johnson, unlike Kennedy, who had never been a Senate insider, had been majority leader, spoken of as the most effective one in modern times; he might be able to pull the party together and energize its vote-getting machinery. He might get the country moving, as Kennedy had failed to do.

12. *Johnson: Roosevelt Disciple*

We have, in 1964, a unique opportunity . . . to prove the success of our system; to disprove those cynics and critics at home and abroad who question our purpose and our competence.

For my part, I pledge a progressive administration which is efficient, and honest, and frugal.

LYNDON JOHNSON,
annual message, January, 1964

. . . as long as others will challenge America's security and test the dearness of our belief with fire and steel, then we must stand or see the promise of two centuries tremble . . .

JOHNSON, annual message,
January, 1966

It was the opinion of Walter Lippmann, after seeing Johnson's early success in persuading the Congress to accept his recommendations, that he had done "what President Kennedy could not have done had he lived" (*New Republic,* April 25, 1964). What the accidental President intended, and very nearly accomplished, in the first two years of his own term, was completion of the New Deal program, stalled for nearly twenty years by conservative opposition; and this was truly an amazing achievement, accounted for, it can be seen in retrospect, by frank acknowledgment of Roosevelt's inspiration, by his twenty-four years of legislative experience, and by the stupidity of an opposition, in the campaign of 1964, that had given him the largest majority in recent history (61.1 per cent of the popular vote, 90 per cent of the electoral vote).

When he became President on his own he had the public support that Kennedy had lacked; also he had carried with him into the Congress enough Rooseveltians to furnish the votes needed for the measures he proposed. It was as though the hundred days had returned; again there was the flood of legislation that called up memories of the earliest New Deal days; and again there was euphoria among all those who had waited so long for a resumption of progress.

One difficulty was that everything was attempted at once, each thing without much relation to others. It was a war—a war on poverty—and the attack was direct and on a hundred fronts. There was no strategy. Not until later was much attention given to coordination, and by then many of the efforts were discredited. There were maladministrations, conflicts among agencies, and not a few attempts to do what could not be done. It was meant well; the needs it sought to meet were real; but it was tragically mishandled.

What was attempted in 1965, then, was a hasty catching-up with what should have been done immediately after the war. When the unhappy assessments began, it was apparent that it had not been what needed to be done in 1965. It was startling to have stubborn opposition to legislation about liberties, education, housing, immigration, and medical care suddenly vanish and to have approval for every proposal. Recognizably, it was irreversible, too, a commitment; the "war on poverty" carried government forward into the full responsibility Roosevelt had so often said it must assume. Putting it all in order, reducing it to workability and with defensible costs was simply postponed.

Mostly, the program could be subsumed under the heading of welfare. Much, however, as the condition of the poor did need to be rectified, there were now more important priorities. The nation had become a vast, incredibly complicated organism whose parts had never been reconciled. It was a vast engine running without governors and with activating machinery that ran aimlessly. It was time for rethinking, planning, and new disciplines. It got none of these from Johnson. He was a son of the frontier; he inherited the Populist tradition; organicism was a conception foreign to his nature. When the Congress adjourned in 1965 Johnson was a proud man. He had proved his political prowess. Most of the liberal agenda was now on the books. Putting it all in order was nothing to be worried about. He proposed merely to let conflicts resolve themselves and order to be worked out gradually. He himself had other business—in Vietnam. He was running a war and running it personally. Both efforts were lavishly funded. They required budgetary deficits; but these were temporary, and the nation was rich.

Both wars, however, went badly; that on poverty caused dissension and resentment; that in Vietnam caused dissension and disillusion. Not much more than five years after his taking charge he was as beaten and frustrated as he had before been satisfied and confident. He withdrew from campaigning for another term because of obvious signs that he would be humiliated.

It was a reversal so unmistakable that neither he nor the closest observers of his performances had doubts about its reality. He did not understand it; but he knew it existed. The growing revulsion about Vietnam could not really account for the completeness of his rejection; after all he had merely gone on in Southeast Asia with what three predecessors had been doing. All had said that we must defend liberty wherever it was threatened; all had extolled self-determination; and all had accepted communism as an implacable and aggressive force to be resisted everywhere as it attempted to push outward. It was not he who had seen China go, seen Cuba become communist, seen the Berlin Wall built; stood by while Hungary was immolated for heresy, or allowed the Israelis to involve the United States in their war with the Arabs. He had gone on with the policies all Americans had seemed to approve.

Nevertheless he was required to pay for his predecessors' acceptance of a mistaken strategy. True, he, no more than they, had seen that it would ultimately fail, that its consequences would multiply until they became unbearable. He happened to be in office when the legendary chickens came home to roost; and he was the one to be punished.

His successor would surely be a Republican, and, in all probability, Nixon, Eisenhower's Vice-President; and Nixon ought to have been the last politician to have profited from Johnson's ordeal. He had labored to bring it about; but voters have no sense of justice when looking for a change; and no sense of participation in guilt. The policies they now saw as so wrong, they had very lately held to be not only justified, but, as Kennedy had said, worth any sacrifice. Suddenly the sacrifice was intolerable. Self-determination in Vietnam became "immoral." The war was "obscene." Johnson was excoriated for its energetic prosecution. Whether or not liberal Americans deserved to suffer with Johnson, they had no intention of doing so. They turned on him as viciously as though he had done it all against their advice.

It was a time now for the arrangements Roosevelt's successors had not accepted—those that came after war, those that victory and affluence had made possible. First, however, the miscalculations had to be corrected and the conflicts resolved. This could not be entrusted to the party and its leaders who had made them (Eisenhower, of course, was forgiven). The retreat and regrouping would take some time; there must be a sorting out. The successor Republicans must learn by their own experiences what the electorate meant by returning them to office. They must learn that they did not have a mandate to liquidate the Roosevelt-Johnson welfare and conservation measures, only to make them more effective, and, most important, they must learn that containment was no longer generally supported. These were the two essentials for American policy in the 'seventies.

The nation must devote its resources to renewal at home after decades of neglect and must attend to neighbors' needs, not to those of distant lands more properly within others' reach. The further future seemed to be a matter of interest only to dissidents; but many of them were by now convinced that change was to be brought about only by violent attacks on existing institutions, not by rigorous thought about reconstituted ones and disciplined effort to achieve them.

It was a question, as the 'seventies opened, whether Nixon and his party could salvage enough for successors to build on when *their* time came or whether all American leaders would be fatally discredited. The quarter-century of failures was now seen clearly for what it was. It was not seen in 1964 or even in 1966; it was unmistakable in 1968.

The Great Society Johnson hoped for when the war on poverty had been won was more than a state of economic well-being. It lights the imagination to consider what might have been accomplished in a few years of regrouping if he had not accepted as a first claim on American resources the costly war on communism, or even if, as part of that war, he had not so far forgotten the elementary military caution —that American troops must not be deployed on the Asian mainland. He vastly overestimated the will of the South

Vietnamese to resist the North Vietnamese; he was led into grossly exaggerating the effects of air power; and, acting as commander in chief, he directed operations as though his amateur judgment and knowledge could be substituted for experience and training.

In his inaugural speech, Southeast Asia had been spoken of only as a minor matter; his mind then was on other issues. It was a year later that escalation began and with it the diminution of progress at home. His many programs undertaken so vigorously a year before presently were crumbling everywhere. Speaking to the University of Michigan community he had outlined his intentions.

The Great Society rests on abundance and liberty for all. It demands an end to poverty and racial injustice. . . . But that is just a beginning.

The Great Society is a place where every child can find knowledge to enrich his mind and to enlarge his talents. It is a place where leisure is a welcome chance to build and reflect not a feared cause of boredom and restlessness. It is a place where the city of man serves not only the needs of the body and the demands of commerce but the desire for beauty and the hunger for community.

It is a place where man can renew contact with nature. It is a place which honors creation for its own sake and for what it adds to the understanding of the race. It is a place where men are more concerned with the quality of their goods than the quantity of their goods. But most of all the Great Society is not a safe harbor, a resting place, a final objective, a finished work. It is a challenge constantly renewed, beckoning us toward a destiny where the meaning of our lives matches the marvelous products of our labor.

This statement would be, in effect, repeated by his critics many times after it had become evident that it had more glitter than substance. Perhaps Johnson's worst miscalculation was his persistent belief that his war on poverty could be financed while a war was being carried on with immense logistical costs in Southeast Asia. By 1967, when escalation was well under way, so much of the available technical talent and industrial capacity were diverted to war, that far too little was left for going on with his Great Society. This, and the insufficiency of funds, together with confusion and conflict among the numerous new agencies, left him presiding over a serious administrative situation; and the immense popular support manifested in his election turned to critical questioning.

Some programs were quickly abandoned because of impracticality or mishandling; others were effectually opposed by those who were somehow discommoded. There were numerous surviving ones, of course, representing social gains, but they tended to be lost sight of in all the publicity concerning the failures. Then, on the whole, the beneficiaries were more resentful than grateful. Hopes had been too high; results had been too meager.

There were, however, other reasons for failure to achieve what Johnson had hoped. One was that the administration was consigned to an executive branch unable to carry so heavy a load; the study of delegation had always stopped short of suggesting the obsolescence of the federal system even though the states were recognized as inefficient. To suggest that they ought long ago to have given way to a regional arrangement was considered to be outside any practical possibility; yet no problem was any longer confined within any state's borders. Much of the legislation for the war on poverty specified, or assumed, that the states were sovereign and must continue to receive and administer the growing flow of funds. They were overwhelmed; and administration broke down everywhere. Government intended for a nation of small farmers was hopelessly insufficient for the duties of an urbanized welfare society.

Then too the Constitution provided that representatives and senators should be elected from districts or states, not from the nation as a whole. The additive theory still prevailed; parts flung together would make up a satisfactory operating system. Technology had long ago determined that the organism required conformist parts; everyone knew it; but the knowledge was not allowed to influence thinking about government any more than it was allowed to influence economic policy.

This alone was bound to make such effort as Johnson's at least wasteful and ineffective, if it did not fail altogether; but other basic difficulties were suddenly critical as the load of responsibilities grew heavier. One of these was the failure to estimate the expense involved and the sources of the necessary funds. Even with the wholly inadequate funding of the Great Society legislation, spending in the Johnson years exceeded by about $57 billion the receipts of the government. This was inexcusable for any but such crises as war or recovery from depression; and during this time there was neither, if Vietnam is accepted as a nonwar. There was, however, a continuous ignoring of the financial reckoning to come.

The Congress must make appropriations and only it can lay the taxes to pay for them. But providing and spending were seldom brought together in one accounting. Again the Constitution could be blamed. It said nothing whatever about departing from balance and spending what did not exist. If receipts were not enough to pay for appropriations, the Treasury simply borrowed what was necessary, and, since then every dollar was worth less, everyone, even the poorest citizens, paid through the resulting inflation. This, however, quickly causes maladjustments everywhere as everyone and every business tries to compensate for rising costs; and such disturbances are blamed on one politician—the one in the White House. The Congress had long since perfected ways of evading responsibility. It fell on the President, who could not escape.

These Johnson years were ones of constantly rising prices. This created hardship for those whose incomes were fixed, it caused organized workers to demand higher wages, often in ways that disrupted production, and added to an increasing burden of interest on borrowings. At a time when government was doing more—far more—for welfare than had ever been attempted before, there was a frightening distrust of its irresponsible financing. This was added to by the failure to produce promised results. The poor, told that they need be poor no longer, were a different people than those who had supposed it to be an unchangeable condition. Even if they were somewhat better off it was never enough.

The budgetary unbalance, the inadequate funding of programs, and inefficient administration were the basic causes; but these were not so much complained of by the critics and the disillusioned, as the spending of such immense sums for the wrong purposes; and, of course, these were obvious. The military sector of the budget was allowed by Johnson and the Congress to rise until it passed half the total, and the spectacular, but doubtfully useful, space program used, at its highest point in the 'sixties, more than went in those years to foreign aid, to education, or to health—and it was given several times as much as the Office of Economic Opportunity, the center for the war on poverty.

It was the Vietnam involvement, however, that gathered to itself more of the growing disillusion and bitterness than any other issue; and the whole blame for this centered in the President, who, indeed, *was* responsible. He was not only the chief executive but also the commander in chief; and in both capacities he was arbitrary and demanding; he dispensed more power than he gathered; and there was an increasing deficit. Since he was a politician, he saw his credit diminishing; but he seemed unable to escape the dilemma he had allowed to clamp itself on him as President. He fell into a defensive querulousness that gradually turned to defiance. He affirmed that he would not be the first President to lose a war. He forgot that troops had not been sent to win a war but to protect the freedom of a people. If that was an impossible assignment for an American army on the Asian mainland he did not recognize it. He was no defensive commander. He took over the whole operation, expecting little of the South Vietnam army and making little effort to improve it. The conclusion come to by observers was that the United States was there to win and to protect after winning. It seemed a long commitment, too long for American patience.

13. *Johnson: Overreach*

. . . It's been very clear to me that I had certain disadvantages . . . upbringing in a poor setting, limited educational advantages, geography, where my mother was when I was born and the prejudices that exist . . . a general inability to stimulate, inspire and unite all people of the country . . .

I don't think that I can ever explain to you or the American people something that's as deeply imbedded in their beliefs as the fact that Lyndon Johnson was an extremely ambitious man who sought power, who enjoyed using it, and whose greatest desire was to occupy the top job in American political life.

I always felt that every job that I had was really too big for me.

　　　　JOHNSON, in the first Walter Cronkite television inteview, quoted in *Newsweek*, January 5, 1970

When in power, Johnson diminished the prestige of his office by putting its credibility in doubt. Now he is reaching back from retirement for vindication. It would be a limited one at best. If he is now being true to the spirit as well as the letter of his and Rusk's discussions

early that March, then there was gross deception at the
time and for motives that are still unclear. If on the
other hand, it develops that Johnson is now distorting
the facts or lying for the sake of historians' notices, the
impact on public confidence in the nation's leaders
could not be worse . . .

Time, comment on second Cronkite
interview, February 23, 1970

A reporter who sometimes went with Johnson on his travels,
said of him that he rode Air Force One like a stallion. The
phrase sticks in the mind. He did ride the airways proudly,
as though he were galloping over the plains. To his mind and
manner the nation was his range. Presently, however, the
watching people had had enough of it. Only if his immense
undertakings had been successful and universally wanted
could his style have been forgiven. For a while it seemed
that they might be; but the disappointments came quickly.
They accumulated; he refused to acknowledge their causes;
nevertheless he began to squirm, equivocate, and try to make
the record look better than it was. It was, as Eric Goldman,
his historian in residence for a time, said, in the book he
wrote afterward, "a tragedy." It ended an era of majorities
for the Democratic Party; and left his successor to reassess,
to reorganize, to retreat, and to liquidate.

It was Vietnam that was unendurable. There had been no
considerable revulsion from that intervention during the
other Presidencies since 1945. Until Johnson's accession it
had been an acceptable program of assistance supported by
a general belief in containment and in self-determination for
nations threatened with subjection. There was a mission to
defend the free world, but missions, costly ones, become
tiresome; and moral reasons are soon found for their abandonment.

Kennedy, of course, had broken into war by sending the

first few combat troops. How the escalation went after that can be seen by noting that 1964 was the year of decision— and also the year of Johnson's election for a term of his own. 1965 was the year when the Vietnamese were pushed aside and Americans took over the fighting, with Johnson commanding from the White House. The official figures of the Defense Department show how the expansion went; in successive year-end reports of troop strength in Vietnam, there were in 1964, 23,000; in 1965, 184,300; in 1966, 385,300; in 1967, 485,000; in 1968, 535,000. Casualties by 1968 were 30,000 killed and 192,000 wounded; and those figures quickly became obsolete; there were well over 40,000 dead by the year 1970.

The President gradually took to directing operations from his bed, his desk, or his plane; he gave orders; he shouted and swore at his assistants; he was furious at any check; he resented any questioning; and he allowed no latitude. The White House reporters found these idiosyncracies interesting of course; and they were rather exaggerated than minimized. They were, however, regarded as unbecoming in a President, especially one whose domestic administration left much to be desired and whose direction of the military was being judged incompetent. He had believed those who told him that bombing would reduce the enemy to helplessness; he had failed to understand the resilience of pajama-clad guerrillas; and he had picked the wrong general to conduct operations in the field. Westmoreland, instead of acknowledging the requirements of jungle warfare, adopted a plan of "search and destroy." It assumed that there were enemy concentrations to be defeated by superior fire power. The fact was that the enemy faded into the jungles when massive armaments ploughed across the terrain. Military planners knew that the guerrillas could accept ten times the losses the Americans could have taken and still maintain the will to fight, but tactics in the field never seemed to admit this. Casualties made no difference to the enemy's characteristic resolution. Neither, as Johnson finally discovered, did reason or blandishment.

Johnson's skills as a professional politician proved to be of no use at all; and since tactics were mistaken, the situation was no nearer resolution in 1967 than it had been in 1965. He became desperate—there is no other word for it—and, as desperate men do, he demanded absolute obedience among his official family and expected concurrence from the public.

By 1968, opposition had become more vocal in the Congress, the press, and elsewhere, and although appropriations of increasing size were provided grudgingly, and although the further increases of troops requested by Westmoreland were pictured as making victory certain, Johnson's resolution collapsed under the weight of public disbelief and disapproval.

The governmental chaos in Vietnam had added to the confusion in people's minds about what Americans were doing there anyway. Their army seemed to be upholding a regime with more disposition to keep an elite in power than to defend their nation. Doubts grew; and it was gradually understood that the strongest nation in the world was, however improbably, unable to subdue one of the weakest.

This conviction, not acknowledged by Johnson and his associates, continued to spread. Growing numbers of citizens protested. Many of these, it is true, had discovered with suspicious suddenness that intervention was immoral. Lives wasted and resources diverted from domestic needs began to be a favorite theme, even among those who had supported Kennedy's eloquent pleas for supporting "the free world" and had acquiesced in establishing a global police force. They now found Vietnam a special case. At any rate, they deserted Johnson. Finally, what he would not admit as commander in chief, he did admit as a politician. He had lost that majority he had so proudly counted on in 1964.

It was the defections that had forced Johnson and his associates—Rusk, McNamara, General Taylor, Bundy, Rostow, and the rest—to defend themselves in doubtful ways. Reports were doctored to make them more favorable; prospects were made more cheerful; the regime in Saigon, after elections, was pictured as democratic. Kept up awhile, these transparent fictions resulted in the famous "credibility gap." There were, after all, many experienced reporters both in Washington and Vietnam who told what they saw; and it was not what was being broadcast from the White House. The persistence of the enemy, the incapacity of the South Vietnamese, the waste of lives and material with no result— all were impossible to conceal. Even the "hawks" were discouraged, and the question began to be insistently asked: what would be gained if the North Vietnamese were kept out of the South and the Viet Cong were decimated. The Thieu government could hardly be said to be actually more democratic than that of the communists in the north. Then, too, questions concerning the national interest were at last being asked after years of concurrence in containment. What *were* Americans doing on the Asian mainland?

Johnson squirmed. He would not withdraw, and he could not make progress. He came finally to humiliating attempts at negotiation. North Vietnamese representatives came to Paris but offered only vituperative propaganda. The bombing of the North was stopped, and reasonable offers for a ceasefire were made. Even admission of the Viet Cong to the Saigon government was suggested—if they could be elected. The communist representatives did not listen; they only talked. They said a hundred times that they would consider a peace only when all American forces were withdrawn. What was even more maddening, the North Vietnamese professed blandly not to have any forces of their own in the South. They insisted that it was a civil war and that the Americans were intervening. What to do with such an enemy ought to have been thought of before the intervention had begun. That could be seen now; but it was not this that sapped Johnson's morale; that resulted from the defection of his supporters. What had once been a crusade for liberty was now a cruel and immoral intervention.

As the elections of 1968 approached, the critics were so numerous and so bitter—demonstrations, often violent, had become frequent—that even if not defeated, Johnson would have been the center of the worst dissensions suffered by the nation since the Civil War. At the end of March, when he capitulated, he announced a decision not to increase the Vietnam involvement as Westmoreland advised him he must do if anything like victory were to be achieved.

It was the end for him. From one of the most popular and admired Presidents in the American line, he had become one whose administration was a failure, and whose costly adventure as commander in chief had led the nation into humiliation. Even at the end he did not admit what by now was widely realized—that he had pictured to Americans a gradually worsening situation as one that was improving. A President had used his resources of communication for deliberate and prolonged misinforming. His reports had been more than merely optimistic. They had been misleading. A President could not survive that kind of relation with the public.

During this time, when Vietnam monopolized attention and polarized public opinion, other containment efforts were less active. Vietnam was the test of that policy. As Vietnam was withdrawn from, the domino theory would be tested. The United States would not again deploy its men and resources across the path of the Russians or Chinese if they did advance toward the south, and perhaps overrun all of former French Indo-China and even the Dutch East Indies. The nations involved would have to do the best they could for themselves. There would be aid, perhaps logistical support, but the incoming Nixon's half-hearted promise to carry out treaty engagements was an empty one. It contradicted any inference to be made from what was actually being done. Anyone could see that Dulles' Southeast Asia commit-

ments would never be carried out. Americans were through
with such involvements. The question was whether the nationalism of Thailand, say, or Malaysia, would withstand the
pressures from China; and whether Pakistan, India, Iran,
and Turkey would maintain their independence or would
become other Hungarys or Czechoslovakias. With the United
States withdrawn from a quarter-century of consistent and
increasing effort something like a vacuum was being created
in all the border areas.

The withdrawal from South Vietnam was only one instance of a failing strategy; but with it went the holding
efforts all around the communist borders. Of course the discovery, belatedly, that the communist bloc was not a mono-
lith, contributed to this. This was another failure of American intelligence. Americans, blinded by the certainty of
Dulles, Nixon, and others, only belatedly understood the inability of the communist ideology to overcome the far older
and stronger bonds of nationalism. The Chinese and Russians had borders to dispute about. Americans had a continent of their own; there was no need to contain what had
no possibility of expansion.

Still, there were defending forces in South Korea; there
was NATO and 300,000 American troops with tactical nuclear arms in West Germany; there was the sixth fleet in
Mediterranean waters and the seventh fleet in the Pacific.
More important, there had been miraculous recovering
among the former enemies, Japan and Germany, now next
to the Americans and Russians in productive power. Both
had profited from being disarmed; but disarmed, the Europeans faced hundreds of menacing Russian divisions; and
the Japanese would be of no assistance in checking the Chinese drive to control Southeast Asia. The problem was not
what the containers had conceived it to be. It was one of
finding friends, or at least cooperators, not one of defeating
aggressors by military means.

Containment, after the outpouring of resources, the deployment of weapons, and the encouragement of resistance among the border states, was ending in withdrawal. Americans were seeing how little different the situation was than it would have been without the quarter-century of effort, the loss of lives, the enormous diversion of resources. Those who asked now whether what had come about was more than could have been gained by an earnest pursuit of coexistence, were at last being heard.

What needed to be contained was the missionary aggressiveness of ideologists and demagogues—not only in the communist enclaves but in capitalist ones as well; and the way to do this was for reasonable statesmen to build and operate a world order strong enough to resist challenge. This was the common interest of the great powers. Roosevelt had known this; now it was beginning to be seen by others as a necessity if genocide was to be escaped.

VI
Return to Roosevelt

The Great Pre-emptor

For the first time since 1932, the White House is occupied by a partisan Republican and a professional politician. . . . Washington's judges of political form have been annoyed and mystified by Nixon's failure to behave like other Presidents in the last 40 years. . . . His object is to create a solid majority for the Republican party and Richard Nixon which will be the mirror image of the Democratic majority created by Roosevelt. Most of the votes will have to come from the Democratic center . . . because that is where most of the votes are. This is why the technique of pre-emption of the liberal Democratic issues is his chief political instrument. To be a good President it is first necessary to be a good politician. Moreover the issues he has pre-empted are good issues— they involve things that badly need to be done. . . .
STEWART ALSOP, *Newsweek*, February 2, 1970

1. *Nixon: The Improbable Victory*

By 1968 there were unmistakable signs of a sharp change in the nation's policies. Going on in the way chosen since 1945 was no longer politically feasible, if indeed it could be sustained by the strained economy. It was time for new strategies and new leaders.

269

When an election is won by a margin of 30,041,582 to 29,817,315, it would seem at first that very little could be said about the superiority of the winner over the loser. But when the loser has managed to turn an indicated party majority of perhaps three to two into a loss, however small, something unusual must have happened. What happened in 1968 was that Democrat Hubert Humphrey had to run on Johnson's record. It was an unpopular record; and he lost. The beneficiary was Richard M. Nixon, who was simply the alternative.

Once President on his own, after 1964, Johnson had undertaken far too much both abroad and at home. His commitments were still in force when he was succeeded by Nixon; and Nixon's problems cannot be understood without reviewing his inheritance. The United States as protector and guardian for the whole noncommunist world must stop disorder wherever it broke out; it must check the communists' thrusts outward wherever they occurred. There had for a while seemed to be a rule about this: the more there was to do, the more there was to do it with. The amazing productivity of the economy created the wherewithal, and the increasing technological competence furnished the means; only, as it began to appear, they were never quite enough. The actual rule was that more would always be undertaken than could be carried through.

The climactic action was, of course, in South Vietnam. This was not Johnson's original initiative; he had only undertaken to finish what his two predecessors had begun; but it was he who found that the enemy was such that he had to withdraw or enlarge; and he chose to enlarge.

It was not a popular choice; and Johnson was not able to make it so. Because there was no progress, larger issues began to be discussed. Why, it was asked, did the nation have this responsibility to straighten out matters in such far-off places as Southeast Asia, or in the Congo and the other African mini-nations? Americans found their obligations spread from Vietnam to India and even to Thailand; included were such countries as Greece, Iran, and Turkey, with India expecting assistance as well. Then there was always South America, where Kennedy had made inflated promises; also the Caribbean, where Cuba had become a bad neighbor and Santo Domingo had had to be disciplined. European countries had recovered but were disposed to let the United States go on defending them. The reach of the mission was very nearly global.

The disillusion of Americans with all this load, carried for other people who were resentful because it was not enough, or because they did not like Americans anyway, got to be just too much. It was a quite understandable reaction that those who did not want help could well be allowed to get along without it; if unprecedented generosity resulted in ill-will, let them see how they liked doing for themselves.

Complete abdication of responsibility might soon have brought the national borders into danger. There was, after all, a rival power, tirelessly, and more and more effectively, working in toward the Americans' outworks, taking over wherever they moved out. In spite of the patent emptiness of the claim, communists everywhere professed to be liberators intending only to promote independence for small sister nations. They had placed themselves solidly in Cuba—it had been part of Kennedy's deal, when the Russian missiles had been removed, that he would leave Castro alone; and Europe had been outflanked by a control of the Mediterranean that the Czars had been trying to effect for centuries, something that left Israel and Greece, protégés inherited from Britain, in perilous positions—but ones the United States was committed to defend. Nothing had gone well.

The United States was self-consciously rich and becoming richer; and contrasts appeared more and more clearly with less productive economies. Among Americans, generosity was an old tradition. Disaster, hunger, or even backwardness were always met with sympathy and assistance; but it was not for such humanitarian purposes that aid was now being given. Very little sympathy was mixed with the self-interest behind the massive appropriations of recent years. Much went to improve the military forces of the recipient countries; a good deal more went to relieve farm surpluses rather than to feed the hungry. Altogether it had become an unpleasant business to be defended only on grounds quite different from those of other times, and it was certainly not worth the continued inflation and other evidences of overstrain.

Johnson had come from the Senate, not the best environment for future Presidents. A senator has constituents somewhere—Johnson's were in Texas—and they have expectations. These do not include assistance for the Vietnamese or the millions of India. Nor do its members see the need for supporting an Israeli thrust into a hostile Moslem world. The people of India—or of Germany or the Congo—do not vote for senators, and senators who do not fully understand what this means soon find it out. It will be recalled that Kennedy, when he was chided for concentrating exclusively on the interests of Massachusetts, answered: "What's wrong with that?" He soon discovered when he became President that a good deal was wrong with it. It assured a hostile reception for everything he proposed that did not promise something more for some locality; and a President cannot be thus confined.

When Johnson succeeded Kennedy, in 1963, he quite suddenly found also that in the Senate he had enemies where once he had had friends. He could no longer trade favors in the customary way; besides, his former colleagues instinctively responded to the withdrawing mood of the electorate. From a time when they were saying about the Russians that they must be taught a lesson, they soon were saying that it had to be done at less expense. They wanted the cake, but they did not want to pay for it. Johnson soon found himself— as many others have—in these impossible circumstances. If the obligations of world power were to be met it would have to be done in spite of growing hostility.

Of course, there was one advantage: the government's income rose year by year. Increasing productivity had this effect. But Johnson presumed on it too much. Besides, confronting the communists, rescuing the weaker nations, and relieving the residual poverty at home were bringing every succeeding budget into deficit. Multiplied welfare measures had been overwhelmed by a rising tide of need. The cities were making demands; so were the smaller towns; something massive had to be done about the migrants. The complaints and demands were continual.

The electorate did not like the disorder but was not inclined to admit its causes. To concede that creating wealth was not enough went against the grain; and someone would certainly be punished for this disappointment; and it would, of course, be the President.

Sympathy for the slum dwellers was distinctly limited by the stubborn fiction that it must be their own fault. Anyway they could not be employed; they lacked the skills. That the catastrophe they had suffered ought to have been prevented by public action was very hard to admit in the land of individual freedom. It gradually—but very gradually—became apparent that many of the migrants' children were running wild and rebellious in the streets. Besides, a large proportion of them were black, and being black made it easier for others first to ignore and then to be outraged by the repeated outbreaks of resentful violence. What was called for was something drastic and expensive.

Johnson was moved to begin; and the home front came first; but what was done was clumsy. Displaced families were often broken and children had no fathers; and this condition was worse among minority ethnic groups, especially the blacks. To begin the education of a child already half grown was not a task likely to have a creditable result. The rebuilding of slums was an enterprise with immense complications, talked about for a generation, started over and over, only to end mostly in futility; and the conditions had not changed. Without public planning for the uses of land and resolutions about racial equality, the urban disorder could not possibly be righted. Reducing poverty was involved with the incapacities of migrants, prejudices against newcomers, and sheer lack of space in the old neighborhoods. Ending poverty was more than a war; it involved a dozen revolutions.

Johnson's was a good-hearted but ill-planned and badly managed effort; and, as always, much more attention was paid to the faults and failures than to the successes. Critics never had to admit that something simply had to be done, that alternatives were not obvious, and that mistakes were inevitable and could be corrected.

The moment was peculiarly difficult. The Vietnam involvement, he felt, could hardly be repudiated, and the only chance of liquidation seemed to be the military decision he was told could be won by enlarged effort. The disorder in the cities could be met by educators and social workers; but they demanded immense appropriations. The bills he sponsored; the funds he allocated; the programs he approved, ran into the hundreds of separate undertakings. Presently everyone could see that something was going on; but most of it was ineffective, wasteful, and repugnant to the American tradition of self-help; besides, it was costing too much.

Johnson got little credit for effort either abroad or at home, and much discredit for failures; and, when Humphrey tried to succeed him, he was unable to establish for himself a separate image.

As the campaign for nomination began in 1968, with Johnson withdrawn, the debacle they had suffered in 1964 seemed a clear warning to such Republicans as Governors Romney and Rockefeller and Senators Javits, Cooper, and Percy. A reactionary could not win; only a moderate would have a chance. Then there was the fact that Roosevelt had left the Democrats a majority if it could be activated.

No more Eisenhowers were in sight. Besides, there was no doubt that half Johnson's handicap—the Vietnam war—was a Republican inheritance. Truman had barely begun it; Eisenhower and Secretary of State Dulles had really got it going; Kennedy had only pursued it; and Johnson had been no more than logical in escalating.

Disillusion among the voters was prevalent by 1968; but it was not something the Republicans could use for campaign material. Luckily, they had only to stand by while the Democrats fought among themselves. A strident faction wanted the war simply stopped. It was impractical; but it was thought good for credit with a tired public. Others were not ready to abandon the Johnson policies. The quarrels were fatal; there were at least a dozen leaders who in effect broke with Johnson on the war issue. Most was heard from Senator Fulbright, who, from his high seat as Chairman of the Foreign Relations Committee, having made a complete turnaround, never ceased from harassment; but there were others. Johnson felt himself deserted; and Humphrey was part of the faltering regime.

The Republicans were somewhat better off as a party. There remained a certain conflict between the extremists of both wings; but since the Democrats were tearing themselves apart they could—and did—moderate their differences in the expectation of a comeback.

What had happened at half-time in 1966 ought to have given both parties warning that internal reconciliation was imperative; but the Democrats only fractionalized further; and the Republicans spawned a half-dozen campaigns for notice, some from one policy corner, some from another. The difference was that the Democrats went for each others' throats, and the Republicans were inclined to accept the necessity for agreement.

There arose a complication affecting both parties; a twangy voice from the South began to attract not only the Republican Goldwater followers, but the more conservative Democrats. George Wallace appealed to all those who resented federal interference in racial matters, who questioned the necessity for going on with the fight against communists, and were generally opposed to all federal proposals. Before either establishment became aware of what was happening, this third candidate held a balance of power. The Democrats after 1966 were in such a sorry state that a ten per cent defection to the new contender would make defeat certain; they had quite evidently lost the old South, and the Republicans could at least hope to become the beneficiaries by stealing support from Wallace. They might outdo him in proclaiming states rights and opposition to the Supreme Court.

In California, too, Reagan had beaten Governor Brown by more than a million votes; and it was the same Brown who had beaten Nixon for the governorship four year earlier. Such a reversal seldom happens. It showed clearly how deep the disaffection really was. The Republicans emerged from their convention with renewed hope.

Since there was some reason for believing that a Republican might win, many prominent politicians were ready enough to accept a call if it should come. There was Romney in Michigan, a big businessman become governor with a righteous aura about him. There was Rockefeller in New York, who had proved both his capability as governor and, by re-election, his ability to get votes. These were the most talked about. Rockefeller professed not to want the nomination, however, and threw his support to Romney. But Romney somehow failed to capture people's interest, and it was soon evident that he would not succeed. In late spring and early summer it was fairly foregone that for the Republicans it would be Nixon; but who would it be for the Democrats?

Until Johnson saw the inevitable and withdrew from candidacy in spring, it was assumed that he would expect renomination. But when he did withdraw there was already a confused struggle in progress. The antiwar issue seemed a

paying one to several otherwise unlikely possibilities, the
most serious of whom seemed to be Eugene McCarthy from
Minnesota who was supposed to have been Johnson's choice
for his Vice-Presidential running mate in 1964 if the remaining Kennedys had not insisted on Humphrey. McCarthy
started in New Hampshire and before the primary was over,
had collected a following of young neophytes with an enthusiasm and dedication strange to American politics. They left
their colleges and jobs and came in droves to work for their
man. The astonished professionals hardly knew what to do
about them, and at first were inclined to bend before the
youthful storm. They—or something—made McCarthy a formidable figure in the preconvention campaign.

When McCarthy became a genuine contender, however,
Robert Kennedy, President Kennedy's younger brother, announced his entry into the race and began to mobilize the
family machine. This was serious for McCarthy. His issues
and supporters would naturally be the same as Kennedy's.
Their contest—unless one of them dropped out—would split
between them what was probably not a party majority anyway. That majority was believed to belong legitimately to
Humphrey. It came to him by inheritance—also, in payment
for faithful services. Neither Kennedy nor McCarthy had any
such accumulation of credits. But Humphrey would have to
carry the load of Johnson's unpopularity; and he had never
repudiated the involvement in Southeast Asia.

The Republicans met first in Miami; and Nixon's easy victory over his rivals gave him a good start with a newly hopeful organization. He had even made a treaty with the
Southern leaders who might have gone to Wallace. Through
Senator Thurmond, they were assured that Nixon would give
them no trouble, a pledge confirmed by the choosing of the
conservative Governor Spiro Agnew of Maryland to be the
Vice-Presidential candidate. In the Democratic states of the
East, Nixon could expect to get all the Republican votes
there were; and he could hope for some that were Demo-

cratic. These would be votes against disorder. The crime rates in the cities had frightened all good citizens; and it was believed that the Democrats (including in this the Supreme Court) were soft on offenders. Law and order promised to be a prominent issue.

The Democratic convention could almost be described as riotous. It was not that Humphrey's rivals ever had any chance of nomination, but that the meeting nearly broke up from internal dissensions about policy. Then there occurred the violent battles between police and protesters in the Chicago streets. It was said afterward that the Democrats had turned their national majority into a minority in those few summer days. This was an exaggeration. What did that was a sense of disillusion descending on a confused and frightened country like a dark cloud. There was a war that could neither be won nor ended; no one's life or property was safe; inflation could not be stopped; government was scandalously inefficient. It seemed that the communists on the other side of the world were gaining strength, and that of the United States was declining. There had to be a change.

If it had been hoped that active dissent had been defused by Johnson's withdrawal, the hope was dispelled at Chicago. A dozen or more organizations, all of minuscule size, mobilized a considerable mob; they associated themselves unasked with the frustrated activists, steaming with resentment at McCarthy's failure and Kennedy's loss. It was their purpose to show that they had some sort of power, even if not within the political organization. They considered, and said, that if no way was open to them but violence, then violence would be used. There was plenty of notice. They had been swarming into Chicago for two weeks before the convention. They invaded parks, crowded the public ways, and enough were disorderly to give all a bad name.

Mayor Daley, the long-time Democratic boss of Chicago, had insisted on having the meeting in his city, and had thereafter been forced to prepare for trouble. He seemed to welcome it. His police were tough; and the national guard was available. He was confident he could make good his promise to keep order. If necessary he would give the dissidents the lesson they had needed for some time. As the convention days came on there were marches and confrontations. The melees in the parks and streets were reflected on television screens; and, when the violence lulled, the television reporters staged renewals. There were reactions to police repressions, and some were reflected on the convention floor. Nevertheless the formalities somehow were got through; resolutions were passed; and Humphrey was nominated, with Senator Muskie of Maine as his running mate.

The Democrats remained divided and furious with one another, much as the Republicans had been in 1964. Humphrey, to have a chance of winning, would have to bring back to his support the entire peace group and those who had wanted Kennedy or McCarthy. The professionals would support him; but funds were short, as always happens when losing seems likely. That meant a preponderance of television time for Nixon; and this by now was the medium of choice for campaigning. Altogether it looked like a Republican year. Still, Humphrey was ebullient by nature, a compulsive speaker, and his record was unassailably liberal. This chance at the Presidency was the climax of a notable career. He meant to turn things his way by sheer energy.

All this might well illustrate an aphorism repeated by the professionals among themselves. Campaigns, they say, are not won; they are lost. There is another, following this, that runs: Campaigns make no difference; they are concluded before they begin. Such remarks are never meant to assert absolute verity. There have been surprises; but not many; and it is usually amateur observers who are surprised. There were no surprises in 1968.

From the first the gambling realists set the odds against Humphrey at five-to-three or worse; and they never conceded an approach to parity. Of course Nixon might make a mis-

take; he had lost an election to Kennedy by less than one
per cent, and it was judged that it was a real loss; he did not
do well on television. Then he had fallen to Brown in that
governorship race; and if he could not carry California now
he could not win. It appeared that the Eastern states would
stay Democratic; and no one knew which candidate Wallace
would hurt most in the South. Middle America and middle
Americans were Nixon's reliance.

What the professionals saw, however, was the fatal probability that the Roosevelt coalition was breaking up. Organized labor, distressed farmers, progressives, all had undergone
change. Labor was now middle class. Farmers, such of them
as had not moved cityward, had returned to their Republicanism. Progressives were now concentrated on peace and
had been nagging Johnson for the better part of four years.
It was suspected that Humphrey was not wholly in accord
with the Vietnam involvement; but he had never openly
opposed it. He could count on a core of regulars from the
city machines, all the racial minorities, and some liberals who
recalled his courage and compared him favorably with
"Tricky Dick"; but these were fewer than they had been a
few years ago.

They proved not to be enough; and there was never really
much doubt. Late in the campaign Humphrey's voluble determination brought him up in the polls; and it was said that
if he had had a little more time, he might have made it, thus
confounding all the wiseacres, as Truman had done in 1948.

The fact was that Nixon almost succeeded in losing again
as he had to Kennedy. It was true that he had full television
exposure; but this had negative value. The more people saw
of him, the more they wondered if they wanted him to be
President after all. His make-up was better than it had been
in the famous Kennedy debates; some cynical reporters
guessed that he even wore it to bed. He was certainly more
at ease; but viewers were sophisticated; and there were dangerous remarks about his supporters, who all seemed to be

lawyers, bankers, and public relations men, especially public relations men.

As for his confidence, that was the result of coaching—and of experience. It was deliberate choice that made him refrain from saying anything he could be held to after the election. Since everyone told him that he could win by being careful, he would be sure of offending no one who could be thought to be inclined his way. This eroded some support from those who wanted comfort about the country's troubles. He did speak for order, but cautiously, because there were those who understood it as a code word for repression; and that was dangerous ground for the old communist-chaser. About the war he would not undercut Johnson, who by now had got negotiations going in Paris. Anyway, conservatives had not yet abandoned containment.

The real question for Nixon was whether his record would be recalled by the Democrats he must attract to win. No one, for years past, had so infuriated them; and it would come hard to accept him as a potential President. Still, he meant to be as nearly as he could an Eisenhower, solid, capable, and trustworthy. It would be a tour de force; but short memories are often counted on by politicians; and Nixon counted on them now.

No substantial claims were available; but his few mistakes lost no votes. What did lose them was again his performance on television. He simply did not appear, to many Americans, as a man who ought to be President; and they very nearly failed to elect him. It was a nearer thing than it should have been. But, if it came out closer than expected, the result was the same. Nixon won.

It was an election that showed a serious defect in the Constitution. There were moments when the electoral college system seemed to threaten no choice at all or one thrown into the Congress. The campaign cost a sum estimated at from $50 million to $70 million; and the Republicans had twice as much to spend as the Democrats, largely, but not altogether, because the polls said they would win—not altogether, because business sources are more easily tapped by the Republicans. This involved the obligation to favor them in all the ways they would invent during the next four years.

Fifty or so millions may not look large to businesses wanting favors; but this can only be because they expect a good return on the investment. The question had long been an embarrassing one: why should the Presidency have this shadow thrown across its validity as a democratic choice? Why not public funds for a public process?

Then there were all the questions about television. First, why should private companies profit from the expenditure for a public event? Forgetting the stupendous amount, the airwaves after all were not theirs. And especially they were not theirs to manipulate. And, if twice as much time for one candidate as for the other did not constitute manipulation, what would?

Nixon, like all his predecessors, might—probably would—honestly try to be President of all the people, not just Republicans, and not just the Republicans to whom his victory had been worth such an enormous expenditure of money. But could he? Why did Americans go on risking the near certainty that no man could?

2. Nixon's Problem

I pledge to consecrate my Office, my energies, and all the wisdom I can summon to the cause of peace.
                              RICHARD NIXON,
                         Inaugural, January, 1969

As I look down the new road . . .
I see an America in which we have abolished hun-
ger . . .
I see an America in which we have checked inflation
and waged a winning war against crime.
I see an America in which we have made great strides
in stopping pollution of our air, cleaning up our waters,
opening up our parks, continuing to explore in space.
                            NIXON, State of the Union
                            Address, January, 1970

In office, by however slim a majority, but, as Kennedy had
said in a similar situation, with the responsibility clear, Nixon
announced at once that he would change, altogether, the
national strategy. He must do it abroad. He must do it at
home. He had no alternative. His task forces and Presidential
Commissions told him so. His able assistants told him so. Besides, he was a professional; and he knew why he had been
elected and why he would be elected again—if he should be.
Two words would be heard again and again, emerging from
the "Churchillian rhetoric" as one commentator called it;
those words were peace and order. Americans were sick of
their opposites.

The rhetoric was meant to reassure his conservative supporters, now enlarged, as he hoped. In fact he spoke of them
as his "silent majority." Still he had no illusion whatever
about what was demanded. He must, even if it was late,
make conciliatory efforts abroad and show that at home he
could re-establish order.

He did not hint that this was a return to Roosevelt policies;
nevertheless it was. He had to go all the way back to 1945
and start over where Truman had gone wrong.

It became apparent, very shortly, that what Nixon had in
mind politically, looking to re-election, was reminiscent of
the Roosevelt maneuver of 1938–40. It will be recalled that
Roosevelt in his first campaign—1932—succeeded in the often
tried but seldom successful political coalescing of South and

West. To do this he appealed to the old Populist sentiment as well as to those Republicans who were ready to abandon Hoover and—for this once—their party. It had sufficed; but there was reason even then to believe that his winning had been more a loss for Hoover than a victory for himself. The voters were tired of Republican excuses. So, in 1968, the voters had been tired of Johnson and Democratic excuses.

The Midwest had not stayed Democratic very long after 1932. Local elections soon began to show losses. Roosevelt, anticipating what would happen in 1936, switched to reliance on the gratitude of those who had benefited from his measures for relief and reform. The unemployed had jobs; the poverty-stricken had relief; homeowners had credit; debts had been eased by devaluation. This was an enormous constituency and a far more loyal one than the one he had first appealed to. It tied to him the labor leaders and the city bosses who might not like to have less hold on their people, but who had lost face in the Depression because it had been quite beyond their ability to do anything about. They found ways to make the most of being Roosevelt's men.

The question for Nixon was whether the drastic changes involved in the withdrawal doctrine would win him a constituency as firm and lasting as the one Roosevelt had put together. His appeal began to change from the hard-line ideologies he had preached so long to a liberalism hardly recognizable as Nixonian. It had to be a cautious maneuver calculated to gain more than was lost, so that sometimes he seemed not to have changed at all; but it was on the whole unmistakable. His new appeal would be more conciliatory, more liberal, wider.

There was real question whether anything he could do domestically would widen his support. He had plans. He meant to balance the budget; to stop inflation; to rationalize the welfare system; to make a start on an environmental clean-up; to enlarge housing; to reduce crime; and, perhaps especially, to find a way for the Presidential establishment to function more effectively. What he lacked was a Congressional majority.

It was a special fortune that he had dependable assistance, something no recent President had had. He had watched carefully, as Truman, Eisenhower, Kennedy, and Johnson had failed in one way or another. Truman from incapacity and small-mindedness, Eisenhower from a negative conception of government and exaggerated admiration for men who had succeeded in business, Johnson from an egomania permitting only yes-men around him. None had been able to find competent assistance for the work he must do, the communication he must keep up with the Congress, and the strategic planning he must at least superintend.

Nixon's watching had gone on for twenty-two years, first from the House of Representatives (1946–50), then from the Senate (1950–52), and as Eisenhower's Vice-President for eight years. He also had learned from his defeats—for the Presidency in 1960 and for the governorship of California in 1962. The loss of the Presidency was so close that the difference was not very instructive; but his loss to Brown in California had been humiliating; and he had reacted badly. In a final bitter press conference he had lost control of himself and told the reporters they should be gratified that they no longer had "Dick Nixon to kick around."

This had seemed to end his political career, and he had at once moved to New York and become a nominal member of one of those law firms whose clients are the most affluent of all American enterprises and where a former Presidential candidate who had sedulously cultivated connections could be of use. It soon appeared, when Kennedy was assassinated and Johnson had succeeded, that Nixon was doing more than watching and waiting. Like Roosevelt from 1920 to 1928, he began to cultivate Republican local leaders from coast to coast and in 1966 was the most active of the campaigners for the party's Congressional candidates. He was at least partly responsible for the defeat of enough liberals to make

Johnson's further progress in his war on poverty impossible.

Kennedy had felt that he could not withdraw from Vietnam at the opening of the 'sixties because he feared reaction from his liberal supporters; Nixon might not be able to withdraw because of embattled reactionaries; they might say he was opening the gates to communism. Could he persuade them, or if he could not persuade, could he afford to ignore them?

His problem was less difficult than Kennedy's had been. Conservatives can often effect a liberal policy and do so without criticism. If an Eisenhower does something it *must* be safe. Nixon might well be able to put American interests above containment. Association with the Russians might be pictured as harmless if it had no internal corollaries. It might make the United States safe for capitalism even if the rest of the world was not made equally safe. If he *could* be convincing about this he might well mobilize the growing antiwar groups and establish a majority.

The same principle that allowed Republicans more leeway abroad also allowed it at home; and there was ample opportunity afforded by disillusion with the welfare system after the Johnson years. Nixon might find some credit too in these domestic efforts.

Not even the Social Security system was in good order by 1970. This was the oldest of Roosevelt's permanent programs for relieving Americans of man's worst fear; and in twenty-five years it should have had its deficiencies corrected. The worst difficulty, of course, was its insufficiency; the income for an elderly couple was not much more than half the minimum required for adequate subsistence and their retirement conditions were scandalous. From time to time the Congress voted increases in the taxes to support them and enlarge its payments; but they were never enough.

Other programs dating from the 'thirties were also in difficulties, and those legislated in Johnson's time had never been well begun. There was a catch-all Office of Economic

Opportunity meant to equalize chances in life for everyone, from infancy upward. With generous allocations its various efforts, given time, might have had the hoped-for effect; but its efforts were essentially half-hearted repairs: belated schools for children from degraded homes; training for youths who had left school and taken to vagrancy; assistance for abandoned women with children. There was, however, a strong tendency to keep assistance below the level of necessity, rooted in resentment that it needed to be given at all.

Besides the welfare organizations, struggling with conditions they could only meliorate, not cure, and not even really relieve, there were more than a hundred lending agencies for all sorts of purposes, large and small, and many others making outright payments. A catalogue of federal assistance programs issued in 1967 by the Office of Economic Opportunity ran to 700 pages. To look through it superficially was to conclude that before Johnson's first years were over every possible need must have been met; but one of the worst difficulties was precisely the variety and scatter. A person in need found it very difficult to get assistance in the bureaucratic jungle; then again it was often discovered that many were getting help from several sources at the same time.

Thus Nixon, again in the same ironic sequence as the containment reversal, must attempt the straightening out of the results—now visible—of Roosevelt's large determination that security and equality should be made certain for all people. He had never missed a chance to denounce this idea. He had always advocated return to the self-sufficiency of individualism. True, he had seen Eisenhower struggle feebly with the disestablishment of the welfare complex and finally settle for not adding to it even when the problems of migration, degeneration of the cities, and the rise of civic confusion were growing worse and worse. Now it was impossible even to consider abandonment or even reduction. If he stopped, the chaos would end finally in primitive battles among citizens in the streets.

He set out to bring order out of the administrative tangle. It was quite clear, however, that much of what was being done would have to go on. Not only that, it would have to be enlarged. For that he would have to find funds only to be had by contracting the military and space allocations. No President had been faced with more difficult strategic decisions.

Giving up containment was not something to be contrived overnight. It remained a stubborn conviction that the Russians meant˙ to foment rebellions and impose communist rule, and that a countering force must be in a constant state of readiness. To substitute for this costly preparedness an arrangement for getting along with reduced armament, or, at least, fewer genocidal weapons, was a task requiring political persuasion at home, as well as Russian concurrence. For the Russians were, if possible, more convinced than Americans that it was the purpose of their enemies to encircle them and destroy their government. Then there was the complication of a newly revivified China, now to be reckoned a superpower.

The conditions for coexistence in 1970 were very different from the conditions of 1945. In 1945 the United States was a victorious power whose strength was at its climacteric; the Russians were decimated by warfare on their own soil, and they did not possess nuclear weapons. By 1970, the Russians approached the United States in weaponry, and the policy of containment was failing. The Russians had not only concluded a treaty with West Germany and were pressing for a European Security Conference, but were extending their sphere of influence in Asia, the Mediterranean, the Indian Ocean, and the South Atlantic. All this *The Economist* (August, 1970) felt was not "the behavior of a country looking for a settlement of arguments with other people." It was the "behavior of a power out to maximize its own position in the world"; and this was a widely held conservative sentiment.

Were the problems at home pressing enough to persuade

Americans that living peaceably with the Russians was possible? Even Republican Nixon would find this situation difficult; but he had to try.

It has always been required of American Presidents that they carry mountainous loads of responsibility; but only a few of them have proved equal to the duty. Fortunately it had sometimes happened that crises corresponded with the most capable leaders; but not always. Fillmore, Pierce, and Buchanan allowed dissension to disrupt the Union, and only an agonizing war saved it. In the present instance, a quarter-century of mistaken strategy and unplanned domestic development had deposited in Nixon's White House the accumulated ills that, if not cured, might destroy the nation. He would not only have to convince his xenophobic followers that a Russian-American *détente* was possible, but that the domestic chaos must not result in mere suppression of the incidents resulting from it. It required reversal of his lifelong reactionary habit—if not his principles—and the exhibition of organizing talents the American people had no right to assume he might possess.

Then there was the possibility that, for one reason or another, a majority could not be persuaded to re-elect him in 1972. By that time his policies could not possibly have matured. He might, however, have withdrawn enough forces from Vietnam, Korea, and Europe to make the Nixon doctrine convincing. And possibly a new set of administrators might have brought some more convincing competence into governmental administration. He would not have shown much progress in legislation; but what he needed to do, during his first term, needed no cooperation from the Congress anyway.

3. *Nixon: Return to Coexistence*

. . . we are moving . . . from an era of confrontation to an era of negotiation. Our negotiations . . . will have far greater chance for success if both sides enter them motivated by mutual self-interest rather than naïve sentimentality . . .

I see an America at peace with all the nations of the world. . . .

NIXON, State of the Union
Address, 1970

This is the doctrine I announced at Guam—the "Nixon Doctrine" . . . the United States will participate in the defense and development of allies and friends, but cannot—and will not—conceive all the plans, design all the programs, execute all the decisions and undertake all the defense of the free nations of the world. We will help where it will make a real difference and is considered in our interest.

NIXON, President's Report to the Congress,
February, 1970

Working closely with two Democratic Presidents in the 1960's I defended [the Vietnam] war publicly. I urged congressional candidates to run in support of the President's efforts in Vietnam. The United States Senate, including many of the most outspoken opponents of this war went along . . .

Our deep, continued—indeed, seemingly endless—involvement in Southeast Asia is wrong.

We need a foreign policy that does not require us to bloody our swords in every civil war around the globe. . . .

LAWRENCE F. O'BRIEN, Chairman,
National Democratic Committee,
July 27, 1970

The failure of American policies could be measured in one way by the loss of confidence in the Democratic Party. It had broken up in dissension among several factions; it had lost the old South; liberals had made Vietnam a divisive issue; its ethnic groups had lost faith in its ability to do much more about civil rights or to implement the war on poverty; the unions were prospering and no longer politically reliable. The durable coalition spoken of by Richard Scammon had not held together during the campaign of 1968—or at least not loyally enough to win the election. It might at last have disappeared altogether.

There was a new consideration as well. Eighteen-year-olds could now vote—unless the Supreme Court reversed the Congress; and it was apparent that their attitude toward ventures involving the draft for military service would be hostile. Young people are always asked to do the fighting when there is any to be done; and that in Southeast Asia had been harder to justify than most such calls. Besides, not many of them shared their elders' fears of a communist conspiracy. Both parties were readjusting their appeals; but the Republicans had the best of this; being in power they could disengage and could claim the defeat was owed to Democratic blunders. Not many voters under thirty would recall the Dulles crusade and Eisenhower's complaisance.

Nixon, in fact, began a reversal of many policies without delay, seeing well enough where the weaknesses had been and knowing that he had not been approved in 1968 so much as he had profited from his opponent's weaknesses.

He moved cautiously at first because of the Eisenhower concurrence in containment, and his own enthusiastic role as Vice-Presidential spokesman for the policy. Without openly repudiating his own record he set out to win the support being lost by the Democrats. For the first time since 1932, polls showed, after a year, then after two years, that the Democrats were now actually a minority party; also that if he had been a candidate in 1970 instead of 1968 he would have won by a much wider margin—almost as wide as Johnson's in 1964 when running against Goldwater, the superhawk.

Nixon the politician understood the world more realistically than those who had watched his career had calculated. During the campaign there had been no hint of what was in his mind. In domestic matters he had made his familiar appeal to the lowest instincts of the voters, aimed principally at attracting those who considered repression a sufficient answer to multiplying ills. His central target had been Ramsey Clark, the Attorney General, rather than Humphrey, his opponent. Law enforcement had been too weak. Criminals had been encouraged. He would set things right by strengthening the police and the courts. The Democrats were vulnerable enough on the crime issue, and the mess they had made of proliferating welfare schemes was a ready target; but their worst record was that in Vietnam, where failure of the Johnson strategy was unmistakable. Nixon would do, he hinted, what Eisenhower had done in Korea—find a way to end the conflict begun by the Democrats and now sunk in endless futility.

In his State of the Union Message, however, there were intimations of change in his whole world outlook. There would be new policies, he said; they would rest on "an evaluation of the world as it is, not as it was twenty-five years ago at the conclusion of World War II." He then announced the Nixon doctrine. Henceforth the defense and the development of other nations would not be primarily an American undertaking. Help might be given, but responsibility would not be assumed.

As for domestic policies, the 'seventies should be a time for reforming—the welfare system, to begin with. Inflation must be stopped; the environment must be cleaned up. The main business of government must be to abolish hunger, provide minimum incomes, make better progress in providing educational and other facilities.

That this was Nixon speaking—a Republican, a conservative—was incredible. He sounded, it was said, almost "like Roosevelt."

During the first months of his term he did little more than choose associates, consult, and organize. Nevertheless he made some beginnings. He somewhat mollified the protesters against Vietnam by beginning a withdrawal and by making it clear to other Asians that they could expect help in defending themselves but that no American combat troops would be available. There would be no more expeditionary forces.

He asked the West Europeans to recognize their obligations, and, now that they were again prosperous, to expect less assistance. Taken together, these nations had as many people as the United States, and their productivity was rising as rapidly. They were shirking. They were expecting to be defended by an ally thousands of miles across the sea and having enormous obligations elsewhere. The three hundred thousand Americans still in Germany would be drastically reduced; this last Nixon did not actually say, but it followed from his plain speaking.

The President, it was clear, was not only withdrawing from the quarter-century of mistaken strategies; he was pushing alternatives. Since Johnson had not been able to find the funds needed for his war on poverty, deficit financing had become a regular resort. There had been no planning about all the new undertakings, and already there was acrimonious discussion of priorities. Between those who were encouraged in expectations that were never met and those who turned sourly away from overseas obligations, Johnson's supporters had grown fewer and fewer.

Nixon hoped to assemble the disappointed and dissident into what would be a lasting majority. He, of course, did not expect—or even want—to reach the extremists; what he was working toward was a widening of the center. The conception was a reasonable one. Enough Democrats had deserted to defeat Humphrey, but only just; Nixon could not count on them again. To be re-elected he must have a majority of his own, earned by performance in office.

It had seemed at first that the apparent convention contract with Senator Thurmond to go easy on the South in racial matters was to be honored. The administration did indeed show signs of weakening the enforcement of integration, especially in the schools; but all this was changed when George Wallace again came uppermost in Alabama. His following was not to be transferred so easily to Nixon. So the "Southern strategy" could be given up. It had all along been a doubtful reliance. It was far rightist, and it would make demands incompatible with moderation. Nixon's strategy could now be redesigned to attract those who were tired of fruitless resistance to the legitimate claims of the blacks. This, together with the turnaround in foreign policy, gave his program a wholly new cast.

There were other accommodations made possible by changed attitudes. The Congress had been willing, in the expansive days of Truman's Presidency, when containment was an accepted policy, to make generous provisions for aid to third world nations. As the promised results failed to materialize and as generosity was more and more met with surly dissatisfaction, it had been harder and harder to persuade the Congress that more ought to be done for ungrateful recipients. In 1969 the total was less than half what it had been even in 1966 (one and three-quarter billion dollars as against three and one-third billion dollars); and earlier aid totals had run to six billion dollars and more (approximate figures). The time was not far distant when aid would be abandoned as a policy supporting containment and would be measured by other criteria—more humanitarian, perhaps; and this would bring it into competition with the needs of the millions in America still living in poverty. Such a comparison was already being made. This enabled Nixon to base his doctrine on the conservative principle that he must economize. Containment was costly.

Another evidence of strategic failure—something Roosevelt's policy would have made unnecessary, and something Nixon could take advantage of—was the nearly three million American soldiers on duty *in foreign lands:* in Europe, 310,000; in Asia (including Japan, Okinawa, Taiwan, the Philippines, Thailand, and South Vietnam), 700,000; in Latin America, 25,000; then there were the fleets: the Atlantic, 255,000; the Pacific, 400,000 (figures approximate and shifting). How containment had worked against American interests could be seen by noting that the Russians had no soldiers serving in actual combat and only those abroad who were deployed in Eastern Europe and the Middle East.

If it may be supposed that coexistence could have succeeded, this immense force might have been reduced to a suitable number serving in an international peace-keeping operation—say half-a-million men and perhaps ten per cent of the ships and planes. This seemed outrageously fanciful in 1969. In 1970 it was the logical result of the Nixon reasoning. At the beginning of that year, as the result of Henry Kissinger's work and his skill in coordinating that of others, a comprehensive statement of foreign policy for the 'seventies was issued. Nothing like this had ever been done before; but there were reminders of the Monroe Doctrine, of the Theodore Roosevelt Corollaries, of Wilson's and Franklin Roosevelt's statements of war aims. None of these, however, had been analyses of global strategy, telling friend and enemy alike what could be expected of the United States.

In President's Nixon's document on the state of the world, he used the phrase "era of negotiation," saying that it must be entered on as the only alternative to continued risk of destruction. These were other words for "coexistence," a recognition that, as Roosevelt had insisted, the world was, in many respects, one, and that treating it as more than one might well be fatal.

It might be said that Nixon had been an unconscionably long time coming to this conclusion. There were those who recalled that he had been a notorious communist-hunter when in the Congress; that, in fact, he had founded his political reputation on xenophobia. He had been an ardent pleader for containment; and, as Vice-President, had urged hostile rather than conciliatory policies whenever the opportunity arose. He met this kind of criticism by a very simple strategem. He said that things had changed. It was not true that they were much different from the position in 1945; but that was a long time ago; they had undoubtedly changed since Dulles' day, when Nixon had been so hot for containment.

It was indeed quite different now that Johnson had fallen on the same issues and that Humphrey had failed because of association with Johnson. As a candidate, Nixon had not been so perceptive. If now, in office, his reappraisal of America's interests abroad had produced a reversal in his views of policy, it was recent. It was, in fact, the result of political sensitivity. Adventures in Asia and elsewhere, far from American shores, were now decidedly unpopular. The professional politician was listening.

He, of course, insisted that the change in his policy was made necessary by changed conditions. First and most important were the heightened perils of resort to force; the developments of two decades, he said, have "magnified the risks of intractable hostility." Thus, in a phrase, he not only repudiated the Dulles intention of maintaining an aggressive vigilance around the Russian borders but gave notice of his intention to abandon policies he had heretofore been so eloquent in defending.

He elaborated:

Twenty years ago the United States and what was then the Communist bloc could be resigned to the mutual hostility that flowed from deep-seated differences of ideology and national purpose . . .

For us as well as our adversaries, in the nuclear age, the

perils of using force are simply not in reasonable proportion to
most of the objectives sought in many cases . . .

We both have learned too that great powers may find their
interests deeply involved in local conflict—risking confrontation
—yet have precariously little influence over direction taken by
local forces.

In this can be recognized the Kissinger advice; but also
the return to Rooseveltian wisdom. First, regardless of ideology, coexistence is essential to national security, and hostility
will not safeguard but will jeopardize it. Second, the quarrels
and ambitions of small nations must not be allowed to set
larger ones against one another; confrontation in support of
local causes may easily become intolerably dangerous.

This possibility had become more real as years had passed:

The nuclear age has also posed for the United States and the
communist countries the common dangers of accident or miscalculation Both sides are threatened, for example, when any
power seeks tactical advantages from a crisis and risks provoking a strategic response.

What followed from this appraisal of the situation existing
after years of containment was the revival of a very old doctrine—that of recognizing spheres of interest, and apportion-
ment of responsibilities. This was put in other words:

First we will deal with the Communist countries on the basis
of a precise understanding of what they are about in the world,
and thus of what we can reasonably expect of them and of
us . . .

Second, negotiations must be the result of careful preparation
and an authentic give and take on the issues . . . We will not
become psychologically dependent on rapid or extravagant
progress.

In addition, as a third essential, there would be "an appreciation of the context of negotiations," the central fact being

"the interrelationship of international events . . . entwined in many complex ways."

How much more sophisticated this statement was than any made by American statesmen since the war! Gone were the threats and boasts, gone too the missionary determination to wrest the free world from wicked communists; gone the crocodile tears about small nations; and gone the proclamations of determination to man the walls of liberty. The iron cutrain, a phrase coined by Churchill and accepted by Truman, was abolished as a controlling fiction.

Soon the American intention was made good by the beginning of direct negotiations, first in Helsinki, then transferred to Vienna, then resumed in Helsinki. The Russians had not followed the Nixon-Kissinger document with one of their own; but they did say that negotiation must take the place of confrontation.

Prospects of a viable coexistence were opened for the first time since 1945. Yet those who doubted the sincerity of Nixon's intentions thought there was ample justification in remarks he made during his many television appearances. For instance, he said, in one of these (in July, 1970): "Anyone who doubts the validity of the domino theory cannot have talked to the dominoes lately." This was a reversion to the old Nixon, who had been Dulles' colleague and supporter. Was it the true Nixon? If so how could it be thought consistent with the conciliatory efforts necessary to coexistence? Or was he doing as Eisenhower had done: keeping xenophobes quiet while exploring the possibilities of negotiation for compromise?

Some sort of answer to this was made when he spoke to the United Nations in October: "One of the paramount problems of our time is that we must transcend the old patterns of power politics in which nations sought to exploit every volatile situation for their own advantage or to squeeze the maximum advantage for themselves out of every negotiation."

VII
A Final Word

"In the inexorable march of history," wrote Hegel, "there occur moments when the sheer weight of accumulating events finally produces a decisive change." August 1970 may well go down as one of those moments, the beginning of the elusive "era of negotiation.". . .

Time, August 17, 1970

For all his deviousness, Roosevelt was a master reassurer (no slouch as a mover and shaker, either, or as king-hero to most). His humor, his air of patrician calm, his simplicity of expression, and his masterful use of intimacy over the radio calmed a trembling nation even when his policies were faltering badly. People who were politically aware then, have that memory with them, that model to hold up against the current reassurers. Indeed we grew up with Roosevelt from 1933 to 1945; over all those years the office and the man seemed to grow together into one thing, one oaken trunk of stability in the midst of national and world chaos.

JAMES D. BARBER,
from a Center paper, September, 1970

Concerning the strategic decisions made at the opening of the nuclear age there is a choice between two views. Either there were colossal American misjudgments, or containment was inevitable because of communist aggression. What is not arguable is that the Russians and Chinese managed their affairs very well, in a competitive sense, and that the United States was committed to excessive efforts, now to be sharply curtailed. This was what Nixon, as President, had to face: finding his way out of an impasse that ought never to have happened and undertaking neglected tasks that ought to have been far advanced.

As to the Southeast Asian wars, it began to be seen generally by Nixon's time that not only strategy but tactics had been mistaken. Presidents, generals—at least those who prevailed—and the commanders in the field seem never to have accepted the condition that American forces were there to train and assist, but not to take over the war and defeat the enemy. It was not until General Westmoreland's service was ended that any serious effort was made to increase the capability of the Vietnamese forces. When, in 1965, half-a-million Americans descended on the country and a search-and-destroy tactic was adopted, the Vietnamese army was neglected. It fell into barracks lethargy, was riddled by corruption, and was so thoroughly demoralized that its disuse seemed justified. It was not until there was a change of field command as well as a change of commanders in chief that anyone seemed to recall what the American mission was supposed to be.

An enemy could not be defeated whose territory was forbidden, who had a long border (Cambodia and Laos) for sanctuary, and who had only a nominal enemy in Saigon. If it should be defeated, what would have been gained? If South Vietnam could not be made capable of defending itself the United States would be responsible for its future.

It must be said that Nixon seemed to be the first President, at least since Kennedy, to understand that it was for the Vietnamese to establish their own independence and that the Americans were to assist them in this: furnishing materials, munitions, and training but not to do the fighting. The cleaning out of the Cambodian sanctuaries after beginning withdrawal caused violent revulsion among those who were already impatient and frustrated; but it could soon be seen to be part of a quite altered tactic. The performance of the

South Vietnamese army in that foray surprised everyone, even those who had known it intimately; and the maneuver had to be judged a success in gaining time for Vietnamization.

The violent reaction occurred partly because there existed no considerable confidence that the Nixon doctrine was actually to be effected, and partly because there was by then so limited a willingness to allow Presidents the authority they had been expanding since the engagements in Southeast Asia had begun.

Not only military management was being questioned; the whole operation of the expanded Presidency was loudly being protested.

Presidents, during the last quarter-century, had too often appealed to people's worst, instead of their best, impulses; had too often asked of people what no people would give; and had listened to those who meant to pursue mistaken policies. The political system, the bureaucracies, the immense business organizations, the military, all needed redirection and did not have it. So many even of the numerous welfare initiatives of the Johnson Administration were failures because of ineffective administration! There were such massive diversions of funds to purposes better not undertaken! Presidents were simply not being leaders in wise strategies.

Dissension in the United States had run in the Johnson years to sporadic outbreaks of violence. No one seemed to understand how this could have occurred; but, of course, misgovernment had made it possible. Potential revolutionists always exist in troubled times; but usually they lack the means for action. The well-meaning expansion of the welfare system, so necessary for other reasons, was simply taken advantage of. The disaffected found ways to be supported, to abstract funds for travel and training, for organizing riots, for defying public authority, and for legal defense. In the 'thirties, when the hardships of depression might have been expected to produce revolutionists, there had been none in evidence; they had had no financing. The affluent society of the 'sixties was cleverly subverted to pay for its own disruption.

If there is reason for protest and those inclined to violence are tolerated or even followed by a substantial minority and then the means are furnished for protesting, it may be expected that sporadic disruption will follow. Such phenomena as the wild excesses of extremists in 1970 do not occur spontaneously. There are always minorities in a democracy and always those who feel oppressed by social arrangements, but ordinarily there are felt to be political remedies available. There is dialogue, perhaps excited and unreasonable; but the majority is allowed to prevail without being attacked. Destruction of property, assassination, and rioting are a repudiation of the going arrangements.

Instead of a proud, wealthy, and orderly nation, the United States had emerged by 1970 to disappointment, disillusion, dissension, and savage reaction. It ought not to have been so; it need not have been so.

It was fancifully suggested, earlier, that Roosevelt might have gone on at least as long as Stalin, Churchill, Chiang Kai-shek, and de Gaulle; and that if he had lived only to be seventy-two this would have seen him through the elections of '48 and '52. He might have been able, it may even be imagined, to have had as his last Vice-President somone other than Truman; and that someone might have been his successor. Eisenhower would not have appeared; and perhaps Kennedy, succeeding in 1956, would have been ready for responsibility; anyway, he would not have been called on to approve a Bay of Pigs or to confront the threat of Russian missiles in Cuba.

To elaborate this supposition is to produce truly amazing contrasts. Some—but not all—of them assume a conceit about what Roosevelt would have done; but, if only the most modest surmises are made, the might-have-beens open out prospects startlingly different from what in fact existed in 1970.

What Nixon—and his successors—must now do would, in

such circumstances, not have been necessary. Liquidating a quarter-century of attempts by each superpower to contain the others involved, not two but three—each carrying into negotiation carefully cultivated suspicions anchored in ideological differences. Yet if one held back there would never be even a secure *détente*. The risks would have to be borne, as they had been borne for so long, until a conjunction of readiness was reached. The negotiators would each be wary of their domestic demagogues with their new willingness to disrupt and destroy whenever they disapproved something done in their behalf.

Even lacking such extremism, leaders would have found it extremely difficult to convince their people that their own national interests were being served. The question would ultimately have to be whether the maintenance of world order and the solution of world problems were more sensible than the strategy of conquest; but could any democratic leader establish the tolerance he would need for long and patient negotiation?

This was not only true of the relations with other nations; patience concerning domestic matters was equally lacking.

Affairs on the American continent would have to be righted against the determined opposition of those who held to the convenient conviction that poverty resulted from shiftlessness and ought not to burden those who were certain that the punishment of crime was an adequate deterrent even though its causes remained untouched.

Facing a reckoning so disastrous it is extremely difficult not to moralize; nevertheless only the most obvious and elementary lesson is insisted on here: whatever the nature of the crisis, power must be consigned by the people only to those who are prepared to use it wisely.

The formula for this reformed selection process was not simple. It would require the revision of many institutions, supported by determined interests who would see them altered only over their fierce objection. The constitutional question would finally be come to; but it would certainly be at a late stage of governmental disintegration.

There had come a time when most Americans could not recall the inspiration of genuine leadership. Twenty-five years is, after all, a full generation. Roosevelt was becoming a legend, a figure in a cloak of courage and success. Every year on the anniversary of his death there were modest ceremonies in Hyde Park and Warm Springs. For many years someone associated with him was found to say a few words at the place where he died or the one where he was buried. By 1970 those left for this were very few; and the press fell back on quoting correspondents who had some less intimate recollections, or historians who knew him only from study.

Averell Harriman was one assistant who still survived at nearly eighty, having had an astonishing number of assignments since his ambassadorship to the Soviet Union, where he had been at the time of Yalta. Reminiscing over the telephone from his Florida home in 1970 he was quoted as saying that history would have followed a different course if Roosevelt had lived:

> For one thing relations with the Russians would have been different—different in our favor. For another, France would have been denied a return to Indochina and there probably would not have been a Vietnam war.

He went on to recall Stalin's emotion at hearing the news of Roosevelt's death. Holding the Ambassador's hand he had spoken of him as "a great leader for peace." Who now associates Stalin with words of that kind? Peace, the first necessity of mankind? Roosevelt, the word suggests, might well have kept the Russians to different courses.

Harriman was involved in some of the events following Roosevelt's death. He thought there was no way of telling whether Roosevelt would have used the nuclear bomb to end the war with Japan. He thought he "would be remembered most for his peaceful revolution—the New Deal . . . he transferred control of the economy from Wall Street to Washington."*

Harriman's loyalty to Roosevelt made him less than a perfect expositor of the orthodox view that the postwar confrontations were inevitable. That view was, however, very well expressed by a senior foreign correspondent of *The New York Times*, C. L. Sulzberger (Sunday, April 12, 1970), who also had some recollections:

> On April 13, 1945, I was in Moscow when the news was received that late the previous day President Franklin Roosevelt had died.
>
> For the only time during many visits to the Soviet capital I saw people weep in public, groping through the streets in dazed sorrow, even though World War II was approaching its triumphant end. It was as if the emotional Russians had lost a personal friend.
>
> Some people now contend that Washington initiated the cold war; that, once he learned of the atomic bomb project, Truman felt strong enough for a tough approach, maintained American troop positions in the Soviet Zone of Germany and attempted actively to intervene in what was to become Moscow's sphere of influence.
>
> The facts are different. Roosevelt himself had another attitude from that with which he is credited.
>
> Just before his death, Roosevelt, disturbed by Soviet accusations of double-dealing, warned Stalin: "It would be one of the great tragedies of history if at the very moment of the victory now within our grasp, such distrust, such lack of faith, should prejudice the entire undertaking after the colossal losses of life, materiel and treasure involved. Frankly, I cannot avoid a feeling of bitter resentment toward your informers, whoever they are, for such vile misrepresentations of my actions."

It is true that Roosevelt, in his very last days, did write in this way to Stalin; but to conclude from this that the two leaders had come to a final parting is to misunderstand the

* San Francisco Examiner, April 12, 1970

relationship they had established. After so long a time as political leaders of continental nations, each understood the problems of the other. Roosevelt must be credited with the probability that he would have carried through any temporary misunderstanding to agreement for the purposes they had in common.

A quiet different summing up was made by Arthur M. Schlesinger, Jr., whose three completed volumes on *The Age of Roosevelt* were the result of long and serious study:

Against the backdrop of Vietnam, Roosevelt's recognition of the power of awakened nationalism in the colonial world looks better than ever. In 1944 he proposed that Indochina, instead of being returned to France, should be prepared for independence. Had his recommendations been followed, [44,000] Americans and countless Vietnamese, now dead, would be alive today.

... Today it is precisely Roosevelt's domestic policy that is under the more persistent criticism; and where the Right led the assault 15 years ago, the Left leads the assault today.

... All he did, a young radical told me the other day, was to "abort the revolution by incremental gestures." At the same time, he "dangerously cultivated a mood for charismatic mass politics, dangerously strengthened the presidency, dangerously concentrated power in the national government ..."

... Roosevelt will survive this assault from the left as he has survived the earlier assault from the right. In another quarter century we will worry over new facets of his glittering and elusive personality, new perplexities in his presidency—a consequence both of his personal complexity and of the remarkably malleable and uncertain days in which he lived.

... His power sprang from his preternatural sensitivity to the emerging social moods and needs of his time—this allied with astute realism and unlimited resourcefulness about means and a generous, buoyant, at times almost ingenuous, idealism about ends. He led our Nation through a crisis of confidence by convincing the American people that they had unsuspected reserves of decency, steadfastness and concern. He defeated the grand ideologists of his age by showing how experiment could overcome dogma, in peace and war.

. . . His policies were imperfect, his solutions incomplete; but the spirit in which he confronted the American condition—that exhilarating combination of gaiety and resolve, that glowing sense of high adventure and high purpose—should strengthen us all as we face our own crisis of confidence today.*

For most Americans Roosevelt the leader and statesman has already passed into the legends of their history. When he was alive there were skeptics; but most people were supporting his progress through war to a peace institutionalized for permanence. It was a credible effort. It did rest on a belief that the difficult Russians could be persuaded to cooperate; but he had reason for that hope—if he could have done it himself.

To say now that he kept a system viable that ought to have been revolutionized is to use the simplistic language of the radical unsophisticate. There are still alive several members of the Brains Trust who recall some differences about this. In the spring of 1933 the banking system was paralyzed; some argued that this was a golden opportunity to nationalize. Never had a group of enterprisers been in such disrepute. There was suspicion that many of them had thought only of their own interests as the crisis came on; and some had not even been honest. Roosevelt listened to it all, then asked a simple question: who would run it? Obviously it would have to be the same people. Amateurs replacing them would make an even worse hash of things; and the country could not stand more years of disorganization. Drastic change would have to wait its time.

This was the Roosevelt way; he felt his way forward, toward adaptations. Those clear objectives for a whole people, ones they would support—like Social Security—he caused to

* *The New York Times* news service, Monday, April 13, 1970

be embedded in an institution. That particular one deserves, if any social arrangement does, to be called permanent; and there are others.

The first years were ones of many starts and some stops. Some beginnings seem strangely naïve in restrospect; but they were meant to accomplish something that somehow must be accomplished.

With the Western world, at least, freed of Nazis and fascists, with China and Russia convinced of safety from another attack, the experimentation at home might have been resumed. All that mighty productive power might have resulted, say, by 1952, in a United States rich, progressive, and helpful to the rest of the world—if still pluralistic and not really socialist, still one directed to planned and humane ends. It might have become one, also, prepared to meet the greater challenges looming like dark clouds over humanity in 1970. There were beginning to be questions whether man could survive; and there were few energies to be spared from contemporary problems for exploring the means for going on in this world more than another generation or two.

If Roosevelt had lived on for a while instead of dying in 1945, the nation would have been in a very different state. So would the world; and Nixon would not have been called on to do what required repudiation of his life-long commit-ments. He was not only called on to return to the Roosevelt polices; as a professional politician he was *compelled* to do something of the sort. For success in what he must do he lacked those qualities spoken of by Schlesinger—gaiety and charm; but he did have those others—resolve and flexibility. For his purposes and for a troubled people, they would have to suffice.

The years since Roosevelt had been wasted ones. In these, study and action had been diverted from the consequences of human proprietorship on the small planet earth to com-petition for control of some parts of it; and larger causes might well determine that these would soon be worthless.

Alexander King, Science Director, NATO, in a Center for the Study of Democratic Institutions paper (September, 1970) described the dimensions of the danger:

We face the problems through a miasma of ignorance and much new break-through research is required if serious progress is to be made. Two separate geo-scientific approaches are predicting on the one hand a serious heating up of our planet by the end of the century, caused by the accumulation of carbon dioxide in the upper atmosphere as a result of excessive combustion and a dwindling proportion of the earth's surface covered with chlorophyl-bearing plants to maintain the oxygen level. On the other hand geo-physicists, alarmed by the discovery of liquid water at the base of the antarctic ice cap, suggest that the ice will, before long, slide into the ocean, devastate the world with monstrous tidal waves and trigger off the next ice age.

. . . It may well be that both or neither of these movements are to be taken seriously but it would be good to know the probabilities. It would be interesting to envisage a US-USSR cooperative scheme for the use of nuclear power to shave off the surface encrustment of ice in antarctica for the survival of the race.

Other scientists, withdrawing from work on weaponry, have similar suggestions for urgent attention. For instance, the chemicals responsible for the upsurge in agricultural productivity have had unexpectedly fatal effects on plant and animal life, and ones not likely to disappear for years to come.

No nation, however rich and powerful, could solve such apocalyptic problems alone even if their solution became a high priority with their politicians. The enemy to be faced at once appeared to be emerging from men's own activities in an ecosystem they had not tried to understand. For the United States, or for the other superpowers, it was not each other they must soon confront, but themselves as disposers of nature's power.

The world and its people need peace and order; they need coexistence and cooperation; they need confrontation within themselves. If they do not soon attain these, survival beyond a few more generations is clearly at hazard.

A Short Chronology of Events, 1945-70

(prepared by Christopher Cogley)

1945

April 12: Franklin D. Roosevelt died at Warm Springs, Georgia.

April 25–June 26: The United Nations Conference, held by forty-six nations in San Francisco, drafted and adopted the United Nations Charter.

May 7: Germany surrendered unconditionally to the Allies at Reims, France.

July 16: The first atomic bomb was successfully tested at Alamagordo, New Mexico.

July 17–August 2: The Potsdam Conference between Truman, Stalin, and Churchill (Atlee after July 28) agreed to the disarming of Germany.

August 6 and 9: The atomic bomb was dropped on Hiroshima and Nagasaki.

August 14: Japan surrendered.

December 27: The Moscow Conference between Byrnes, Molotov, and Bevin released preliminary plans for the establishment of atomic-energy control, the drafting of peace treaties, and the unification of Korea.

1946

February 28: Secretary of State Byrnes hinted in a speech the beginning of a new "firm" policy toward the Soviet Union.

March 5: Winston Churchill commanded wide attention with his "iron curtain" speech delivered at Fulton, Missouri.

July 26: The McMahon Act was signed by President Truman vesting control of the development and use of atomic energy in a civilian five-man Atomic Energy Commission appointed by the President and confirmed by the Senate.

November: In the first postwar Congressional elections, Democrats lost control of the House and Senate.

1947

February 10: Peace treaties for Italy, Rumania, Bulgaria, Hungary, and Finland were signed in Paris.

March 12: President Truman in a plea for assistance to Greece and Turkey outlined the Truman Doctrine, declaring it the policy of the United States "to support free peoples who are resisting subjugation by armed minorities or by outside pressures."

June 5: Secretary of State Marshall proposed the European Recovery Program, a massive economic plan to prevent economic and political chaos in Western Europe.

November 29: The State of Israel was authorized at the United Nations by a proposal sponsored by the United States and the Soviet Union.

1948

February 23–25: A communist bid for power in Czechoslovakia was successful when President Benes yielded to demands to install a pro-Soviet Cabinet.

April 19: In Italy, the Communist Party was narrowly defeated in Italy's first postwar elections.

April 26: An Inter-American Conference in Bogota adopted a charter setting up the Organization of American States.

May 14: The State of Israel was proclaimed in Tel Aviv; it was recognized by the United States and three days later by the Soviet Union; the first Arab-Israeli war began.

June 21: The Western Allies responded to a Soviet land blockade undertaken on April 1 by beginning an airlift of food and fuel to West Berlin.

June 28: The first rift appeared among the communist alliance when Stalin broke with Tito of Yugoslavia.

November: President Truman upset all expectations by defeating Thomas Dewey in the Presidential election; Democrats regained control of both houses of Congress.

1949

January 7: A cease-fire was imposed in Palestine.

January 21: Dean Acheson replaced Marshall as Secretary of State.

January 29: President Truman inaugurated the policy of granting American aid for the world's developing areas by proposing the Point Four Program.

April 4: The North Atlantic Treaty was signed by the United States, Canada, and ten West European nations, establishing the North Atlantic Treaty Organization. Greece and Turkey would join in 1952.

August 6: Secretary of State Acheson in a White Paper blamed Chiang Kai-shek's "reactionary clique" for the impending defeat of the Nationalists in the Chinese Civil War and barred further aid to that government.

September 12: The Federal Republic of Germany was proclaimed in Bonn.

September 23: The Soviet Union detonated its first atomic device, ending the United States monopoly.

September 30: The Berlin airlift ended when the Soviet Union suspended the land blockage of that city.

December 7: The Nationalist Chinese Government fled to the island of Formosa, ending the Chinese Civil War with victory for the communists.

1950

January: Russians boycotted Security Council meetings.

February 7: The United States recognized the State of Vietnam, organized under French auspices in 1949, in opposition to the Democratic Republic of Vietnam, organized by Ho Chi Minh in 1945.

June 25: North Korean troops crossed the 38th parallel into South Korea.

June 27: President Truman ordered United States air and sea support for the South Korean Army and U.S. troops in Korea; he also announced that the United States was sending a thirty-five-man Military Assistance Advisory Group to the State of Vietnam to instruct troops there on the use of weapons, the first material evidence of U.S. involvement; the United Nations Security Council called on U.N. members to help repel the North Korean attack.

November: The Congressional elections reduced the Democratic margin in both Houses of Congress.

November 3: The United Nations Assembly passed a resolution presented by Acheson authorizing the Assembly to deal with breaches of the peace if a veto prevented the Security Council from taking action.

December 23: The United States signed a Mutual Defense Assistance Agreement with the State of Vietnam.

1951

January 5–April 4: A debate in Congress resulted in approval of the President's power to defend Europe with ground forces.

July 10: Truce talks began in Korea.

September 7: The United States agreed to provide direct economic assistance to the State of Vietnam.

September 8: A peace treaty between Japan and forty-nine nations was signed in San Francisco.

1952

February 20: A NATO conference approved a European Army with German contingents.

May 27: A treaty founding the European Defense Community was signed in Paris.

October 3: Great Britain successfully detonated an atomic bomb.

November 1: The first U.S. hydrogen bomb was set off at Eniwetok, an island in the Pacific.

November: Dwight D. Eisenhower defeated Adlai Stevenson in the Presidential election and Republican majorities were elected in the House and Senate.

1953

March 5: Premier Stalin of the Soviet Union died.

June 17: East Berliners revolted but were crushed by Soviet forces.

July 27: The Korean Armistice was signed.

August 14: The Soviet Union detonated its first hydrogen bomb.

1954

April 26–June 21: In a Geneva Conference, France, Britain, the Soviet Union, the United States, the Democratic Republic of Vietnam, the State of Vietnam, Laos, Cambodia, and Communist China agreed on a formula for ending the Indo-China war: the accords divided Vietnam into two zones along the 17th parallel, the Democratic Republic of Vietnam administering the northern zone, and the State of Vietnam administering the southern zone; a ban on new troops or bases was imposed, and elections for the reunification of the two zones were scheduled for July, 1956; Laos and Cambodia were made independent; an International Control Commission composed of members from India, Poland, and Canada were to supervise the accords. All parties signed except the United States and the State of Vietnam; the latter two gave verbal assent.

May 8: The French stronghold in Vietnam of Dien Bien Phu fell to Viet Minh forces.

September 8: The Southeast Asia Collective Defense Treaty was signed in Manila by the United States, Britain, France, Australia, New Zealand, Pakistan, Thailand, and the Philippines.

October 23: West Germany was granted sovereignty and admitted to NATO.

November: Congressional elections yielded a Democratic House and a slim Democratic control of the Senate.

December 2: The Senate ended the McCarthy era by censuring the Senator from Wisconsin.

1955

January 28: Congress approved the Formosa Resolution, President Eisenhower's request for emergency power to permit U.S. forces to protect Formosa and the Pescadores.

May 14: A mutual defense treaty was signed in Warsaw by Albania, Bulgaria, Czechoslovakia, Hungary, Poland, Rumania, East Germany, and the Soviet Union. It was called the Warsaw Pact.

July 18–23: The first Summit Conference was held at Geneva with President Eisenhower, Premier Bulganin, French Prime Minister Faure, and Prime Minister Eden, resulting in no agreement but setting precedent.

October 23: A referendum in the southern zone of Vietnam established a Republic of South Vietnam with Ngo Dinh Diem as its first President; Diem declared that the elections slated for July, 1956 would not be held.

1956

February 24: In a secret speech at the 20th Congress of the Soviet Communist Party, Nikita Khrushchev denounced Joseph Stalin's method of rule.

July 19: The United States withdrew its offer to help Egypt build the Aswan High Dam on the Nile.

July 26: Egypt announced the seizure of the Suez Canal.

October 23–24: A popular revolt began in Budapest, Hungary, and spread throughout the country. After eleven days of wide resistance, Russian forces defeated the revolutionists.

October 29: Israel launched an attack on the Sinai peninsula, driving toward the Suez Canal.

October 31: The United States condemned the Israeli attack.

November 4: The United Nations voted to establish a military force to end the Egyptian-Israeli war.

November 5: British and French paratroopers invaded Egypt at Port Said.

November 6: American protests forced British and French troops to halt their Suez advance.

November: President Eisenhower was elected to a second term; but Democrats increased their leads in both Houses of Congress.

1957

January 5: President Eisenhower articulated the Eisenhower Doctrine in a speech before Congress, asking for power to use military and economic aid to combat Soviet penetration into the Middle East.

March 25: Treaties were signed in Rome by France, West Germany, Italy, Belgium, the Netherlands, and Luxembourg establishing the European Economic Community.

October 4: The Soviet Union launched into orbit the first manmade satellite.

1958

March 27: Nikita Khrushchev became Premier of the Soviet Union.

July 15: President Eisenhower ordered marines into Lebanon at the request of the Lebanese government to prevent an overthrow; they began withdrawal within a month.

November: Congressional elections resulted in a Democratic sweep in the House and the Senate.

November: The United States and the Soviet Union began an unpoliced three-and-a-half-year moratorium on nuclear-weapons tests.

1959

January 1: Fidel Castro assumed control of the government in Havana, Cuba, as the Batista regime collapsed.

September 15–27: Premier Khrushchev visited the United States and talked with President Eisenhower, inviting him to visit the Soviet Union.

1960

February 13: France tested its first atomic bomb in the Sahara.

May 16: The Paris Summit Conference was ended before it began as President Eisenhower refused to apologize to Premier Khrushchev for U-2 spy flights. Eisenhower's visit to the Soviet Union was canceled.

November: In a narrow victory, John F. Kennedy defeated Richard M. Nixon for President; Democrats retained a reduced control of the House and the Senate.

December: Meetings in North Vietnam between the government and dissident elements from South Vietnam resulted in the formulation of the National Liberation Front.

1961

January 3: The United States broke diplomatic relations with Cuba.

March 13: President Kennedy proposed a ten-year plan of economic aid to Latin America, called the Alliance for Progress.

April 17: The invasion of Cuba by anti-Castro elements, aided by the United States, was crushed at the Bay of Pigs.

June 3–4: President Kennedy and Premier Khrushchev conferred in Vienna.

August 13: East Berlin began construction of a wall separating East from West Berlin and preventing people from leaving or entering East Berlin.

September–November: The Soviet Union broke the moratorium on nuclear testing with the detonation of a series of nuclear weapons, the largest ever exploded.

December 11: Two U.S. Army helicopter units arrived in South Vietnam, the first direct U.S. military support for South Vietnam.

1962

October 22: President Kennedy announced a United States air and sea blockade of Cuba to halt the introduction of offensive nuclear missiles under Soviet auspices in Cuba.

October 28: Premier Khrushchev offered to take offensive missiles out of Cuba if the United States would promise neither to invade Cuba nor to permit others to invade Cuba.

November: In the Congressional elections, the Democrats lengthened their lead in the Senate, retained their lead in the House.

November 21: President Kennedy lifted the blockade of Cuba.

1963

May 25: Thirty nations in Africa established the Organization of African Unity at a conference in Addis Ababa, Ethiopia.

August 5: The United States, Britain, and the Soviet Union signed a treaty to ban nuclear testing in the atmosphere.

August 28: 300,000 blacks and whites held a demonstration for passage of Civil Rights legislation in Washington, D.C., at which Martin Luther King made his "I have a dream" speech.

November 1: President Diem of South Vietnam was assassinated; a series of coups followed.

November 22: President Kennedy was assassinated at Dallas, Texas.

1964

July 2: The Civil Rights Act of 1964 was signed by President Johnson.

July 18: The first of a series of inner-city riots took place in New York City and Rochester, New York.

August 2–4: President Johnson reported that the U.S. destroyers *Maddox* and *C. Turner Joy* had been attacked by North Vietnamese torpedo boats; he ordered immediate retaliation.

August 7: Congress approved the Gulf of Tonkin Resolution giving the President power "to take all necessary measures to repel any armed attack against the forces of the United States and to prevent further aggression."

October 15: Premier Khrushchev was ousted as Premier and First Party Secretary of the Soviet Union.

October 16: Communist China set off its first atomic bomb.

November: In one of the greatest electoral landslides in history, Johnson defeated Goldwater and carried huge Democratic majorities in the House and Senate.

1965

January 4: President Johnson outlined a blueprint for the "Great Society" before Congress and the nation.

February: Continuous U.S. bombing of North Vietnam by air and sea forces began.

February–March: Martin Luther King and more than 2,600 blacks were arrested in Selma, Alabama, for demonstrating against voter registration rules; President Johnson ordered army units to protect a Selma-to-Montgomery march.

April 28: President Johnson ordered the marines to land in the Dominican Republic as fighting persisted between political factions in that country.

June 9: The White House confirmed that United States forces were undertaking combat assignments in South Vietnam.

September 9: President de Gaulle announced that France would withdraw from NATO.

1966

November: Congressional elections revealed Republican gains; Democrats continued to hold control of the House and Senate.

1967

January 27: The Soviet Union, the United States, and 60 other nations signed a treaty to limit military uses of space.

February 10: The 25th amendment to the United States Constitution was formally ratified; it dealt with Presidential disability and succession.

June 5–10: The six-day Arab-Israeli war resulted in the expansion of Israeli military occupation to four times its former size and an uneasy truce.

July 12 and 23: There were extensive riots in Newark and Detroit during the summer.

August 3: President Johnson announced that U.S. forces in Vietnam would be increased to 525,000 by June, 1968; he also asked for a 10 per cent surcharge on income taxes to finance the war.

1968

February–March: The Viet Cong and North Vietnamese attacked South Vietnamese cities during the Tet offensive.

March 31: President Johnson ordered a partial halt to the bombing of North Vietnam and proposed peace talks with the North Vietnamese. He said he would not seek re-election.

April 3: The North Vietnamese agreed to begin peace talks in Paris.

April 4: The Reverend Martin Luther King was assassinated at Memphis, Tennessee. The event touched off profuse urban rioting throughout the country.

June 5: Senator Robert Kennedy was assassinated at Los Angeles, California, shortly after winning the Presidential primary in that state.

July 1: The United States, the Soviet Union, and fifty-eight non-nuclear nations as well as Britain signed a treaty prohibiting the spread of nuclear weapons.

August 20: Czechoslovakia was invaded by Warsaw Pact forces to depose a liberal Communist regime.

October 31: President Johnson halted all bombardment of North Vietnam and invited South Vietnam and the National Liberation Front to the expanded Paris peace talks.

November: Richard M. Nixon narrowly defeated Hubert H. Humphrey for President; third-party candidate George Wallace received 13.5 per cent of vote; Democrats held control of both houses of Congress.

1969

January: President Nixon's inaugural announced an "era of negotiation."

June 8: The President ordered the first U.S. troops be withdrawn from South Vietnam.

July 20: The first astronauts landed on the moon.

October 15: Large peace demonstrations throughout the country urged withdrawal from Vietnam.

November 3: President Nixon appealed to the "silent majority" for support while the South Vietnamese took over their own defense.

1970

April 29: President Nixon ordered joint U.S.–South Vietnamese assault on North Vietnamese arms depots in Cambodia, and wide protests erupted.

September: Cease-fire effected between Egypt and Israel at U.S. suggestion.

September 28: President Nasser of Egypt died suddenly.

October–November: Withdrawal of American troops from Vietnam continued.

October 26: President Nixon, at the United Nations, invited the Soviet Union to "join us in a new road" to peace.

November: After a bitter off-year election campaign in which President Nixon and Vice-President Agnew actively participated, the Democratic majority was slightly decreased in the Senate but increased in the House. The Democrats, in addition, regained a majority of the governorships.

November 9: Former President Charles de Gaulle died at his home in Colombey-les-Deux-Eglises.

Index

REXFORD G. TUGWELL, Senior Fellow at the Center for the Study of Democratic Institutions, was recently principal drafter of a model for a new U.S. Constitution. He has also been a member of Franklin Roosevelt's "Brains Trust," Governor of Puerto Rico, and a professor of economics at Columbia University and of political science at the University of Chicago. He received the Woodrow Wilson Award of the American Political Science Association for his *The Democratic Roosevelt* in 1956 and the Bancroft Prize for *The Brains Trust* in 1969.